TARGETING

THE NEW

PROFESSIONAL

Woman

How to Market and Sell
to Today's 57 Million
Working Women

Gerry Myers

PROBUS PUBLISHING COMPANY
Chicago, Illinois
Cambridge, England

ISBN 1-55738-549-1

Printed in the United States of America

BB

CTV/BJS
1 2 3 4 5 6 7 8 9 0

Dedication

Targeting the New Professional Woman: How to Market and Sell to Today's 57 Million Working Women is dedicated to Howard Putnam, a wonderful mentor and friend. Howard exemplifies a true professional who believes in sharing what he has so successfully earned himself. I thank him for his encouragement, his support, and his belief in me and my ability to parlay my marketing background and expertise onto the platform as a professional speaker, consultant, and author. This book is dedicated to you, Howard, a very special person whom I have had the honor and privilege of knowing.

Table of Contents

 **Overview**

Part I—The Foundation

Chapters 1 and 2 lay the foundation for the book. Chapter 1 discusses the physiological differences between the genders, as well as the effect society has had on the development of the sexes by its definition of male and female roles. The term the "glass wall" is introduced. Five traits that distinguish men from women are presented. The evolution of the new professional woman between 1970 and 1990 is explored. The chapter concludes with the integration of the 4 Ps (price, product, place, and promotion) of the marketing mix with three additional elements. Chapter 2 focuses on myths businesses hold in regard to marketing to women and dispels them with reality. The chapter includes selling skills, follow-up procedures, and goal setting.

Part II—Successful Marketing Strategies

Chapters 3, 4, 5, and 6 comprise this section. Chapter 3 showcases industries that have developed successful marketing strategies resulting in increased sales to women. Nike, Jockey International, Samsonite, Gillette, and Southwest Airlines are just a few of the corporate giants discussed. Chapter 4 divides the marketplace into three hypothetical areas: women as the prime market, women as the growth market by design, and women consumers as they enter the once male-only domain. This chapter investigates the dramatic changes that have occurred in the last few years in the medical field, the gun industry, and the financial sphere. Facts, figures, and the rationale behind the new marketing strategies of Smith & Wesson, Doubletree Clubs, and Merrill Lynch are presented. Chapter 5 concentrates on the automotive industry. What the Big Three are doing—is it working? Who is gaining and who is losing in the race for market share? What impact are women having on the design, marketing, advertising, sales, and service of vehicles? Aftermarket products, innovative marketing ideas that work, and 20 marketing tips complete this chapter. Chapter 6 features advertising designed to win sales, as well as examples of advertising women find offensive. Numerous illustrations are given. There is a section on the portrayal of women in advertising by decades, beginning with the 1920s. Effective advertising in the 1990s concludes this chapter.

Part III—Demographic and Psychographic Differences

Chapters 7 and 8 underscore the demographic and psychographic differences between women. The commonalties and diversities of single women versus married women and managerial versus non-managerial or non-working are delineated. Age, income, and lifestyles are woven into a discussion of the purchasing habits of women. The differences in the buying patterns of men and women are also illustrated. Condoms, cigarettes, and beer: How are these industries marketing to women? Chapter 8 focuses on the relationship between the workplace and the marketplace. The roles education, marital status, and lifestyle changes have played in the development of today's professional woman are examined.

Part IV—The Marketing Environment of the Future

The concluding section contains Chapters 9, 10, and 11. Chapter 9 questions what university marketing departments are doing to prepare college students for the marketing environment of today and the future. It features the woman buyer in another role—as purchasing agent for a corporation. Poignant anecdotes are related by women about their buying experiences. Chapter 10 showcases customer satisfaction and explains how women differ from men in this area. Letters, illustrations, and experts in the field communicate the importance of building a long-term customer relationship. The book's final chapter relates the past to the future. Advertising, politics, and retailing are three areas depicted, with a glimpse into the twenty-first century. Women—how have they affected the marketplace? Learning how to gain an edge with this powerful and lucrative market segment today and tomorrow is the essence of *Targeting the New Professional Woman: How to Market and Sell to Today's 57 Million Working Women.*

Acknowledgments

I would like to acknowledge the following people for their help and support in writing *Targeting the New Professional Woman: How to Market and Sell to Today's 57 Million Working Women*.

A special thank you goes to my three children and their spouses who, during the writing of this book, not only provided inspiration and reassurance but continually checked on my progress:

❖ to my son Richard, his wife Donna, and my beautiful granddaughter Victoria, who will find the marketplace a better, friendlier environment for women as she grows from a toddler to womanhood;

❖ to my daughter Debbie and her husband Mike Richman, who not only offered encouragement, but helped edit the book, as well;

❖ to my youngest son Kenneth, who understood my scarcity of time throughout the many months I worked on the book.

I want to express my appreciation to the wonderful people I interviewed, who generously shared their time, insights, successes, and failures with me as I was gathering data, illustrations, and anecdotes for the book. Your insights and participation will enable the marketing process to continue to evolve into a more effective system that will benefit both businesses and women consumers.

I wish to acknowledge three very special friends who exemplify the real meaning of friendship. Thank you Ruth Teich and Jo Lynne Merrill for the hours you devoted to proofreading and editing my book, and Wanda McPhaden for your continual support and help.

Lastly, my thanks to Probus Publishing, who provided the venue and the opportunity to transmit this crucial information to the marketing community.

Introduction

The Economic Impact of Women

Too often, a "glass wall" separates the manufacturer, marketer, and salesperson from the woman customer. They can see her, but they can't quite reach her.

T he dramatic impact of the newly dominant and increasingly growing segment of women in the workplace is a well-documented phenomenon. The issues involved in the transformation of the once primarily unisex working environment haven't been ignored by the media or by corporate America as it struggles with change. Headlined frequently in newspapers, explored and debated countless times on television, and talked about in corporate boardrooms daily, the influx of women into the workplace has left its mark. Unequal wages, sexual harassment, and the glass ceiling vie for attention from the media, executives, and employees.

This book explores the logical, but neglected, corollary: the enormous impact women are having in a far wider business sphere—the consumer marketplace.

Targeting the New Professional Woman: How to Market and Sell to Today's 57 Million Working Women acknowledges the endless debate among marketers, retailers, and advertising gurus. One faction argues that the female consumer is a separate marketing niche, while the adversarial stance defends the position that the woman customer should be part of the mainstream marketing strategy. It is the contention of this book that while the female consumer may not be a special "niche" in every sense of the word, for many products she is unequivocally a different market "niche" than the male consumer. In order to successfully market to her, the people creating effective campaigns must recognize her unique characteristics and respect the dissimilarities as well as similarities between her and her male counterpart.

Businesses must realize that not only is she different from men, but today's woman is unlike the female consumer of 20 years ago. She has evolved as divorce, single parenthood, and full-time employment have altered her lifestyle. Marketers and sales personnel must comprehend and master the way women think and understand the circumstances that make them unique. They must take into account what offends a woman, how she reacts, what to avoid, and what to emphasize. Costly mistakes are made when there is a lack of knowledge of the woman consumer and her buying process. Few people can completely put themselves in someone else's shoes and experience the walk in the same way—especially when the essence of the individuals is as diametrically different as it is with men and women. That's why corporations must seek to gain this lifelong experience from the only credible source—women.

To fully understand the woman buyer of the 1990s, one must identify the dramatic changes that have taken place in the last two decades.

Young and Single

In 1970, only one-third of the women between the ages of 20 and 24 had never been married; today, that figure has nearly doubled to approximately six million single young women.[1] These women are choosing to begin careers rather than opting for early marriages. They are independent, assertive, and have disposable income. As a result, they are the sole decision-makers for all of their purchases; whereas, 20 years ago these same decisions may have been made jointly or by the husband alone.

Divorced and Single

A second major factor that has significantly affected the marketplace is divorce. Today, nearly 50 percent of all marriages end in divorce, triple the number 30 years ago.[2] Many divorced women, who once may have made joint decisions with their spouses, are forced to make their own, whether they want to or not.

Women are entering the work force in record numbers. Most are not "pinch-hitting" for a few months—saving up for new furniture or a trip, or bringing in a little extra spending money through part-time employment. The majority of these women, whether married or single, will remain in the work force until retirement.

Women and Work

As a result of increased employment and marital status changes, women's needs have changed and, therefore, their buying criteria have shifted. In 1950, only one out of three women worked. By 1980, more than one out of every two women were in the work force, and by 1990, 58 percent or nearly 57 million were employed. Between 1985 and 2000, women will be the largest single group entering the workplace. It is projected that by 2000, 65 percent of all women will bring home a paycheck, more than half the work force will be women, and 80 percent of prime women consumers (those between the ages of 25 and 54) will be employed.[3] They are buying everything from automobiles to computers and from sports equipment to expensive gold jewelry.

Many of these women are courageously climbing the corporate ladder and making important financial decisions at the office. They are extending this newly acquired power into their personal lives. In the showroom, they expect to be treated as valued buyers.

Other women, frustrated by the glass ceiling, have chosen to enter the world of entrepreneurship rather than remain in corporate America. This trend has grown to a significant level. By 1992, women-owned businesses employed more workers than *all* the Fortune 500 companies combined.[4]

More than 10 million women earn annual salaries in excess of $30,000 and more than 2.1 million take home $50,000. Forty-five to 50 percent of middle managers are women. In the last decade, female entrepreneurships grew 82 percent, and revenues for these businesses rose 129 percent.[5] These numbers can no longer be ignored by the business community. Companies hungry for market share have awakened and found the female consumer to be the most lucrative—and the most forgotten—entity in the marketplace. As they scramble to gain her loyalty and her dollars, they often fumble the ball by insulting her intelligence and discounting her authority as a buyer.

The most vivid example of an industry-wide misfire lies with the American automotive industry. Detroit has come to grips with her presence, but is still struggling with the best approach to this previously ignored, and still frequently mishandled, customer. Recognizing that women now have an enormous impact on the future of the automotive industry, manufacturers have begun to design their cars and advertisers are attempting to create campaigns to attract them. However, as the Big Three tackle many of their internal problems, they fail to commit enough resources to the needs of women customers. The courting of the female automotive consumer—designating her as a priority—just hasn't happened in Detroit.

The paradigm shift needed by the male-dominated management to accept and welcome this precious resource into the inner sanctum is well overdue. Women's potential contributions to the industry cannot be minimized. They must be given more power in the decision-making process at the manufacturing level if they are to be successful in having a positive influence on the sales projections. Whether Detroit acknowledges it or not, their inability to meet the needs of female consumers has had a detrimental effect on domestic car sales. The downturn in domestic car sales, while partially due to the economic conditions in the country, also reflects Detroit's deafness to women's voices. To continue ignoring their needs or minimizing their influence is foolhardy.

The indisputable fact is that women are the purchasers of nearly 50 percent of all automobiles, and they influence more than 80 percent of all automotive purchases. In 1990, they purchased 4 million vehicles, accounting for more than $65 billion in sales. These figures are growing annually.[6]

In other realms, women are gaining strength at equally impressive numbers. They now account for 37 percent of all business travelers, and by 2000 they will account for 50 percent.[7] They purchase airline tickets, rent cars, eat in restaurants, stay in hotels, and use other travel-related products in record numbers. These industries must recognize the female market and must seek to win its business. For many, it represents the only growth segment in an otherwise flat economy.

Targeting the New Professional Woman profiles companies and programs that have successfully attracted this growing new market segment—and those that have failed. It examines the strategies behind the triumphs and the miscalculations that lead to failures. It reflects on the importance of both the manufacturer and the salesperson in their distinct, but related, roles as they address the issues and needs of the female buyer. The female consumer is perhaps the most powerful, least recognized being in existence today. She is no longer a peripheral consumer to be courted casually, but a valued individual to be intensely pursued.

Targeting the New Professional Woman hits at the heart of marketing. Relegating antiquated theories and strategies to their proper place and accepting the demographics and psychographics of today's woman are the first steps to effectively marketing and selling to her. By glancing inside board rooms, design areas, advertising creative departments, and sales training programs in many enterprises, one can begin to see the source of many of the problems. Male executives and male managers meet with advertising and marketing men to create campaigns for products designed by men, yet specifically targeted to women.

Corporate America has been stunned by the realization that it can no longer impose its attitudes and values on the female consumer. She is tired of being ignored and forgotten. She is fighting back with her strongest, most effective weapon—her dollars. She glories in her victory when she buys elsewhere—from the competition—knowing that while companies may not be listening to her words, her dollars speak loudly. As the battles mount, she composes a memoir, a tale of woe she will tell time and time again, about her ill-treatment, her dissatisfaction with the product, or her disgust at an advertisement she found offensive. With each retelling, she will feel a new victory and be secure in the knowledge that her words and advice will be listened to by her friends, neighbors, colleagues, and acquaintances. As millions of dollars are spent in advertising to try to lure her back, she will gradually, but consistently, chip away at the sales revenue of many companies. She knows her powerful word-of-mouth message will make her the victor.

Interestingly, women are more prone to nurture and help a business than to destroy it. Given the chance, the same woman customer will be an ambassador of goodwill, spreading corporate praise and consumer satisfaction in eloquent prose. She is eager to tell her network of the fine service she received, the top-notch treatment she experienced and the product designed with her in mind. Her loyalty is uncompromising. Her referrals are qualified customers pre-sold on the product or service. Her voice remains firm in its conviction for the wonderful business she is recommending.

Given this new, growing consumer populace, it would seem inevitable that corporations would be dedicating vast resources and tailoring strategies to insure they gain their share of this market. Currently, corporations are not doing nearly enough to entice her business. I challenge companies trying to master the art of marketing to women to read and absorb the concepts set forth in this book. It will enable them to take advantage of the growth opportunities that women customers provide, to prosper, and to understand and meet the needs of today's professional woman so that she will be a valuable, loyal, long-term customer.

Women will make the difference between profitability and demise for many companies in many industries. They are no longer token players, and their needs must begin to be reflected in the product design, sales training, and advertising. If corporations refuse to address the female consumer challenge, they are likely to become extinct before the turn of the century.

Notes

[1]U.S. Department of Labor, Women's Bureau, December, 1989. Bureau of Census, Current Population Reports, 1991.

[2]Ibid.

[3]U. S. Bureau of Labor and Statistics.

[4]National Foundation of Women Business Owners, 1992 Study.

[5]National Association of Women Business Owners. Patricia Aburdene and John Naisbitt, *Megatrends for Women* (New York: Villard, 1992), 65.

[6]J. D. Power and Associates. National Association of Automobile Dealers.

[7]American Hotel and Motel Association.

Part I
The Foundation

Chapter 1

The Difference in Women Buyers

There are no differences between men and women and what they want." I have heard this or read it numerous times, usually in connection with a failed marketing or promotional effort aimed at female buyers. Marketing and selling successfully to women is essential in today's competitive marketplace. *Targeting the New Professional Woman: How to Market and Sell to Today's 57 Million Women* is a practical approach to marketing to women that will produce profitable bottom-line results. It clearly illustrates concepts and techniques that work, and defines those that have failed.

When marketing strategies designed to attract female buyers have produced disappointing results, researchers, product managers, advertising executives, or designers often assumed it was because there is no difference in marketing to men and women. This isn't the case and only leads to the next marketing problem: How to get women to buy the product? The usual solution is to revert back to traditional marketing efforts that have experienced some measure of success in the past in lieu of developing an appropriate and highly effective marketing program. It seldom occurs to the marketers with preconceived, as well as ill-conceived, ideas that the theory of creating marketing efforts and products to appeal to women was correct, but that the implementation was the problem. Otherwise, they could not have so easily dismissed the "theory" that "women have different needs" as ridiculous. It is far easier to continue the stereotypical views of the past, even though they have led to failure, than to change in order to succeed. Companies must look introspectively and realize what worked in the past just isn't working anymore. Innovative approaches need to replace old rules. If old traditions continue, they will lead to the demise, or at least the downsizing, of many more companies before the turn of the century.

Best-selling books, *You Just Don't Understand* by Deborah Tanner, *60 Significant Differences Between Men and Women* by Cris Evatt, *Brain Sex* by Anne Moir and David Jessel, and *Men Are from Mars, Women Are from Venus* by John Gray are a few of the books examining the differences between the sexes. Interestingly, most, if not all, of the books currently in print that deal with the differences between the way men and women think, communicate, and react are in the "relationships" section of the bookstore. This leads one to surmise that while it is generally accepted that there are significant differences between men and women, these differences only manifest themselves in personal relationships. In other words, the premise seems to be that men and women communicate and relate on one level in interpersonal relationships, but that their thinking, logic, and rationale is totally different in a business environment. Obviously, that premise is preposterous.

Just as women and men bring different characteristics to personal relationships, so do they to business relationships. The same traits, innate or learned, that make communication between the sexes difficult on a personal level can also hinder it in a buying situation. *Targeting the New Professional Woman* is dedicated to providing the business community—brand managers, product managers, advertisers, market strategists, and retailers—insights into the thinking of today's woman consumer. Achieving marketing success with the female customer is based on understanding her communication styles, networking system, and thought processes, and then putting this knowledge into action. Marketers must meet *her* needs as *she* sees them.

The differences that exist between the sexes shouldn't be a barrier, but a positive tool to build a long-term, solid business relationship. Too often, a "glass wall" separates the manufacturer, marketer, and salesperson from the woman customer. They can see her, but they can't quite reach her.

Breaking the glass wall between the customer and company is essential. Companies must realize that men and women are innately different in their thought processes, as well as their physical characteristics; one isn't right and the other wrong—they're just different. To work together successfully, each must understand and respect the dissimilarities, know how to compensate for them, and be able to bridge the gap.

Before we examine some of the key differences that influence a woman's decision to buy, or not to buy, take a few minutes to fill out the brief quiz on the following page.

MEN OR WOMEN

While the following phrases describe traits of both genders, each phrase better describes either men or women. Put an "M" for men or a "W" for women before each phrase.

____ 1. Are more loyal customers

____ 2. Talk more about feelings and relationships

____ 3. See money as status

____ 4. Share information with more people

____ 5. Talk about things, gadgets, tangible items

____ 6. Are more competitive

____ 7. Like to negotiate more

____ 8. Are more sensitive to their treatment

____ 9. Usually do their homework better in a buying situation

____ 10. Build relationships on cooperation and trust

The answer to questions 1, 2, 4, 8, 9, and 10 is women. The answer to questions 3, 5, 6, and 7 is men. If you scored 80 percent or better, you are consciously or unconsciously aware that there are many valid distinctions between the sexes. If you scored 60 or below, you need to change the way you view women. It will be necessary for you to dismiss the antiquated stereotypes you have and to replace them with a new understanding of women that will make you more successful in marketing and selling to the female consumer. This book will help you focus on how understanding these differences can improve your marketing objectives. It will suggest tactics to increase sales with the female buyer.

The Network Effect

To understand the strength of the woman's network is to realize that she doesn't view her network as a means to a promotion or as power. She thinks of it as an extension of herself, an integral part of her existence. Sharing is just part of who she is. She sees sharing information as a way to enhance others' lives, not as a source of power to guard closely. Women discuss far more things with many more people than men do. Their perceptions and styles are foreign to the male gender.

She is inclined by nature to share her experiences, relationships, and decisions with other women. She makes recommendations and offers advice; she listens to the recommendations and opinions of others. A woman's network is a powerful tool.

Realizing how women network is essential to understanding the importance of providing fair treatment, good customer service, and excellent follow-up. Women network in a much broader arena than men do. *The Female Advantage* by Sally Helgesen described the management style of Frances Hesselbein, National Executive Director of Girls Scouts of the U.S.A. Her system was circular, like a web, with her in the middle, rather than a hierarchical organization. She wanted to be in the middle of things, not at the top removed from the others.[1]

Carol Gilligan, author of *In a Different Voice,* noted that those who perceive the best place to be is at the top are uncomfortable with the web concept because "the most desirable place in the one is the most feared in the other."[2] In other words, if you want to be at the top, set apart and above the others, the fear of being in the center, or middle, is great. On the other hand, if your management style is to be in the center of things—you like receiving information from everyone, and you feel free to disperse data the same way—you would be uncomfortable distancing yourself from information with structured channels as in a hierarchy management system.

According to numerous studies, it appears that men tend to be hierarchical leaders, while women prefer to be in the center. "Women emphasize keeping relationships in an organization in good repair," said Helgesen. She quotes *The Managerial Woman* as saying that "women in the workplace tend to 'assume without thinking that the quality of relationships is [their] most important priority.' " Helgesen goes on to say that "women structure their days to include as much sharing as possible. It was a deliberate process, a major goal of every day."[3]

A marketer must realize that a woman will sit in a business meeting with people she doesn't know and verbalize a positive buying experience she has had, or vocalize in lethal language how she would never shop at a particular establishment or purchase a particular product again. She will expound on the same tale at a dinner party or call friends just to tell them. Retailers should assume that when a woman walks in the door, she will leave and tell her story to numerous people, people who may or may not be future customers, depending on what she says.

Many authorities have said if a person is happy with the service he receives, he will tell five people, but if he is unhappy, he will tell 16. I believe that women tell many more.

Recognizing the differences in the way men and women network should emphasize the need for the woman customer to have a good experience in your store every time. She'll spread the word. Make sure it's the message you want to convey.

Generalizing and Individualizing

There are many differences between persons of the same sex, just as there are between the two genders. Men are short, tall, fat, thin, smart, business oriented, mechanically inclined, blue-eyed, brown-eyed, blonde, brunette, and bald. Women are short, tall, fat, thin, smart, business oriented, mechanically inclined, blue-eyed, brown-eyed, blonde, brunette, and red-headed. Yet, we all can distinguish between the genders. We don't confuse thin men and thin women as one gender and fat men and fat women as another. The same distinctions apply to men's and women's innate traits and learned characteristics. Some men are aggressive, money oriented and goal driven, while others are less so. Some women are more business oriented than other women.

While market segmentation by demographics and psychographics is essential to properly position products and services for the female buyer, it isn't necessary at this point to focus on the categories that might make up the total universe of female consumers. That will be addressed in Chapter 7.

Comparison between the genders creates distinctly different profiles of women and men that are beneficial for manufacturers, marketers, advertisers, and retailers to consider in the development of their products and services. While it is understood that not all men nor all women are the same, there are sufficient similarities so that the generalizations made in this book are accurate for our purposes. The design and premise of the book are to clearly and concisely demonstrate the broad differences between male and female customers and the effect misjudging or ignoring these differences has had on many industries. It is not a marketing textbook designed to discuss all the various market segments complete with models. Rather, I intend to present a comprehensive understanding of how meeting the needs of the new professional woman will positively impact businesses in the marketplace and a manufacturer's bottom line.

There are nearly 97 million women in the United States, and 57 million of them work. If they were placed on a continuum to determine personality and buying traits, a few women would be at each end of the spectrum. The vast majority exhibit a cluster of behaviors that are more likely to be feminine rather than masculine. Unfortunately, many of these feminine behaviors adversely affect how men and women work together toward a common goal—whether it is a personal relationship or a business endeavor. Understanding the differences between the genders is the first step to meeting the needs of the professional woman consumer.

Create Loyal Female Customers

Targeting the New Professional Woman describes how many of the traits discussed in best-selling books on personal relationships can actually be converted to the business environment and used to create loyal female customers.

Trait Number One: Women think more about others, while men are more self-focused.

When the male viewpoint is the only one taken into consideration in the design, features, and advertising of the product, the female customer's needs are frequently ignored or misread. Products often come to market that demonstrate what she should want and should buy, not necessarily what she does want or will buy. Male designers erroneously assume that women place the same value on a particular feature of a product that men do. Women simply don't. For example, in purchasing a car, performance is a key element to a man. How much horsepower it has, how quickly it will go from zero to 60, are features of interest to him. But safety is the number one concern for her. Dependability, reliability, and the overall package are more important to a woman than horsepower. (The automotive industry is discussed in detail in Chapter 5.) Advertising and marketing efforts must be sensitive to a woman's needs—and reflect her concerns in meaningful language that she will relate to.

Trait Number Two: Women view money as a goal, while men see it as status, a way to keep score.

When marketing financial services or selling large ticket items, it is crucial to understand how women view money. This in no way implies women aren't interested in money or what it will buy, just that women put a different value on it than men do. Women see money as a medium of exchange, a way to achieve security for the future. They seldom see it as a total measure of their success, but rather as a tool to purchase what they want and need. They put less emphasis on the power and status associated with money than men do. Women, in general, are more conservative financially and take fewer risks. These subtle differences are very important to developing marketing strategies aimed at female clients. (Women and finance is presented in more detail in Chapter 4.)

Trait Number Three: Women talk more about their feelings, experiences, and relationships, while men talk more about things, gadgets, sports, and cars.

This trait has perhaps the largest impact on present and future sales. Women share more information with their network of friends, business associates, and acquaintances. Therefore, a few caustic words can go further to undermine an entire marketing campaign, product, or company. Understanding that women have a wider range of people with whom they share a greater amount of information, regardless of whether it is good news or bad, is vital to comprehending the true force of the woman consumer. Women talk about their experiences with other women at business lunches, at the office, and in neighborhood groups. They don't guard information as a source of power, believing as men often do, that "He who knows more has more power." Instead, women see information as a tool that will allow them to make the best possible decision. The more information they have, the better their decisions will be.

Men talk about business, sports, cars, and gadgets—nonpersonal topics. They discuss how things are put together, how they work, how to take them apart, and how to fix them. Women are less versed in these areas and tend to focus their conversations more on interpersonal topics—how they are treated, how they feel about something, and their attitude about the people involved. Selling successfully to a woman requires that the salesperson cultivate a level of trust, build rapport, and be professional and knowledgeable. Taking time to listen to the customer, really listen, is very important, especially to female customers.

Trait Number Four: Women gather more information before making a decision, while men are more narrowly focused.

"A woman's strength, and her weakness, is her capacity to perceive, for example, the human dimension of a business decision. Her mind, with its greater sensitivity to personal and moral aspects, and the greater facility with it which connects the elements to be considered, makes the decision altogether more complex than it is for the man, who relies more on calculated, formulaic, deductive processes," said Anne Moir and David Jessel in their book *Brain Sex*.[4]

Women tend to take more information into account when making purchasing decisions, especially on large ticket items. They generally don't buy expensive items or goods they know little about on their first visit. When advertising these types of products, plenty of information should be included in the campaign. Women read these ads in order to increase their knowledge of the product. They do their homework. They will check a number of retailers that carry the product in order to gather more information. They feel comfortable asking for opinions, suggestions, and approvals from their friends. Men rarely seek such assistance.

A salesperson should understand that when a woman leaves the store, it doesn't necessarily mean she isn't going to buy. It may mean she is still seeking information. Even though she is not buying your product right now, she may return to buy from you in the future. A great deal depends on how she was treated while gathering the information. Understanding this and realizing the importance of building rapport and creating a positive environment that will bring women customers back is the secret to long-term growth and profitability.

Accept her for who she is—someone who may anguish over choices, shop for alternatives, and ask for confirmation from friends and colleagues. She takes more time in the decision-making process and responds negatively to high-pressure tactics; but she almost always bases her decisions on sound information. While women shop and compare more, spend time gathering information, and are concerned with their treatment, they are also more restricted by time constraints. Working full time and balancing a family has taken its toll on women. They have less time for many of the pleasures they enjoyed in the past. Although information gathering is essential to her peace of mind in many circumstances, so is the importance of convenience and the appreciation of her busy lifestyle.

Lastly, salespeople should be knowledgeable, professional, and well-versed about the products they represent. They should provide plenty of information, but avoid giving too much advice or being patronizing. She will see that as high-pressure or implying that she cannot make a decision. That would be grossly inaccurate. She can make decisions. If treated improperly, her first one will be not to buy from you.

Trait Number Five: Women are relationship oriented, while men are goal oriented.

Men value power and attainment. In school they played sports—games with distinct winners and rules. Girls participated in group activities without the same type of structure. Men focus on ways to gain power. They pride themselves in being self-sufficient. Autonomy is a symbol of manliness. The series of jokes about men refusing to stop and ask directions is no joke. Being self-sufficient is all important.

By contrast, women need interaction through communication and relationships. They value sharing and working as a group. Women who are in their thirties and forties today are more likely to have been encouraged to play in groups and to learn to work together peaceably. They don't see the need to produce a clear winner. They thrive on sharing information and are comfortable asking for help or seeking answers to questions they don't fully understand. This is often hard for men to comprehend.

Just as these diverse values and goals impact an intimate relationship, so do they affect a business relationship. Learning to communicate with women customers is essential to marketing and selling to them. This has distinct ramifications for product managers and advertising executives in charge of creating a product marketing message.

After an effective message has been produced and conveyed, the sale is ultimately made in a one-on-one situation. If the salesperson sees his role strictly as a conveyor of information about the product, hands the woman brochures to read in place of verbal interaction, or spouts technical information, he may lose a buying customer. She is looking to "connect" with the salesperson. She is not looking for an intimate or personal conversation, but one that shows his concern for meeting her objectives by understanding her needs. He does this by asking open-ended questions and by finding out what her needs are, not by telling her the features of the product. Selling to women is discussed in greater detail in Chapter 2. It is only mentioned here to emphasize the importance of understanding key differences in the genders and how they affect sales. If the salesperson doesn't connect with the woman through conversation, and someone else does, from whom do you think she is going to buy? And to whom is she going to refer her network?

To sell successfully to women, you must master the art of asking open-ended questions. Men often are too direct. They see the mission and try the fastest way to achieve it. Women often want to be sure that the salesperson understands *exactly* what they want.

No one likes to waste time with useless questions. Women don't want to discuss the weather or how their weekend was. But they are more than willing to describe what they want, why they want it, and how they plan to use it—if asked. This information, along with the answers to other product-specific questions, will assist the salesperson in providing the services that will sell to women.[5]

Innate Versus Learned Differences

Brain Sex vividly describes the physiological differences between men and women. While many of our characteristics and actions are learned, some are innate. This section examines the role that some of these physical differences play in our buying decisions. It is included to further reinforce the concept that men and women think, react, communicate, relate, and buy differently, in part because of their physical differences.

For instance, it's a scientific fact that women's hearing is superior to men's. They see better in the dark and have a more acute visual memory.[6] Because women have wider peripheral vision, and therefore have a larger visual field, they see more in the showroom than do male customers. Women are more keenly aware of the appearance of the store—cleanliness, tasteful decor, what other salespersons are doing, the salesperson's body language, as well as the words. She interprets that and integrates it into her mental process. "A woman understands, better than a man, what a man or a woman means, even when he or she is apparently saying nothing," said Moir and Jessel.[7]

"Women are better at picking up social cues and important nuances of meaning from tones of voice or intensity of expression," said Moir and Jessel.[8] Again, this will affect a woman's perception of the buying situation. How she feels about the salesperson's tone of voice, body language, and facial expressions will have a far greater influence on her decision to buy, or not to buy, than it will on a man's.

According to Moir's and Jessel's research, the construction of the brain is not the same in men and women. Males have a thicker cerebral cortex (a rind-like covering of the two hemispheres of the brain) on the right side only. Females have thicker cerebral cortex on the left side. From other anatomical differences, psychologist Herbert Landsell deduced that language and spatial skills were each controlled by centers in both sides of the brain in women. In men, however, spatial skills are centered primarily in the right side of the brain, while verbal skills are controlled from the left side. The structure of their brains is one reason for the disparity in the way men and women communicate.[9]

In 1989, the journal *Brain* reported that neuroscientists had noted structural differences between men's and women's brains. According to a study by neuropsychologist Sandra Witelson, male and female brains are actually a different shape, and the same parts of the brain perform different functions in men and women. "These results suggest that the female brain is not just a scaled-down version of the male brain," said Dr. Witelson in an interview with the *Dallas Morning News.*[10]

There is agreement among scientists that the corpus callosum, connecting fibers between the two halves of the brain, are different in men and women. The corpus callosum is more plentiful and thicker in women, allowing more information to be exchanged between the two sides. This lends credence to the theory that women are "gatherers" of information from many different sources. It strengthens the argument that women express their emotions more easily than men. A woman's ability to easily impart her perception of her treatment to her network can be an asset or a liability to a business.

Men's preoccupation with power, things, profits, and independence and women's concerns for people, relationships, and harmony need to be more closely coordinated in order to have successful interaction between the two—whether on a personal or business level. Having the necessary components for a sale—a salesperson and a customer—isn't sufficient. Understanding and meaningful communication need to exist.

What Happened Between 1970 and 1990?

Now that we have discussed some of the differences between men and women, let's explore the changes that took place between 1970 and 1990 that have directly affected women's buying habits. In 1970, only 36 percent of women between the ages of 20 and 24 weren't married. By 1990, that figure had almost doubled (61.1 percent), totalling nearly 6 million women (Table 1-1). Approximately two-thirds of young women were finishing school and choosing to begin careers rather than marriages. These women were becoming a dominant force in the marketplace. They cannot be classified simply as Generation X, or profiled only as young with disposable income. They must be recognized as female purchasers, as well. Many Generation X women are first-time car buyers, as well as purchasers of a number of other products and services. Their initial experience will affect both their networks' buying habits and their subsequent buying decisions. It will influence where they buy, what they buy, and how they buy in the future.

TABLE 1-1 Percent of Females Never Married by Age Group				
	20–24	25–29	30–39	40–44
1970	36%	11%	12%	5%
1988	61%	30%	25%	6%

Source: Marriage and Family Statistics Bureau.

* In the text, information and statistical data reflecting 1988 to 1990 is described as 1990. This is done to clarify the message and avoid any unnecessary calculations that would have no measurable significance on the statistics and their relevance to the discussion.

Women between the ages of 25 and 39 who have never married more than doubled from 1970 to 1990. As these women mature without a mate, they will make financial, real estate, and entertainment decisions based on their own criteria. The fashion industry, sports and fitness businesses, financial institutions, medical, and legal practices and even travel agencies need to be aware of the numbers of women who are prospects for their products and services. During the next decade, many companies will realize the vast effect the new professional woman is having on their market share and profitability, and they will take aggressive steps to make her a brand-loyal, happy, satisfied customer. Let's look at what's happened to marriages over the last three decades, and again relate it to the marketplace (Table 1-2).

As divorce rates climbed in the 1970s and 1980s, so did women's independent purchasing. With 50 percent of all marriages ending in divorce by 1990, many divorcees were confidently and eagerly making their

TABLE 1-2 Number of Divorces	
1960	400,000 per year
1990	1.2 million per year
Source: Marriage and Family Statistics Bureau	

buying decisions alone. Others, who no longer had a spouse to share this responsibility, had no alternative. As a result, these women relied more heavily on their friends and their network for support and help. They listened to other women's recommendations about which product brands to purchase and which retail stores to patronize, and they heard where not to go and what not to buy, as well. Divorced women are a diverse group. Many have less money than when they were married and must shop more carefully now. Others have achieved success in the business world and have more disposable income than before. Whatever her financial situation is, she is now one of the 39.5 million single women in this country over the age of 18 who are making sole decisions on a variety of issues.

As 57 million women entered the work force, some becoming entrepreneurs, others making the tough climb up the corporate ladder, they faced obstacles never encountered as homemakers. Having fought for respect and recognition in the workplace, they will demand it in the marketplace.

The new professional woman has emerged during the last two decades.

The Four Ps and the Woman Consumer

Manufacturers and retailers must oust age-old stereotypes and accept that differences do exist between the sexes. Corporations that have formulated their marketing decisions on the traditional role of women as homemakers, and that perceive the only differences between women today and those of 20 years ago is that part of their time is spent in the workplace, will suffer a measurable decline in market share in this decade. While "traditional" women still exist, their numbers are diminishing, and their roles are changing. Women are entering the workplace at younger ages and with more education. They realize that being in the work force is an economic lifestyle they will have for most of their adult life. This lifestyle has precipitated a very different buyer than the traditional woman of the past. Corporations must now focus on the new professional woman.

Understanding that men and women value things differently is critical for success in marketing to women. Corporations must:

1. receive input from women on what their needs are prior to the design stage, and manufacturers and distributors must abandon the "push" or forced marketing theory of products to women, and instead provide products they want;

2. create marketing strategies and advertising campaigns based on what women value; and

3. see that sales staffs are adequately trained in the skills of selling to women.

The marketing mix consisting of the 4 Ps—price, product, place, and promotion—isn't adequate today. The competitive marketplace and the more astute consumer have changed the environment so that what was once considered the essence of marketing strategies is simply not complete any longer.

Customer Satisfaction + Product + Sales Training + Promotion

(marketing/advertising) + Price + Place = Sale

As you can see, additions have been made to the four Ps to accommodate aspects that are mandatory in order to sell effectively to women. Promotion, which includes advertising and marketing, if done inappropriately, has a detrimental effect on sales to the female consumer. This is in keeping with what Dick Berry, a professor from the University of

Wisconsin, discovered when he surveyed marketing managers, customer service managers, production managers, and senior executives. He found that the four Ps are no longer considered sufficient. Berry analyzed the results and noted that the elements of the marketing mix managers considered important included three additions to the traditional four Ps— customer sensitivity, customer convenience, and service. In fact, except for product, Berry found that the three additions (two "Cs" and an "S") scored above the other three Ps in importance in making a sale. Berry found customer sensitivity to be number one, followed by product, customer convenience, service, price, place, and promotion.[11]

This mirrors my belief, and the results of other studies, that price, while an important factor, is not the determining component much of the time. Promotion ranked last in importance in Berry's study. This is consistent with my theory regarding the significance of promotion (advertising and marketing) to women. Unfortunately, bad advertising can lose a sale. Good advertising, however, won't always convince a woman to buy. Word-of-mouth advertising is far more meaningful to women than the strategically created and properly executed advertising message. This is not meant to minimize advertising, but to put it in its proper perspective. (Chapter 6 discusses advertising designed to win sales.) Advertising should convey the essential information to the consumer that is needed to make the buying decision. Far too often, billions of dollars are spent to persuade consumers they will be more successful, more beautiful, or more relaxed if they purchase a particular product, rather than to elucidate the features of a product. Advertising definitely has its strengths and is a fundamental part of the marketing process, but it has its limitations as well. No amount of advertising dollars can change a bad buying experience into a good one.

Customer sensitivity is the number one priority in Berry's survey. In my experience, customer sensitivity and satisfaction rank number one as well. Unfortunately, too many companies still think only of the traditional four Ps as they develop their market strategies.

While product, price, place, and promotion are important, I chose to present the formula with promotion broken down into marketing and advertising because the tone, visuals, and language of the message is as crucial in selling to women as the concept. Many businesses still "just don't get it." They haven't yet acknowledged women as a market they need to understand and cultivate. This rigidity will prove to be damaging to those corporations' health and prosperity.

The discussion of the four Ps would be incomplete without some dialogue on price, since it is often the center of corporate strategy. In surveys of women consumers, price rarely is the only deciding factor. Price is part of the total package. If the product is a luxury item with numerous amenities, women, as well as men, expect to pay more. If it is sold by a discount establishment with low overhead and minimal service, customers expect to pay less. It is, however, a real misconception to believe that women buy primarily on price. They don't. They are value-added customers who consider far more than the lowest price point. In fact, because men like to negotiate more, and they view money differently, price plays a larger role in a purchase by a man than a woman. If your women customers are buying primarily on price, it is because someone in the channel from the manufacturer to salesperson has failed to provide any other credible reason for the sale. Women are interested in service, features, convenience, and a whole range of other tangible and intangible aspects, as well as price. When price is negotiable, as with automobiles, women consider the fairness of the price and the overall tone of the negotiation process as part of their treatment. Negotiating a fair price for a woman prospect is paramount to the sale if a loyal, satisfied customer is the goal. Suggesting a much higher price, because she is a woman, doesn't fit with her concept of good treatment. Even if she buys, she won't remain a customer for long or refer her network—two goals a salesperson should strive for.

A salesman must communicate to a woman customer that he is sincerely interested in her well-being. To do this, he must put aside his desires for immediate profit and winning at any cost. She must believe that his goal is to match her needs with a product that will be of benefit to her. That's what sells to women.

Notes

[1] Sally Helgesen, *The Female Advantage: Women's Way of Leadership* (New York: Doubleday/Bantam Doubleday Dell Publishing Group, Inc., 1990), 43–60.

[2] Carol Gilligan, *In A Different Voice: Psychological Theory and Women's Development* (Cambridge: Harvard University Press, 1982), 62.

[3] Helgesen, *The Female Advantage*, 27.

[4] *Brain Sex: The Real Difference Between Men and Women* by Anne Moir and David Jessel. Copyright © 1989, 1991 by Anne Moir and David Jessel. Published by arrangement with Carol Publishing Group. A Lyle Stuart Book.

[5] Cris Evatt, *He & She: 60 Significant Differences Between Men and Women* (Emeryville: Conari Press, 1992).

[6] Moir and Jessell, *Brain Sex*, 100.

[7] Ibid.

[8] Ibid, 48.

[9]Ibid, 42.

[10]Tom Siegfried, "Brains and Sex," *Dallas Morning News,* (November 26, 1990): D6–7.

[11]Alexander Hiam and Charles D. Schewe, *The Portable MBA in Marketing* (New York: John Wiley & Sons, Inc., 1992), 19.

Chapter 2

How to Achieve Greater Success in Selling to Women

As you read this book, you will be able to identify a common pattern that is significant to the successful development, marketing, and advertising of many products. Companies that have experienced prosperity with the new professional woman are constantly reacting and adjusting to fit the ever-changing needs of the marketplace. While many factors contribute to the success or demise of a company, one of the most significant commonalities is that companies that have been successful have involved women early in the design and marketing process.

Gillette's Sensor for Women was designed by a woman; the Chrysler Voyager had design, marketing, and advertising input from a committee of women; the phenomenally successful Nike campaign was created by two women who, working with other women, fought to create a campaign women could relate to. The successful LadySmith gun was designed after Smith & Wesson conducted focus groups with women. And the Double-tree Hotels built the Doubletree Club chain after listening to the needs and wants of both businessmen and businesswomen.

Women as Influencers

The Big Three in Detroit (I am including Chrysler prior to the formation of its women's committee) didn't ask women, didn't listen to women, and didn't sell very effectively to women. Japanese and European car makers adopted a different philosophy. Wanting to capture the very lucrative female market, they took the time and trouble to find out what women wanted. They designed these features into their products and advertised them as benefits. Sales to both men *and* women made Honda's Accord number one in 1987, 1988, and 1989. Without the large percentage of women buyers, Honda's Accord wouldn't have achieved that position.

"While women have helped make certain makes and models number one, they don't always respond to the same features or advertising in the way men do," explains Shelley Hobson, editor of the newsletter, *Marketing to Women*. "Women and men have a different relationship with cars. Women are more interested in safety features and service, and men are more performance oriented," said Hobson. To reach women successfully, a company can't just take its already established male formula, modify it slightly and think it will meet a woman's needs. When Reebok entered the women's market, Nike's share to women dropped. Nike altered their successful male campaign slightly to attract women; it didn't work. Substituting female athletes in place of men just didn't appeal to women. However, the Dialogue campaign specially aimed at women and their needs experienced unprecedented success. The campaign dialogued with women—about their feelings, thoughts, lifestyles, and early years. It stirred emotions and memories, but most importantly, it sold shoes. (More details on the Nike campaign are in Chapters 3 and 6.) "Messages must be tailored to women. They must communicate and project an understanding of her needs and values," advised Hobson.[1]

Corporate America has a new respect for the purchasing power of women. But recognizing the power and knowing how to harness it are two different matters. Many corporations are still searching for the right formula that will attract women to their products and will make them loyal, long-term customers. According to Hobson, the woman's market can be a gold mine for many companies. Not all products are gender related. Even makers of unisex products need to be aware of the female consumer. Prudential doesn't design special brochures for women, but they make sure women are in all the brochures they produce.

"The mission of our newsletter," stated Hobson, "is to try to provide information on the woman's market to Fortune 1000 companies, news organizations and women's studies programs. We help companies understand how women feel about certain issues, what their hot buttons are and what's going on in their lives. For instance, women used to see cosmetics as a way to cover up their imperfections. Now, more advertising messages stress cosmetics as a way to enhance positive attributes."

Marketers need to understand that today women want to be considered as whole beings and that their talents are as important to them as their looks. The decade of the superwoman is dead. Women don't want to be pressured to excel in everything. They want to obtain balance in their lives between their jobs, their families, and their leisure time.

The Pink Myth

If a marketing professor queried students by asking, "What three things do hotel rooms, running shoes, tool sets, guns, typewriters, cars, and tires have in common?" few, if any, would know the answer. But accomplished marketing professionals should. First, the manufacturers of each product realized that female consumers could greatly improve their profitability. Second, they all designed a product they thought would appeal to women without asking women what they wanted. Instead, the manufacturers and marketers asked *themselves* what women wanted. "Pink" was the unanimous answer. Third, none of the pink products have achieved much success. Pink was not the solution to a complex problem that deserved a more intense analysis.

Women customers are worth pursuing. They are worth hundreds of billions of dollars annually to American companies. Women are staying in more hotels, but they are not choosing pink rooms, nor are they selecting pink cars or pink-walled tires. Office equipment manufacturers also tried pink. In 1959, the Royal typewriter casing came in pink. In 1986, Canon used pink as if the copier was a fashion accessory.[2]

"Color it pink," while tried by many, just isn't the answer. Corporate America definitely subscribed to the old adage, "If at first you don't succeed, try, try again."

Admittedly, some products have succeeded with pink. Mary Kay, the guru of direct sales cosmetics, built a pink empire—but that is a different product that achieved its phenomenal success in a different era. Women buy pink lingerie, pink blouses, and pink flowers. It's not that pink is unappealing. The difference between a pink blouse and a pink hotel room should be obvious to marketers: One is tasteful, the other offensive. Pink hotel rooms, pink-walled tires, and pink office machines are a result of men stereotyping women.

The main problem is that when the focus is on color, it's not where it should be, on the other and more important features of the product. For instance, in 1989, when General Motors designed a car with a pink-and-white scheme, they still hadn't gotten it! Having noticed that their attempt to attract the woman's market ended in failure, they compounded the mistake by declaring, "there are no differences in designing and marketing products for women," rather than looking at real features that women wanted in cars.[3] Designing a product with a woman in mind is very different than patronizing her by making it pink.

Marketing Realities

Besides the ominous *pink myth* that seems to show its color in a multitude of inappropriate products, there are also many other falsehoods that marketers must come to grips with if they hope to win the women's market.

Manufacturers, researchers and advertising agencies can increase demand for products by designing them to fit the needs of consumers and creating advertising messages that sell. The 4 Ps (product, place, price, and promotion) can only get the customer into the store; after that the sales staff takes over. The salesperson either begins to build the foundation for a lifetime customer or loses her forever.

It is imperative that the sales process is positive. This chapter explores selling to women—one-on-one. Manufacturers cannot rely totally on the retailer to educate the sales force. They must begin to take responsibility for training the staff to understand and meet the needs of women consumers, because ultimately they are the ones who will reap profits or suffer losses from the transaction. Informing retailers and sales personnel to be sensitive to the female market just isn't enough. Telling them to treat women with respect, or as they treat male customers, is too superficial to do the job. Salespersons need to understand how their words and actions affect the sales process with women. As long as the glass wall divides the female customer from the sale, businesses will continue to lose millions of dollars. While invisible, the glass wall keeps women from buying when they are mistreated or not taken seriously as customers by the sales staff. Knowing that women are important customers isn't the same as knowing how to win their business. It's time for manufacturers, marketers, advertisers, and retailers to learn how to market and sell most effectively to women.

Myth: You will lose male customers if you target women.

Reality One: Targeting women doesn't mean you will lose your market share with men.

Manufacturers, marketers, product managers, and brand managers must recognize a woman's desire, perhaps even demand, for a different design or look if she is to buy the product. This concept has brought fear into the hearts and minds of the upper echelon of management who rationalize that incorporating women's recommendations into a product's design would eradicate the male market they have spent years cultivating. Contrary to this commonly held belief, most companies have found just the opposite to be true. After hotels responded to women's requests by adding more open areas, better lit corridors, a more secure entry system, and hair dryers and other amenities to the rooms, they were surprised when male guests began to comment on how much more they enjoyed these added amenities. What would lose male sales would be decorating the room with frilly curtains, floral accessories, or a pink or pastel color scheme. But then, that would turn women patrons away as well. The few who tried this approach failed. By conducting focus groups with both men and women, staffing marketing and design departments with some women, and implementing concepts that appeal to both sexes, manufacturers, developers, and marketers can avoid costly mistakes.

Women's opinions have generated a number of improvements, even in the most unlikely of areas. In the male-dominated firearms industry, many changes to the standard line of handguns were made after information from female focus groups was evaluated, and the LadySmith line was successfully introduced. According to Chris Killoy, director of product and market management for Smith & Wesson, "Some of the changes we made in the gun as we developed the LadySmith eventually found their way to our other firearms. The data gave us insights on ways to improve the product for all of our customers, not just women. We found out that what was good for the women's market was good for others."[4]

The management of Jockey International, a name synonymous with men's underwear, feared it would tarnish its image if it produced a woman's line. The consensus was that men would no longer see the company as manufacturing a product for them, and women wouldn't think of Jockey when they thought of underwear. "After all," reasoned many of Jockey's upper management, "women want silk and lace, not comfort and quality."[5] The dismal forecast that was predicted for the company as a result of the decision to introduce Jockey for Her to the marketplace instead became an enormously profitable product line.

Nike also worried about shattering their male image if they introduced a women's line of athletic shoes and apparel, but it didn't happen. What did happen was that Nike went from 10 percent of the aerobic-shoe market in 1991 to 13 percent in 1992. In specialty stores, the growth was far more dramatic. They went from 8 percent to 26 percent, making their women's line one of the fastest growing segments of the company.

Each of these companies had been living with set paradigms. Each needed a paradigm shift—a way of perceiving the marketplace a little differently. Each needed to get out of their comfort zone, explore the marketplace, and adjust their way of viewing, evaluating and thinking about today's woman consumer.[6]

Myth: Manufacturers know what the woman customer wants; they don't need to ask her.

Reality Two: Manufacturers need to ask the female customer what she wants, then give it to her.

Today, the push-pull theory is less effective. Designing the product and then trying to force it onto the marketplace is less and less successful, especially with women. Women are more sophisticated buyers than in the past, and they know what they want.

Before Jockey launched the Jockey for Her line, they asked women what they wanted. Other women's lingerie manufacturers watched their market share decline as they continued to receive their input from male marketers, retailers, advertisers, and corporate executives, who assumed they knew what women wanted and presumed women would buy what they gave them. In 1987, the sale of teddies fell 31 percent, panty sales dropped by 40 million units, 9 million fewer bras were sold and the overall sales of chemises, slips, and teddies declined $4 million in two years.[7] As women's lingerie manufacturers continued to subscribe to the adage that customers will buy what you give them, they left the sales counters open for Jockey to walk in and seize the customers and market share.

Myth: You can never be successful by creating and positioning a product just for women.

Reality Three: Creating a product with its own identity will sell to women if it is positioned properly.

Virginia Slims, the LadySmith handgun, the Sensor for Women razor, and Jockey for Her all identified women as their target market in their name. Although Virginia Slims doesn't say "for women," the name does imply the market. Advertisers and marketers must be careful not to patronize women in the name, design, package, or advertising of the product as they attempt to focus their attention on her and her dollars.

In the mid-1950s, Dodge produced a lavender car with a floral interior to appeal to women. The Dodge LaFemme and Ford Ms. Mustang didn't work for several reasons. First, women saw the color and interpreted the manufacturer's message to be, "We think all you care about in a car is the color, so we made a pretty car for you—in soft pastels." Second, not all products need to be identified as "For Men" or "For Women." Automobiles are basically a unisex product. By listening, automakers have been able to build a vehicle that better fits her needs.

There is considerable difference in making a product *for women* and one designed *with women in mind*. Creating a car with features that are important to women and advertising it in a sensitive, informative way, is what women want, not a car designed and painted only for them.

Myth: There is no difference between men and women.

Reality Four: Walk in her shoes for a while, and see if you still agree with that falsehood.

To understand a woman's motivation to buy, marketers need to understand as much as possible about the woman's thought process. Reading magazines she reads and watching television programs that appeal to women are just two ways to put yourself into her world. Imagine getting into a car wearing high heels, feeling the alarm as the hotel desk clerk loudly announces your room number in a crowded lobby, or understanding the resentment when you are ignored in a store where electronic or high-tech equipment is sold. This will give you some insights into the experiences women bring into a buying situation.

Realize how a woman feels when she works full time at the same job as a man, knowing she is only earning 72 cents to his dollar, and at the end of the day, she still has the responsibilities of the house and children. Try to feel as she feels when she reads women pay more than men for cars, dry cleaning, and a host of other products and services. Women are denied membership in some golf clubs or don't receive prime tee times even when the membership may be in her name. Doing business in a man's world isn't always equitable, yet many companies preach that if you treat women as equal in a buying situation, that is all they want. I don't think so. When she walks into a store, sees a commercial or looks at the package design of a product, all the years she has been a woman play a part in her thought processes and her reaction to the situation. It would be foolhardy to believe otherwise.

Myth: Women don't react any differently than men do in a given situation.

Reality Five: What a difference a word or two makes.

One night, I arrived home late. As I wearily exited my car, I heard the sound of a motor under the hood. With keys in hand, it didn't take a mechanic to know something was very wrong. The last thing I wanted to do was deal with the situation, but my instincts told me that waiting until morning was not a good plan. Standing there, pondering what to do, I suddenly remembered the 800 24-hour Roadside Service number I had been given when I purchased my car.

I retrieved the number from my glove compartment and made the call. A man answered, and asked me a few basic questions concerning the type, model, make, year of the car, and what the problem was. He immediately knew what was wrong.

"I'm going to walk you through how to fix it," he calmly stated.

"Me!" I responded, not nearly as calmly. Although I am talented in many areas—I own a public relations, marketing and advertising firm that specializes in consulting and training sales personnel and management on how to successfully sell to women—mechanical projects are not my forté. Even though I work a lot in the automotive industry, my knowledge of cars and my inclination to fix them are limited.

"You can't leave it until morning," I heard him say, as if he truly believed I was going to fix the problem. "Take a kitchen spoon out to the car, open the hood, and locate the battery. You will see three black boxes. Tap on them gently, and the motor will stop," he instructed.

He waited on the phone while I opened the hood and located the battery. But I was unable to find the three black boxes. I went back in and relayed that information to him. He thought for a minute, then said, "Stand next to the hubcap on the driver's side. Look down and turn your head to the right. They will be about 8 to 10 inches from you. I did, and there they were! I don't know how I missed them the first time. I tapped on the first box, as I had been instructed, and the noise stopped!

Now, my adrenaline was really pumping. I rushed back in and grabbed the phone. "You're a genius," I shrieked with excitement. "I can't believe I fixed my car myself," I continued before he had a chance to interject.

By now, I had visions of my friends calling me "Ms. Mechanic." After all, I had fixed my car! I barely paused in my accolades to this marvelous man to write down the nature of my problem as he explained it, so that I could convey the information to my dealer.

Once I had taken the necessary notes, I returned to my lavish praising. The elation I felt at my accomplishment was tremendous. Having to deal with numerous car problems over the years, as most women have, and knowing these situations are generally not pleasant encounters, I felt I had earned the right to be proud of a job well done.

Energized by this unexpected, positive experience with my car, I was anxious to hang up and spend the next hour or two telling this incredible story again and again until I ran out of friends. While this might seem like a minor feat to many—to me it was a triumph worth boasting about.

As I paused for breath, he made his last comment. "Your husband will be so proud of you," he said. Stunned, limp, and deflated, I slowly sank into my chair and quietly hung up the phone. Those eight words— "Your husband will be so proud of you"—echoed in my head.

This man, who one minute and one sentence earlier was my hero, now had crushed the very spirit he had created. He had not only made my day, but my entire week—before he burst the bubble.

Why, I wondered, did he feel compelled to say that?

It had taken him only eight words to go from hero to zero in my eyes.

Had he been a salesperson who had said anything as insensitive, he would have lost the sale. The time invested by both of us would have been wasted. The significance of this scenario might escape some. After all, how could something said so casually make such a big difference? Why would I leave over a few ill-chosen words?

The answer is simple: I am a woman. How I am treated has a decisive influence on where I do business. I want to be respected as an individual regardless of my marital status or gender. I don't need any other reasons. After all, *I am the customer.*

While I would like to end with that story as a testament to the impact that a few words can have, I would be remiss if I neglected to mention some other words that women find offensive—words that will also lose sales. A recent survey conducted by Art Spinella of CNW Marketing Research of Brandon, Oregon, documents how one or two words can lose a sale.[8] Most salesmen are amazed that they can lose a sale simply by addressing the prospect as "honey." When CNW sent out 50,000 questionnaires to female new car buyers, 26,195 women responded. This phenomenal response, more than 50 percent, demonstrates how eager women are to share their car-buying experiences and to air their grievances. Of the respondents, 39 percent said they had been subjected to "terms of endearment," such as "honey" or "babe." Of those, 71 percent said they bought the car elsewhere for no other reason. That is an appalling reason to lose a sale, but it continues to happen.

Whether men agree with this, whether they believe it is petty or ridiculous, isn't the issue. It isn't up for discussion. It's a fact. To a woman, a few words are all it takes to lose the sale.

Sharon Roberts, manager of sales and business training for the education department of Lennox Industries, provides training to the sales staff.[9] "When selling heating, venting and air conditioning equipment, one salesman told me he explained to the husband in great detail about the maintenance and installation of the duct work. 'I really thought I had the sale,' he said. Then he told the wife how nice it would be for her because she wouldn't have to dust so often," said Roberts. He lost the order. Again, a few innocently said words killed a once viable sale.

Myth: Little things aren't as important to women as big things.

Reality Six: Little things are big things to women.

How a woman is treated can be as critical to the sale as the product, price, or color. In fact, most of the time, it is more important. Women want a salesperson who is knowledgeable about the product, who isn't intimidated if she has done her homework and asks technical questions, and who doesn't feel the need to spout extremely detailed and highly technical jargon in order to appear superior.

The astute marketer knows women relate to money differently than men, they value their treatment more and, for the most part, they prefer not to be in an argumentive or unpleasant situation. Women dread confrontation, high-pressure tactics, and negotiation more than men. Understanding these characteristic differences are important in honing your marketing and selling skills to women.

Women value little things more than men. Price is seldom the only criteria to a woman buyer. Value-added services are paramount. They look for someone they can build rapport with; someone they can trust; someone credible. Women connect through conversation. To establish rapport and trust, it is important to ask open-ended questions and to listen to the answers.

Open-ended questions provide you with insights you would not have any other way. Close-ended questions provide pertinent information for you, but they don't show an interest in determining what is important to your customer. Close-ended questions are for the salesperson's benefit, not the customer's. Open-ended questions give the salesperson an opportunity to find out who the customer is, what the motivation for buying is, and why they selected you or your product. Open-ended questions provide a limitless source of information that will make salespersons better able to sell to customers because they will understand their customers' needs.

EXERCISE 2-1

Open-Ended Questions

Write five open-ended questions you would ask a customer who is interested in your product.

1.

2.

3.

4.

5.

Sample Open-Ended Questions

Converting "yes-no" and one-word answers into meaningful information just requires asking the right questions.

❖ How did you hear about us? This type of question tells you if the customer responded to an ad or came as a result of a referral. Or was your store chosen because the customer works or lives close by? These clues make you more aware of the customer and the motivation for the purchase from you.

❖ What features are you looking for? What did you like best about your last _____? (whatever the product—car, stereo, computer)

❖ What did you like least? Why are you buying a new one? Again, you will learn what features are important, and why. Knowing what the customer liked and didn't like about a previously owned product, will help you position the features of your product to be benefits to the customer. Is the customer buying a new one because of a promotion, or because of trouble with the last one?

You can gather a wealth of valuable data. It's yours for the asking.

However, before information can be exchanged between you and the customer, two things have to happen. You must:

1. Ask open-ended questions.
2. Listen to the response.

Listening Is a Selling Skill

A good listener hears what the person is saying; an effective listener hears, understands and takes action, when appropriate.

It is imperative that the salesperson connect with the customer through meaningful dialogue. Better communication occurs when the people involved each have an open mind and try to understand the other person's position.

Salespeople cannot listen if they are doing all the talking. They cannot be listening to what is important to her. Listening, asking open-ended questions, clarifying when you are unsure of what she is saying are all important in establishing rapport. Salespersons must know what features of the product are benefits to her. They should understand her lifestyle, why she is buying the product, why she is purchasing from you. Is she a referral? Is she shopping around? Has she been to other retailers or are you the beginning of her list? How do you compare with the competition? Knowing these answers can provide you with invaluable insights that will assist you in making the sale.

Myth: The customer is always right.

Reality Seven: The customer is always the customer.

While this myth has prevailed through time, I'm not in agreement with it. Experience tells us that customers make mistakes. But whether right or wrong, the inevitable truth is that the customer is always the *customer*. Without them, where would you be?

There are situations where a retail establishment, manufacturer or salesperson must say no to the customer and, therefore, risk losing their business. While some situations can't be resolved, there usually is a viable solution that will sustain a continued relationship with the customer. In Chapter 10, customer satisfaction is discussed. Examples of letters written by customers who have experienced problems are presented. Many of these letters went unanswered. The customer was asking to remain a customer, and the manufacturer or executive turned his back. That is inexcusable. If this is happening in your company, spending millions of dollars to advertise won't change a declining sales trend. Advertising and marketing strategies can only accomplish so much. Corporations need to understand the human side of business. Many have lost touch with the most vital element of their success—the customer.

Many customers are lost because of poor treatment or negative experiences with the store. Others, simply because they didn't feel appreciated. Advertising and marketing budgets must include proper training of the sales staff as part of the marketing mix. Customer satisfaction and service is as important as—if not more important than—price, product, place, and promotion. The importance of the human element cannot be overstated.

In the following chapters, I describe some of the abuses and injustices suffered by the customer because of a lack of caring on the part of the organization. Poor service doesn't lose just one buyer, but many potential buyers and future sales. The message your salespeople communicate may be sending your customers to your competitors.

America has experienced the industrial revolution. Now, we are encountering the service revolution. In the 1990s, customer satisfaction will reign supreme. Those who provide it along with the proper marketing mix will survive, prosper, and grow. Those who don't, won't.

Myth: Selling styles of the 1960s, 1970s, and 1980s are working today.

Reality Eight: Successful salespeople understand the new rules.

When a couple looks at a product together, both are customers. It can be living room furniture, a computer, stereo equipment, or a car. When the salesperson isolates the man as the customer, ignoring the woman, he runs the risk of losing the sale. Often, the reason for ignoring the female customer is that the salesman may feel ill at ease with her. He may think she doesn't understand the product, or he should, as has been traditional, make his sales pitch to the man. However, traditions are changing.

Sharon Roberts, of Lennox Industries, concurs.[10] "Our salesmen frequently misinterpret what women mean. When a women says 'I need to think about it' she frequently means 'I need more information.' Good salesmen know how to listen to and interpret what she says."

Roberts admits that selling heating, ventilating and air condition (HVAC) equipment to women is often difficult for men to do. They tend to give the technical information to the husband rather than the couple.

If a woman is the only buyer, salesmen are uncomfortable and don't know how to communicate with her.

Roberts is conducting sensitivity training sessions at numerous Lennox meetings in order to educate the sales staff and make them more effective in their jobs. "It used to be that when they entered a home, they would shake only the husband's hand. Now with a limited, and often-times dangerous, amount of information on the female customer, a salesman may bypass him entirely in an effort to shake her hand first," said Roberts. "I tell them to shake whomever's hand is closest."

Roberts says the training sessions have been very productive and popular. "Once they 'get it,' the salesmen begin to calculate how many sales they have lost in the past because they were using outmoded techniques."

The more uncomfortable the salesman is with the female customer, the greater is his need for sensitivity and sales training. It is not the responsibility of the customer to make the salesman feel at ease, but the other way around. Understanding the female buyer will be a big step to becoming comfortable with her. Being cognizant of her needs, what angers her, and what she looks for in a salesperson and product will facilitate a smoother, more pleasant sales process for all concerned.

Myth: A thank-you note is always appreciated.

Reality Nine: Salespersons frequently send an unappreciated thank-you note.

Often, even though the sale was made and the woman was happy, a salesperson's actions can ruin any chance for future sales either to the woman or her network. One such action is to send the thank-you note only to the man. This is very common in the automotive industry and probably in many other areas. As mentioned in Myth Eight, when a couple comes in to buy, both are customers. When the thank-you note doesn't include her, it turns the joy with the new product into rage at the salesman. The salesperson has clearly discounted her importance or value. I wonder how a man would feel if he was the customer—he spent the time shopping, made the selection, did the negotiating, and earned the money for the product—but only his wife received the thank-you note.

When you multiply the number of times this happens to women and the number of women friends who hear the story, many manufacturers can count thousands of lost sales by a gesture that was supposed to provide a positive bond with the salesman, not lose future business. Yes, write a thank-you note, but write it to both people. Either one is capable of killing the sale.

Dos and Don'ts with Women

Do address her by name;

Do treat her with respect;

Do listen to what she is saying;

Do answer *her* if she asks the question;

Do project confidence and knowledge;

Do allow her time to gather information;

Do understand how women network;

Do realize that women are loyal customers;

Don't call her honey, dear, or sweetie.

Don't patronize or talk down to her.

Don't do all the talking.

Don't just talk to her husband or male companion.

Don't think charm is a sustitute for product knowledge.

Don't use high-pressure tactics.

Don't think of her as an isolated sale.

Don't lose her and her network.

Sales Checklist

After the prospect leaves the retail establishment, frequently the salesperson dismisses the customer from his mind. What he should do in the next few minutes is give some serious thought to why the customer reacted as she did. "Did she buy because I was courteous to her and knowledgeable about the product? Did she leave because I angered her in some way? If so, what did or didn't I do?"

While this exercise is more beneficial for higher-priced items such as computers, stereo equipment, cars, or financial services, it is useful for all salespeople to reflect how their treatment of customers affects their sales ratio.

On the next page are two checklists that will facilitate this process.

Obviously, in a department or specialty store where the salesperson has numerous customers per hour, this written exercise would be inappropriate. However, the same information can be processed mentally to improve customer satisfaction and sales performance even on low-ticket items.

Whatever the price of the product, both men and women enjoy good service in a pleasant atmosphere. Businesses that provide this, along with a quality product at a competitive price, will win the market in the 1990s.

Checklist #1—After the Customer Leaves

Review your presentation.
____ I was appropriately dressed/appearance okay.
____ I greeted customer promptly, warmly, but professionally.
____ I had good body language.

I did well on the following (Add 2–3 things you think you did very well.)
____ After greeting, I asked open-ended questions.
____ I listened attentively, didn't do all the talking.
____ I transitioned smoothly from asking questions to explaining the product features as benefits to her.
____ I handled objections and concerns (asked for feedback).
____ I closed effectively.

If the customer is a couple:
____ I answered her questions attentively.
____ I needed to pay more attention to her questions and needs.
____ I handled both parties professionally.
____ I addressed my answers to whomever asked the question, and I asked my questions to them both.

Next time I would not:

_____

Did customer buy?   ____ No   ____ Yes
Why, why not? _____
Will she/he be back? _____
What am I going to do to follow up with the customer? _____
_____

Do I need to check back? _____   **When?** _____

Checklist #2—Follow-Up Report
(For Large Ticket Items)

Prospective buyer:
Name(s) _____
Address _____
_____

Home phone number _____ Work phone number _____
Status: Bought _____   Did not buy _____
Note Sent: Yes _____   No _____   Date: _____
Date to check back _____
Comments:

_____

Follow-Up
Date _____   Time _____
How contacted: In writing _____   By phone _____   Other_____
Comments

_____

Date _____   Time _____
Comments

_____

References and Referrals

References and referrals are a key component to growth and expansion. While the power of the press and advertising to reach the masses with hard-hitting, continual messages is certainly acknowledged, an owner or manager should never underestimate the effect word-of-mouth advertising has on his or her business. Whether a product is a one-time purchase or it is bought frequently, whether it is less than a dollar or sells for several hundred dollars, women share their buying experiences with their friends, neighbors, relatives, business associates, and people they have just met. Women can be, and should be, a referral source to build your business.

When to Ask for Referrals

There are several times when it is appropriate to ask for referrals. The conclusion of the sale is the first opportunity. If you or your company follows-up with an evaluation of the product or service either by phone or by mail, you have another shot. If you follow-up and there is a problem, solve the problem first; then, ask for the referral. This will demonstrate that you are responsive to her needs. When sending reminder notices for maintenance, new software updates, etc., you can personalize it, and ask for referrals at that time.

When asking for referrals, be sensitive, tactful, and helpful. If the customer expresses appreciation for the way she was treated, let her know that you would welcome the opportunity to provide the same type of service to her friends or colleagues who might be in the market for your product or service now or in the future.

Always thank your customer for a referral, and if that referral becomes a customer, be sure and thank her again. Depending on the cost of your product or service, a gift to show your appreciation might be appropriate.

Don't think that referrals are exclusive to high-ticket products. They are not. I have referred women to the salesperson I buy make-up from, the salesperson in the career clothing section of a department store who really cared about my needs and to many professional people including accountants, lawyers, and bankers.

Remember three things:

❖ Women share more information with a far greater number of people than men do; they give more referrals;

❖ Women want to help both your business and their friends. A happy, satisfied customer will send you business;

❖ Don't overdo it; be sensitive to the difference between good follow-up and being a pest.

Customer follow-up may seem like a lot of work, and it is, at least at first. But the dividends are great. Once you establish the routine of following up and asking for referrals, you will do it automatically. After all, if someone is willing to do half the work for you—selling the customer on you and the product before she ever enters the store, why wouldn't you want to do everything possible to get and keep that customer and her network?

Big Ticket Items

Many salespeople believe that once the sale is complete, the transaction is concluded. But the salesperson's job isn't finished; in fact, it has just begun. If the product is an item that will require routine maintenance, making sure the customer receives good treatment in the service area is as important as the initial sale. That is, if you hope to sell her or her network in the future.

There are many ways to make sure your customer is satisfied, and that the product is performing as expected.

Smaller Everyday Sales

Not everyone sells big ticket items, but everyone can build loyalty and repeat customers. Good service is not limited to high-priced items. Wal-Mart and McDonald's are excellent examples of stores that pride themselves on providing good customer service for low-priced merchandise. Nordstrom is another example of outstanding service. While the average woman's blouse is considerably more expensive at Nordstrom's than at Wal-Mart, it is still not considered a big ticket item. Yet Nordstrom's reputation for service is nationally known. People pay extra for that service—again demonstrating that price is not the determining factor much of the time.

Stew Leonard's markets in Connecticut made selling produce and dairy products a fine art, and it has paid off with loyal, repeat customers, who send or bring their friends, relatives, and even out-of-town visitors. Imagine a dairy and produce market so special it is someplace you would take an out-of-town guest.

Building loyal customers is important no matter who you are, because without customers, there is no paycheck.

Most of us would provide exceptional service if the wife of the owner or CEO of the company came in to the store because he signs our paycheck. We also know that she has a direct pipeline to the boss. Each customer who enters the store has something in common with the boss' wife. Even though the signature on your check is not the customer's, without her you may not get another one. Any customer can take a complaint to the manager. Many do.

Manufacturers need to make sure customers receive fair treatment and that the sales staff is listening to the customers' needs and helping them select products that fit those needs within their budget. This is as much the manufacturer's responsibility as making sure that there is product on the shelves.

How Differences Between the Genders Affect Sales

According to the *Sports Illustrated* "The American Male '91" study,[11] men place much more emphasis on power, achievement, athletics, and leadership—to be the best at what they do. In the survey, "being a winner" and "being a leader" were twice as important to men as to women; being athletic was nearly three times as important to men. When asked what fantasy profession they would choose, being a famous athlete was number one with men, with a score four times higher than with women. Men also selected being a famous scientist or political leader far more than women. Women placed more emphasis on being responsive to others.[12] Men are more likely to work on cars, build things from scratch, and have dinners out that cost more than $35 per person. Women, by contrast, will prepare more full-course meals, work on crossword puzzles, and buy more books than men.[13]

While this list is only a sampling of the incongruities, it illustrates the dissimilarities between the sexes in undeniable terms. These differences affect the buying styles of the sexes and make the purchasing process different for men and women. For instance, a woman may not buy in a particular place if she is unhappy with the way she is being treated. A *PC Week* article was titled "When Retailers Patronize Women, Women Won't Patronize Their Stores."[14] While the title just about sums up the message, the article went on to examine some of the problems women encounter in a computer store. Even though corporate information centers, PC training divisions, and software companies all have a number of female managers, women are often ignored when they enter the retail computer store.

The article tells of one woman's experience. In it she described how she was in the market for a printer. Upon entering the section of the store with printers, she waited patiently for the salesman to finish with a male customer. When she realized they were just visiting and had no intention of concluding their conversation, she interrupted to ask a question. She received only a partial answer to her query. She left the store vowing never to return again. While male readers may say, "I would have left, too," the truth is they probably wouldn't have had to leave. They would have been seen as a valued customer and waited on.

Let me assure you that the store lost more than one printer sale. She will never buy anything from there again, and neither will her network. In this particular case, she worked in the field professionally, and all her colleagues will hear her "don't ever shop there" story.

The article concludes with a thought-provoking statement: "In a retail market that has become so fiercely competitive, who can afford to turn away customers at the door with such a backward, boorish attitude?"

By 1990, however, the computer industry was beginning to look differently at women. According to *Business Week*, IBM, Apple, Hewlett-Packard and Epson all started including women in their ads—"not as sex objects, but as customers." Computer companies are buying more ad space in women's magazines. From 1988 to 1989, computer advertising in *Working Woman, Redbook, Savvy, Working Mother,* and *Ladies Home Journal* increased from $818,700 to $1,425,740.[15] As more PCs are being sold to women with offices at home, to female middle managers and to women business owners, manufacturers have taken a second look at this growth segment. Like other industries, they tried pastel, then abandoned that idea. Now, they are searching for just the right approach; one that neither panders to nor ignores women.

Women as Valued Customers

Women not only share more information in building and maintaining relationships, but they rely on cooperation and trust. This is ingrained in females from birth. Numerous studies indicate that as they are growing up, girls participate more in group activities in which cooperation with each other is stressed. Boys, on the other hand, participate more in competitive activities, such as sports, where winning is the goal. Building rapport with women customers will establish a foundation for future sales.

Women may not know much about a product or service when they first recognize their need to purchase it, but many do their homework better than their male counterparts. It is inexcusable to make the mistake that the salesperson did in the computer store. Even if the woman customer were a layperson with no professional computer expertise, she deserved better treatment. She very well might have done her homework to learn what she needed and would have been able to ask intelligent questions and understand reasonable answers. Even if she knows nothing, she has a right to expect intelligent answers to her questions—and common courtesy.

Set a Goal

Selling to women can be:

- ❖ Profitable
- ❖ Rewarding
- ❖ An asset to building a business

Losing sales to women that should have been made can be:

- ❖ Costly
- ❖ Frustrating
- ❖ Detrimental to future growth

The best way to make sure that you and your sales staff sell to as many women as possible is to set a goal. Most businesses have a business plan, with certain goals and objectives: how much revenue they project they will earn in six months, a year, or five years. When developing goals, be sure to include the following:

1. What percentage of your business should be sales to women?
2. What percentage of women prospects you want to convert to customers?
3. What percentage of women customers you want to give you a referral?

Then equate this exercise to dollars.

To sell more effectively to women you need to:

❖ Understand their needs.

❖ Understand their thought process and buying style.

❖ Make it a priority.

Selling successfully to women is a conscious decision. You can decide to do it, or not to.

Notes

[1]Shelley Hobson, editor, About Women, Inc.—*Marketing to Women*, interview with author, 31 August 1993.

[2]Ellen Lupton, *Mechanical Brides*, Cooper-Hewitt National Museum of Design Smithsonian Institution (Princeton: Architectural Press, 1993).

[3]*The Wall Street Journal*, August 23, 1989.

[4]Chris Killoy: director of production and marketing management, Smith & Wesson, interview with author, 18 May 1993.

[5]Howard Cooley, former president, Jockey International, interview with author, 25 May 1993.

[6]Joel Arthur Baker, *Future Edge: Discovering the New Paradigms of Success* (New York: William Morrow & Company, Inc., 1992).

[7]Susan Faludi, *Backlash: The Undeclared War Against American Women* (New York: Crown Publishers, Inc., 1991): 192

[8]"Women and Cars," *Adweek's Marketing Week* (10 February 1992): 14.

[9]Sharon Roberts, manager of sales and business training, education department, Lennox Industries, Inc., interview with author, 7 July 1993.

[10]Ibid.

[11]Lieberman Research, Inc., *Sports Illustrated*: "The American Male '91" (New York: The Time Inc. Magazine Company, 1991): 11.

[12]Ibid, 15.

[13]Ibid, 24.

[14]"Women As Consumers," *PCWeek* (11 August 1987): 30.

[15]Mark Lewyn, "PC Makers, Palms Sweating, Try Talking To Women," *Business Week* (15 January 1990): 48.

Part II

Successful Marketing Strategies

Chapter 3
Important Insights from Corporate Giants

Many corporations have successfully adapted to the changing marketplace. As the demographics of the female consumer changed and women's roles evolved from stay-at-home wives to new professional women, companies have had to re-evaluate their positions and adjust accordingly. From the fashion industry, which has always catered to women, to companies that had never before thought of manufacturing and selling to women, transformations have occurred that will have lasting effects on corporate America. New businesses have emerged to fill the gaps left by corporate dinosaurs unwilling or unable to change. Companies that for years had thrived in the marketplace have lost market share that they will never be able to recover. Women are making a lasting impression on the corporate world and on the bottom line of many businesses.

Fashioning Market Strategy

" 'What's the matter with American women?' a French fashion designer snapped at John Molloy, the author of *Dress for Success*, while he was touring design houses in the mid-1980s. 'They don't do as they're told anymore. We tell them how to dress but they just don't listen,'" wrote Susan Faludi in her best-seller, *Backlash*.[1]

This statement is indicative of the new independence women have been expressing in the marketplace since the early to mid-1980s. "Give us what we want, or we won't buy," became a prevalent attitude toward the fashion industry, as well as many other businesses.

According to Faludi, in the early 1980s Wells Rich Greene conducted one of the largest studies of women's fashion-shopping habits. They found that the more confident and independent women became, the less they liked to shop; and the more they enjoyed their work, the less they cared about their clothes. If this conclusion is accurate, as more and more women establish careers not just go to a job, they will view fashion in a different light than previous generations of women. The fashion industry must adjust to women's new lifestyles and stop clinging to traditional concepts from the past. As *Backlash* documents, the money women spent on apparel in the past will be allocated to different merchandise. From 1980 to 1986, even though they were purchasing more houses, cars, and dinners out, women spent far less on apparel, voicing their dissatisfaction with the fashion trends. In 1987, dress sales dropped 4 percent. Conversely, men's apparel sales rose 2.1 percent the same year.[2]

As women expressed approval of the use of real women in ads, rather than young, ultra-thin models, so have they spoken out against very youthful fashions made for anorexic women. The average woman is 32 years old, weighs 143 pound and wears a size 10 or 12 dress. If fashions are not designed for the average American woman, she will withdraw her dollars from the marketplace. In the late 1980s, that is exactly what she did. "How could the industry make such a marketing blunder?" Joseph Ellis, a Goldman Sachs retail analyst, asked.[3] Ellis's conclusion was that the designers, manufacturers, and retailers went in exactly the wrong direction because they lacked appropriate consumer research studies.

With women going to work in such large numbers, women's needs shifted from stay-at-home clothes to work clothes. In 1987, more than 70 percent of the skirts purchased were for professional wardrobes. Professional women were making their presence felt. Patricia Aburdene and John Naisbitt recognized that the professional woman would affect the fashion industry. In *Megatrends for Women* they wrote, "The movement of women over 40 into positions of corporate and political leadership will revolutionize fashion and retailing. As presidents of their own firms and corporate vice presidents, fortysomething women will be the first generation to define and perfect the female executive image of elegance and authority."[4]

Regardless of their position, today 57 million women need something to wear to work. Designers like Donna Karan carved a niche by designing comfortable, elegant professional clothing for executive women. Karan understood professional women, what they wanted, and what they needed for their new lifestyle. Being a women, she had the unique ability to understand fit, unlike her male colleagues. Male designers who once ruled Seventh Avenue began to topple. Karan wasn't the only female designer to take advantage of the opportunity to provide working women with what the male designers were ignoring. "Liz Claiborne generates almost four times the women's clothing sales of the top three male designers combined," wrote Aburdene and Naisbitt.[5]

Shop-at-Home Trends

Today's educated, savvy female consumers have clearly spoken to the fashion industry. However, innovative shopping techniques have emerged that target the working woman who isn't in the executive suite. For working women who may not have an acceptable wardrobe but who have limited funds, factory outlet malls have proven to be a wonderful solution. This phenomenon is the fastest growing segment of the retail industry, with more than 300 malls, up from just 32 in 1982. Discount malls now house more than 8,500 stores. This growth trend is projected to continue for at least the next couple of years.[6]

The other growth segment is the $2 billion a year shop-at-home cable channels. "Joseph Segal, founder and chairman of QVC (Quality, Value, Convenience) cable channel, was the first to recognize that shopping could be part of the entertainment industry." In 1991, sales were about $1 billion. Operating 24-hours a day, the flexible format allows the busy career woman to shop at her convenience. The shows are seen in more than 45 million homes.[7]

In 1993, QVC and HSN (Home Shopping Network) merged. The estimated $2 billion business is nearly 99 percent controlled by this cable giant. Major retailers—Saks Fifth Avenue, Macy, and Nordstrom's—are all investigating home shopping programs on cable.[8]

Seventy percent of QVC customers are enterprising women who don't want to stop on their way home or go out again to shop for themselves and their families. With less leisure time, home shopping fills a growing need in the marketplace.

Catalog buying is another option that allows working women to shop at their leisure. Between 1984 and 1989, direct mail retailers experienced an average annual growth in apparel sales of 25 percent. During the 1990s, Saks Fifth Avenue, Neiman Marcus, and Bloomingdale's all experienced significant revenue growth from their direct marketing efforts.[9]

According to the Direct Marketing Association, more than half the adult population orders merchandise through the mail or by phone. In the past decade, the number of adults using direct shopping increased 77 percent, while the population increased only 16.2 percent (Table 3-1).

Table 3-1	Direct Marketing		
Year	Population	Direct Shoppers	% of Population
1992	184.1*	101.6*	55.2
1990	181.1	98.6	52.6
1985	164.9	76.2	46.2
1983	158.4	57.4	36.2

*In millions

Sources: Direct Marketing Association
            Simmons Market Research Bureau

In 1992, consumers spent $51.5 billion on catalog merchandise, compared to $48.8 billion the year before. The average household received approximately 1.8 catalogs per week and 1.8 direct mail pieces per day, totalling approximately 13 billion direct mail items. Each year more than 8,500 different catalogs are published. More than 88 percent of Americans read and look at catalogs received in the mail. Slightly more than 77 percent read direct mail advertising, which includes materials from non-profit organizations, financial institutions, contests and sweepstakes, and records, magazines, and book solicitations. Two-thirds of those who received the material found it interesting and useful. More than 90 percent of consumers who utilize direct mail and phone shopping are satisfied with the experience.[10]

Direct mail, catalogs, and home shopping channels are having a monumental impact on retail shopping as we knew it in the 1980s and early 1990s. Marketers that are not utilizing this approach as part of their total marketing and distribution mix may find themselves shut off from a large segment of women shoppers in the twenty-first century.

Marketing to Women in the Nineties— JC Penney and Sears Roebuck

Monitoring trends, listening to customers, and meeting their needs are what maintains and increases market share. Women today are demanding more. They look for companies that show concern for women's issues and have programs that support women. Manufacturers who do more than just make a product—those that have a social conscience as well— appeal to professional women.

With more women working, smart businesses have adjusted their advertising and marketing strategies to accommodate the working women's busy schedule and new interests. "We run a lot more ads and pre-prints on Sunday rather than during the week," said Gail Duff-Bloom, executive vice president and director of administration at JC Penney.[11] "Women are too tired when they get home from work. Our readership is larger on Sundays." Penney also advertises on radio and targets television shows that are most popular with women.

"Nineties women shop with a company that supports women and women's issues," said Duff-Bloom. Penney sponsors the Memorial Day Women's Golf Skins Game on national television, as well as Lyn St. James, the only woman race car driver in the Indy 500.

"On a local basis, we provide leadership seminars or co-sponsor events in 21 major markets. A two-day program like Visions draws between 15,000 and 35,000 women, depending on the market."

Penney gears its promotions to the diverse communities in which it resides. The Mother's Day in-store displays featured a variety of lifestyles, age groups, races, and nationalities, including young mothers, grandmothers, African-Americans, and Caucasians. "We want our advertising to reflect our customer base," said Duff-Bloom. "In the Sunday tabloid pre-prints, our focus is on lifestyle rather than price points. We hope our customers find value in the story copy connected with the merchandise, and are not just looking at price."

Sears Roebuck and Company is also developing programs it believes will be attractive to the woman shopper in the 1990s. According to Jerry Welsh, president of Welsh Marketing Associates Inc., Sears recognizes that women between 25 and 54 are the primary decision makers in the purchases of home furnishings and apparel.[12] "While Sears has developed a strong reputation for its durable tools and automotive area, it is interested in developing the reputation of being female friendly as well," said Welsh.

Sears is launching a major program to increase the awareness of women as the primary caretaker of the family. "The Women's Wellness program will offer fitness, nutrition, and screening information to women at its stores. It will start in five cities in 1993 and expand to more than 30 in 1994.

"Our goal is to encourage women to be the primary advocates for their own wellness and to promote their own well-being through proper eating and lifestyle changes," said Welsh. Sears will be creating events to promote the program in various cities they have targeted. They are hiring prominent female spokespersons to help deliver the message. In addition, the "cause-related marketing" effort will benefit local charities, which will receive a percentage of all monies charged on the Sears credit card during a given time parameter. The last phase of the program involves training college students to disperse much of the lifestyle-enhancing and medical information that will be given out at the stores.

"There will be tote bags filled with information and other gifts given to women who participate in the program," said Welsh. "We really think the inter-generational approach of using college students will have a significant impact on the program. It will also provide a forum for young women to develop a sense of wellness early."

From a marketing prospective, the most important aspect of the women's wellness effort will be to position Sears as the one store most closely in touch with the lifestyles and interests of multi-generations of women.

Give the Customer What She Wants— Jockey International

Howard Cooley, president of Jockey International, didn't believe in abandoning an idea he knew was right. For years Jockey had received letters from women asking them to make a women's line of underwear, but the company ignored the request.[13]

In 1982, shortly after Cooley became president, he proposed the concept at a high-level marketing meeting. The idea met with rejection on all fronts. His senior advisors were horrified, his advertising agency was aghast, and retailers said NO. Everyone agreed this move would destroy Jockey's strong masculine image. "Women won't buy underwear without lace," they told him, "and they certainly won't buy panties with the male Jockey label on the waistband."

Cooley was undaunted by the pessimism. He refused to let this totally male input decree what women wanted and what they would buy. Instead of backing down, he instructed his managers to solicit women's opinions and advice. Unlike his predecessors, he believed that the female customer knew better what she wanted than the male-dominated boardroom.

Cooley didn't believe that the lingerie currently on the market was well designed. "It just didn't fit women's bodies," he said. He reasoned that a better fitting product would sell better. Jockey carefully selected materials for their new product that would accomplish this goal. The elasticity of the material enabled the women's underwear to have the same durability and fit as the men's line. Even though Jockey made some design changes to make the product more appealing to women, Cooley felt it was important that women know what brand they were wearing.

The Jockey name was on the waistband in muted tone-on-tone printing rather than the bolder type of the men's briefs.

Winning over his executive board and getting the product manufactured weren't the only obstacles Cooley had to overcome. The marketplace was as resistant to change as was his company. Even after Jockey discovered the market was viable, and even after the product was designed and manufactured, getting it into stores was another hurdle to overcome. Retailers criticized the packaging concept, as well as the product. "We were told that women wouldn't buy underwear in packages. That they had to hold it up," said Cooley. "My belief was that if women could trust the size on the package, that process would be unnecessary. After little success with retailers who wanted nothing to do with Jockey for Her, a woman merchandiser at Bloomingdale's gave us a try. She promoted it with ads and decent space in the store. It was very, very successful, and Marshall Field's quickly added the line," said Cooley. "After that, all the others began to buy."

Since 1983 when Jockey for Her was introduced, the product has experienced tremendous success. The initial advertising campaign was created to appeal to all women. It featured young women, grandmothers, and all types in-between, from size 4 to size 10. "We got a lot of thank-you letters from older women who appreciated being part of intimate apparel ads. The most letters we got for any one ad was for the grandmother ad," said Cooley. "We didn't use professional models in any advertising, at least while I was president," he commented.

Within five years of its introduction, "Jockey for Her" became the most popular brand of women's underwear in the nation and garnered an incredible 40 percent share of the market. Manufacturers who had traditionally made women's lingerie watched their market share continue to decline. Unwilling to change their product to fit the needs of women, they preferred to remain isolated in their predominantly male-managed environment, producing what they thought women should buy, rather than what women were clearly saying they wanted.

"Today other companies like Fruit of the Loom and Hanes have copied the product," said Cooley. Traditional lingerie companies have also added cotton panties to their product line, but they will never recapture the market share they once enjoyed. Jockey, who is still listening to the consumer, introduced a second version of Jockey for Her. "Some women want the silky feel of traditional lingerie and the fit and comfort of Jockey for Her," said Cooley. In 1992, Jockey International created a new product, Jockey for Her Soft Elegance. Though Cooley has since retired, he definitely left his mark on the company.

Making Bigger Better—
Mothers Work and Executive Mother

Christine LaBastille and Rebecca Matthias had two things in common: They were pregnant professional women, and they had nothing to wear. When Matthias became pregnant in the early 1980s, she couldn't find appropriate clothes. "Before I was pregnant, I wore a lot of navy suits with ties. I needed that look, but I couldn't find professional looking maternity clothes."[14] As a result, she decided to start a mail-order maternity business. That way, she could stay at home with her baby and still work. What she hadn't counted on was not being able to find suitable products to sell. That's when she realized that manufacturing would have to be a part of her plan.

Mothers Work opened its first store in 1984. Within a short period of time, there were 22 franchised retail outlets. While franchising generated the cash-flow necessary for expansion, it diminished Matthias' control. By 1992, she had bought back all but two franchises. In March 1993, she took the company public. The company now operates 72 Mothers Work locations and 25 Mimi's stores.

She attributes her success to many factors. As department stores and mom-and-pop operations began to drop maternity lines, specialty maternity stores flourished. Her keen business insight let her take advantage of the opportunity to be a key player in this developing industry.

The second, and probably most important reason, for her success is the customer service she provides. With her husband's computer expertise, they designed a system that provides daily feedback on sales. "We know what is selling and what isn't," said Matthias. "We listen to our customers and adjust our product line accordingly." In addition to talking directly to their customers and watching the daily computer data, Matthias, along with everyone in the company, works four to six hours each week selling in the stores. "We make sure the garments fit properly, among other things."

Her success also can be attributed to the product. "We offer things in the store that pregnant women who want to dress professionally can't get other places," said Matthias.

Matthias advertises in local newspapers in areas where stores are located and nationally in women's magazines, such as *Glamour* and *Self*. Their customer base is comprised of upscale professional women, who often bring their husbands with them shopping. "We try to make the shopping experience approachable for men."

Christine LaBastille's company's customer profile is a pregnant woman in her thirties looking for business attire. "I had trouble finding things to wear when I was pregnant," said LaBastille.[15] While her store, Executive Mother, located in New York, has all types of maternity wear, from casual to evening apparel, it has a larger selection of business attire than most maternity stores. Conservative dresses and separate skirts and jackets are stocked for the woman who prefers a suited look. In addition, the store markets items for newborns, including baby gift baskets, which are displayed in front to catch passersby's attention.

LaBastille opened her store in November 1988. Sales were just under $1 million in 1992. Her mix of maternity apparel, infant clothing and toys add to the revenue and appeal. The merchandise mix expands the customer base from just mothers to grandparents, godparents, and friends. "My target market is dual-income women who spend between $100 and $200 on an outfit," said LaBastille.

LaBastille enhances her visibility by speaking at conferences on women's issues and sending out public relations write-ups and letters to the editor. She also advertises in local business publications and the Yellow Pages.

Dialogue Makes a Difference— Nike and New Balance

Nike, Inc. created an extremely successful ad campaign to launch their women's line of shoes and apparel, but not without a struggle. Kate Bednarski was Nike's Women's Marketing Manager during the creation and launch of the products and accompanying advertising campaign.[16]

Bednarski's mission was to convince the male-dominated Nike management that it would be profitable to target the women's market, and that it would not diminish their sales to men. Good marketing strategies indicated that it would be opportunistic to take advantage of the growing female market. Yet, among the male executives, the fear that Nike would somehow lose its prestige as a young male brand was omnipresent.

Bednarski saw real benefits for Nike and for women. Her goal was to change Nike's flat profit line by adding a profitable women's product line. She also knew that they could garner a lot of media attention when the product was launched if it was done properly. In addition, she was motivated by the goal of making a better product for women.

While the management team all agreed in theory, they didn't support their words with actions. Bednarski recalled, "They paid lip service, but when it came to supporting the program with dollars, the advertising budget and staff for the woman's effort always got cut." Meanwhile, Reebok was making a name in the aerobics shoe business with women.

"Nike's original products weren't attractive. They didn't fit well and were launched under another name, Side One. Women wanted Nike; they didn't want an off-brand," remarked Bednarski.

After the first ad campaign that merely substituted women athletes in place of male jocks was a dismal failure, Charlotte Moore and Janet Champ were put in charge of creating a campaign that would appeal to women. According to Champ in an interview with *Lear's* magazine, "The most disastrous ad, one especially tailored for women, showed triathlete Joanne Ernst sweating her way through a hard-core training regimen, then turning to her audience and saying, 'While you're at it, why don't you stop eating like a pig?' "[17]

"Eighty-five percent of the population was really turned off," said Champ.

"Even though both Janet and I live in the world that women live in," said Charlotte Moore, art director for the project who is now associate creative director at Wieden & Kennedy, "we spent a lot of time thinking and researching for the campaign. We wrote copy that we would want to read. We spoke to the female audience the way we wanted to be spoken to."[18]

Champ and Moore spent days just reading women's publications to see the messages that women were being bombarded with, and to craft a rebuttal. They discovered that there was a tremendous amount of information continuously preaching to women that they had to be perfect beings. "Both the ads and the articles were geared for quick fixes. Lose weight in 10 easy days, and so on. The magazines made it seem easy to have it all, and that's just not true. It's not easy," said Moore.

Moore and Champ believed that, while demographic data has its place, total dependence on statistics misses the human element in the marketplace. Even looking at psychographic information and lifestyle trends isn't always enough.

"Good advertising has instinct as well as quantifiable data," stated Moore. "The human element is important." Of course, Moore, Champ, and Bednarski had an advantage in understanding and thinking like the women they were targeting. "Men would not have created the same campaign," added Moore.

Bednarski seconded that statement. In fact, she had a tough time getting the campaign approved. "The women on the marketing team were all emotionally moved; the men just didn't get it. They called it 'The Empathy Campaign,' when it was really 'The Dialogue Campaign,' " asserted Bednarski. "Our strategy was to create ads that really communicated with women, ads that encouraged them to do something good for themselves, to raise their self-esteem."[19]

Nike conducted research with approximately 20 focus groups around the country; they did in-home interviews and direct mail surveys. They were amazed to discover that women placed themselves last on their list of priorities.

"I was alarmed by this," said Bednarski. "Women in our society need to be talked to differently in the media than they presently are. They need to be marketed to differently."

Headlines that read, "Why are we so hard on ourselves?" and "Did you ever wish you were a boy?" captured the inner feelings of women. Four, eight, and twelve-page inserts were designed to create a mood, not just to showcase a product. "Falling in Love in Six Acts: A passion play" was the first of twelve pages. The copy went through the six stages, from "Lust" to "The Finale." (See one of the Nike ads in Chapter 6.)

Nike's marketing strategies included an 800 number women could call to communicate with the company. It provided two-way interaction for the customers. Women could, and did, share their feelings on the campaign—in record numbers. By calling the same 800 number, they could also receive a Nike Women's Source Book picturing Nike's other products. The book contained a listing of their dealers, nationally by state, brief bios on some of the models featured, and other tidbits of information from Nike staff members.

The campaign initially ran only in print. But in February 1993, Nike launched a two-month $13 million advertising effort, including TV, aimed at women.

Revenue from the women's line for fiscal year 1993 is projected to be around $400 million.

New Balance, another manufacturer of athletic shoes, is pitching many of their ads to women with a headline that reads, "Presenting shoes designed by women, built by women and tested by women. All to ensure one thing: They fit women." New Balance's target is obvious. Another ad in the series will feature a female engineer who spent 12 years building jet aircraft, and then decided to build a shoe.

New Balance's unique niche has been its width sizing. This feature of customized fitting is not available in other athletic shoes. "In the past, we haven't paid as much attention to the look of the shoe as the fit. Now, we are concentrating on both," stated John Donovan, manager of marketing services for New Balance Athletic Shoes, Inc. "Our consumer has typically been older, in the 25–50 range. Now, we are marketing to the younger woman, as well, and the appearance of the shoe is very important."[20]

New Balance also is aware that women respond to cause-marketing. Among other things, New Balance participates in the Susan G. Koman's Race for the Cure run each year. Another approach to the socially conscious consumer is the "made in America" pitch. According to *Inc.* magazine, New Balance produces the majority of their shoes in this country versus the mega-brands, Nike and Reebok, which produce overseas.[21]

Like many products, the athletic shoe is heavily market-driven. Nike's and Reebok's combined sales to men and women last year were $3.3 billion, more than half of the total market. With Nike spending around $120 million in advertising and Reebok about $100 million, New Balance will be hard pressed to compete in this area. In 1993, Jim Davis, chairman and CEO of New Balance Athletic Shoe Inc., plans to spend $6 million, up from $1 million in 1990. His media buys—*Self, Glamour,* and *Working Woman*—are all part of the company's strategy to attract the female buyer.

No More Male Baggage
Samsonite

Samsonite has realized that as more women travel for business, they will need more luggage. Their Silhouette line is very functional and comes in a variety of colors that appeal to both women and men.

"Some of our businesswomen customers thought our tapestries were too loud. They asked Samsonite for more subtle tapestry fabrics, and we responded," said Paige Miller, director of marketing service.[22] As a result, the company created the Esteem Professional Collection geared especially to women. The garment bag is longer to better accommodate women's dresses, but when it folds for carrying—it folds in thirds, instead of in half—it is actually shorter than other garment bags. It has a special pouch for jewelry and a softer look. The hardware on it is almost jewelry-like in design. The pieces are light and on wheels to make them easier to transport.

"The line has done very well," said Miller. "It was designed by a woman, with features that women like and need. It's not real bulky and has a lot of nice touches. Our intention is for our luggage to meet the needs of today's women. If our present lines aren't doing that, then we need to create something that does."

After Samsonite produced the luggage, they placed ads in women's magazines with an attention-catching headline: "We think women should carry their own bags." The copy tells the reader that: "After all, for years the shapes, styles and designs of the luggage you carry were geared to 'fashions' dictated by men. But now, to a world of men's luggage comes the Esteem Professional Collection by Samsonite." The ad ends with an 800 number.

Samsonite is just one of many companies that has experienced a positive impact on their sales revenue by tailoring both products and advertising to capture a piece of the professional woman's market.

Some Do It Right—
Southwest Airlines

Southwest Airlines is a shining star in the airline industry. As major carriers continue to post record losses, Southwest's profit line continues its upward slope. Southwest, founded as a commuter carrier, has maintained its niche marketing and, as a result, has continued to prosper. With three women vice presidents, Southwest understands the businesswoman's needs. "I travel four days a week," said Camille Keith, vice president of special marketing. "I talk to a lot of passengers to find out what they like and don't like."[23]

In her position, Keith is concerned with attracting and keeping women business travelers. One program that was created in Dallas is "No Pumps, No Pearls, No Pantihose." Professional women are invited to the Southwest facility for a 9 to 2 Saturday meeting. The day consists of business speakers, community issues, and group exercises. An aerobic instructor helps the group wake up with a brisk, but brief workout. The casual apparel and the format of the program lend themselves to productivity and networking. In addition, the event benefits the Women's Center of Dallas.

Keith's department participates in regional and national conferences, especially those related to the role of women in society. She speaks to approximately 50 groups annually, many of which are women's organizations, and she meets with key customers and influential women in Southwest's 37 markets. "Women aren't shy. They don't mind telling me what they want. They like the on-time, low cost, high frequency that we provide. They also like the 'friends fly free' program."

Keith finds many of the things that are attractive to the female consumer, men like as well. But that seems to be true in most industries. Where Southwest targets female customers differently than males is in its special programming, not in the air. "Our airline magnifies the changes in America," said Keith. "With more women traveling, we include them as a part of our overall company's marketing strategies, as we always have."

Price Isn't Always the Determinant— American Airlines

Some airlines don't understand the woman's market as well as they should. Since American is not a commuter airline for short destinations, the female customer's needs are different. Getting to and from the parking area is a problem. Managing luggage is a problem. Security, especially at night, is a problem.

Kristin Fullingim travels a lot.[24] As a frequent traveler, she has seen many improvements in hotels, but few on airlines. "Some airlines have added a few healthy meals, but not many." In fact, she misses some of the services she previously enjoyed. For instance, the Express Valet Service, once available at Dallas/Fort Worth International Airport, isn't there anymore. "Remote parking is dangerous. Most women park close, right by the terminal," said Fullingim. Although I called American Airlines' corporate communications person to inquire about this, or to ask if they had any plans that women business travelers would perceive as helpful, I never got an answer. I spoke briefly with him twice; both times he promised to call me back, but never did. My only assumption is that American Airlines sees nothing it can do to try to capture the woman's market—a faulty assumption. Many other industries have succeeded, but American hasn't even noticed this is a market it should be addressing. But then, again, if its PR person finds dealing with customers too bothersome, no wonder American is in trouble.

When a company decides that price is the only variable by which a customer makes a purchasing decision, either it is not offering value or it doesn't understand the woman's market. At a recent speech I attended, Ted Tedesco, American's vice president of corporate affairs, explained that price is the only factor that people use to determine the airline they fly.[25] This is not true of the women I have talked with. Most would willingly, even eagerly, pay a small additional charge for more security and assistance. But American is locked in its corporate world, deciding what passengers want and don't want. And frequently it is not guessing right. One could surmise that a shift in strategy is needed.

Asking customers what they want and giving it to them is a proven method that leads to success. Unfortunately, often other concepts are developed and implemented first.

Services Helpful to Women Travelers—
Super Shuttle and ExecuCar

As the travel industry grows, companies such as Super Shuttle and ExecuCar have developed. Getting to and from the airport isn't as easy as it used to be, and women travelers are reluctant to park in remote areas. They prefer the door-to-door service these companies offer.

According to Terry Merrick, director for ExecuCar and Super Shuttle, their services are now offered in about a half dozen cities.[26] There are a number of men and women who are frequent users of this service. "Women usually park in short-term parking, close to the terminal because of security. Our service offers much greater security and service, although it is more expensive." Women whose companies pay for these expenses, or who can afford it, frequently opt for the easier, safer service where available.

Being on the Cutting Edge—
Gillette

When Jill Shurtleff, the Gillette Company's only female industrial designer, was given the assignment to research the market and create a new razor for women, she began by looking at the competitions' products.[27] After studying the primarily T-shaped razors for women, that except for color, size, or other slight modifications had basically the same design as men's razors, she knew a radical change was needed. She realized that men and women shave very differently. Men shave standing up while viewing their faces in well-lit mirrors. Women, on the other hand, often shave in dimly lit showers and in awkward positions. Understanding that the same design was unsuitable for a woman's needs, Shurtleff designed the flat, broad handle Sensor for Women. Within six months, the company had sold 7.7 million units. Even with its mid-year introduction, sales topped $40 million the first six months and garnered 60 percent of the market.

The Sensor for Women is the best selling razor on the market, including both men's and women's lines. According to *Business Week*, one reason for its spectacular success is its unique design. That design solved an unmet consumer need—when women tried it, they liked it.[28]

Entertaining Women

Like many other industries, the Hollywood film industry is male dominated: Hollywood movie executives are mostly male, the films' story-lines are male-oriented, and the biggest stars are male. Despite the fact the two top-grossing films in 1990 earned the big bucks they did because of female ticket holders, Hollywood executives are slow to respond to this growing and profitable market. While many contend that movie executives are good businessmen and will build on this untapped market of women viewers, only time will tell how much they actually will invest.

Pretty Woman and *Ghost* are considered "women's pictures." *Pretty Woman* grossed more than $172 million in ticket sales; *Ghost,* nearly $150 million. Pitted against successful male thrillers the results were very impressive. *Die Hard 2* made $112 million in ticket sales. *Total Recall* sold $117 million. However, both these films were almost twice as expensive to produce as either of the two "women's films."[29]

The *Rambo* series shows the bottom-line impact of women as ticket buyers for the so-called male thrillers. According to David Rosenfelt, executive vice president of marketing for Tri-Star Pictures, about 40 percent of the audience for both *Rambo II* and *Rambo III* was female. That equates to about $60 million. Approximately, the same amount spent by women to see *Love Story* and *Terms of Endearment.*[30]

Still other movies whose main audiences were women, rather than young males 25 and under, were *Rain Man* and *Three Men and a Baby.* *Rain Man* grossed approximately $150 million. Fifty-five percent of the average audience was female, and two-thirds was over 25. *Three Men and a Baby* grossed more than $167 million, and 61 percent of the audience was female. (All figures are for this country and from income in movie theaters only.)[31]

The development of movie theaters in shopping malls and the mega-theater facilities have undoubtedly been factors in attracting more women to the movies. Women are comfortable with the atmosphere. They know where the malls are; they can shop and take in a movie on the same trip, and they feel safe.

Women are looking for entertainment and escapism from the week's work—work that has provided discretionary income for entertainment and rewards. The fact that more women are single also contributes to the rise in the number of female moviegoers. Whatever the reason, savvy movie marketers need to re-examine their strategies. Women as major consumers in the entertainment industry is a concept worth careful attention. Movie executives interested in expanding their prime market beyond the young male under 25 should produce movies and advertising messages to reach this previously under-targeted market segment.

Notes

[1] Susan Faludi, *Backlash: The Undeclared War Against American Women* (New York: Crown Publishers, Inc., 1991), 171.

[2] Ibid, 169–174.

[3] Ibid, 171.

[4] Patricia Auburdene and John Naisbitt, *Megatrends for Women* (New York: Villard Books, 1992), 188–192.

[5] Ibid, 189.

[6] Ibid, 210.

[7] Ibid, 211.

[8] Joan Warner, *Business Week* (26 July 1993): 54–60.

[9] *Bobbin*, no. 33: 20–24.

[10] Deborah Zizmore, director of public relations, Direct Marketing Association, news release, May 1993.

[11] Gail Duff-Bloom, executive vice president and director of administration, JC Penney, interview with author, 27 May 1993.

[12] Jerry Welsh, president, Welsh Marketing Associations, Inc., interview with author, 22 September 1993.

[13] Howard Cooley, former president, Jockey International, interview with author, 25 May 1993.

[14] Rebecca Matthias, founder/CEO, Mothers Work/Mimi Maternity, interview with author, 12 July 1993.

[15] Christine LaBastille, president/owner, Executive Mother, interview with author, 18 May 1993.

[16] Kate Bednarski, president, Dialogue Marketing Concepts, interview with author, 29 June 1993.

[17] Eva Pomice, "They Just Did It: Nike's Bold Campaign to Women Strikes a Chord," *Lear's* (March 1993): 129–130.

[18] Charlotte Moore, associate creative director, Wieden & Kennedy, interview with author, 22 June 1993.

[19] Bednarski.

[20] John Donovan, manager of marketing services, New Balance, interview with author, 7 July 1993.

[21]*Inc.*, May, 1993.

[22]Paige Miller, director of marketing services, Samsonite, interview with author, 30 August 1993.

[23]Camille Keith, vice president of special marketing, Southwest Airlines, interview with author, 24 April 1993.

[24]Kristin Fullingim, executive account manager, AT&T, interview with author, 15 June 1993.

[25]Ted Tedesco, speech to D/FW National Association of Women Business Owners, 1993.

[26]Tessy Merrick, director, ExecuCar, interview with author, 28 July 1993.

[27]Bruce Nussbaum, "Hot Products: Smart Design is the Common Thread," *Business Week* (7 June 1993): 54–57.

[28]Mark Maremont, "A New Equal Right: The Close Shave,"*Business Week* (29 March 1993): 58–59.

[29]Dottie Enrico, "Leading Ladies After a Summer of Successful 'Women's Pictures,' Hollywood May Target a Female Audience," *Sun Sentinel* (13 October 1990): D–1.

[30]Nina J. Easton, "John Rambo—Mr. Sensitive? 'Un-macho Rambo III' Ads Aimed at Women, " *Los Angeles Times* (10 June 1988): 6–19.

[31]Ibid.

Chapter 4

Industries Women Are Impacting

What industries are women impacting? In some way or another, almost every industry will feel the influence of women during this decade. Automotive, breweries, cosmetics, country clubs, fashion, financial, fitness, golf courses, hotels, magazines, medical, movies, newspapers, politics, sports, toys . . . the list is endless. Most will have to realign their marketing strategies if they hope to capture the new professional woman's dollars.

Many corporations have welcomed the professional woman and have already experienced tremendous growth as massive numbers of women consumers have entered the work force. Others have suffered as they try to cope with issues affecting women. Understanding and meeting the needs of the new professional women is essential to businesses that hope to grow and prosper this decade. "Business as usual" is a cliché that doesn't reflect the current marketplace.

What designs appeal to women? What features do women want? What is the best way to reach them? What are they buying and why? What impact will advertising have on them? These are just a few questions confronting manufacturers, retailers, marketers, and advertising agencies.

Dividing a number of industries into a few categories will facilitate a look at these and other issues. This chapter will discuss only the first three categories:

1. Manufacturers that have always considered women their prime consumer.

2. Manufacturers that make products for which the male market is saturated. Their new strategy: produce a product to sell to women.

61

3. Products that once were almost totally male-consumed, and through no efforts of their makers, now have a significant number of women buyers.

4. Products, equally appealing to either gender, that have other criteria for market segmentation.

5. Companies that have no clear idea who their market is and if it has changed. They probably won't live long enough to tell their story.

Women as the Prime Market

Medical services, cosmetics, and household cleaners are just the beginning of a long list of businesses that have always considered women their major market. But even in these fields, marketing executives and advertising gurus have realized that, as the lifestyles and living patterns have shifted, there must also be a paradigm shift if the company is to thrive.

Not all women are entering the workplace. Some stay home because their economic situations allow this choice, and they have chosen to be full-time mothers, community leaders, or homemakers. But, full-time homemakers are becoming a rare breed. While many women work part-time or leave the workplace for a few years to rear young children, most women entering the work force this decade will work for the majority of their adult lives.

Revamping the party or door-to-door sales concept was important for a number of companies. Tupperware restructured its home parties to "value for time" classes run by consultants not hostesses.[1] Tupperware watched its sales continue to drop as women had less leisure time for either "party" or "class" buying. In addition to the decline in the number of in-home shoppers, 12,000 saleswomen left the company for other employment between 1982 and 1987. The company that had experienced phenomenal success for three decades saw sales plummet from $878 million to $777 million in just two years.[2]

The party concept lost even more ground as covered storage dishes and similar products became readily available at grocery stores. Tupperware, in an attempt to recapture these once-loyal customers, has taken its programs into the workplace with "work site parties." There now is a toll-free number for customers to request a catalog or place an order.

Another problem facing Tupperware's marketing was its image—the outdated products colored in frosted pastels were not a reflection of today's tastes. As a solution, industrial designer Morison Cousins was hired to soften the look. Cousins believed that rounding the product's edges would better reflect the popular styles of many of today's commodities, including computers and the Ford Taurus.[3]

Another home sales company affected by the increasing number of working women is Avon. Avon's recent ads that read, "By Phone . . . By Fax . . . By Mail . . . By Rep" epitomizes a company that has seen the marketplace evolve and has consciously offered consumers options that fit their busy lifestyles. To minimize declining revenues, many companies have modified their sales and marketing strategies to accommodate the customer who no longer stays at home.

Marketing to Women Is More Important Than It Used to Be

Until recently, the medical profession consisted of primarily male doctors and female nurses. Women patients felt their symptoms were often minimized, and their complaints were taken less seriously than a man's; their frustration with the medical system continued to grow. As more women became doctors rather than nurses, women had choices they never had before. Today, 50 percent of primary care physicians, 20 percent of the 31,000 members of the American College of Obstetricians and Gynecologists, and 36 percent of all U.S. medical students are women.

Two forces created the new direction. As more women became physicians, patients had a new choice—they could select a woman doctor. And, as more women entered the work force, they became politically active and began to stand up to a system of healthcare that treated them as second-class citizens. Women, tired of hearing that their menstrual symptoms were all in their heads, when they knew very well that wasn't where the pain was, had alternatives that didn't exist 10 or 15 years ago. Until very recently, medical research focused almost exclusively on male patients except for "women's problems." When heart attacks and the impact various medication and dosages had on a patient's recovery were studied, the majority, if not all, of the participants were men.

In *Megatrends for Women*, a recent study on heart attacks was cited. "Four years ago, a major research finding was splashed across the front pages of newspapers around the country: take one aspirin every other day and lower your risk of heart attack. A remarkable finding—for half the population anyway. The research behind this headline-grabbing conclusion involved 22,000 physicians. There was not one woman among them," wrote Patricia Aburdene and John Naisbitt.[4] Aburdene and Naisbitt made some other startling discoveries. Women have been neglected in the clinical research of new drugs, fewer dollars are spent on diseases unique to women, and women are treated less aggressively when they have the same or more serious symptoms than male patients.

According to Aburdene and Naisbitt, these disparities have existed for some time. For the first 20 years of studies on aging conducted by the National Institutes of Health, only men were studied. The logical rationale for this gender-biased study is the theory that women and men age exactly alike. But obviously the hormonal differences in the two sexes invalidates that conclusion. Since women make up two-thirds of the elderly population, the accuracy of the study would be questionable.[5]

Today, much of the bias is changing as the medical profession admits to what women have known all along—there are physical differences between the sexes. Hard to believe, doctors, of all people took this long to figure out something that simple.

While physicians continued to warn women about breast and cervical cancer, very real and serious problems, little attention was focused on the number one killer of women—heart attacks. More than half a million women die annually from heart attacks and strokes, far more than the number that die from all cancers combined. Educating women to these statistics is the responsibility of a woman's personal physician, and the medical community as a whole.

Many doctors have recognized the need to tailor services and procedures to women. As a result, facilities like Houston's Women's Hospital of Texas are springing up everywhere. Providing better services to women is their key concern. Doctors who continue to provide the same mediocre levels of service to women that they always have will notice their practices diminishing. Women want more intellectual answers to questions, not intimating or partial responses. They want better explanations of what's wrong, and they want to be a partner in making decisions on their bodies. Doctors must present the problem along with the options available and, together with patients, decide on the best procedure. Today's woman doesn't want a cookie cutter approach. Just as women do their homework in a car-buying situation or when purchasing financial services, they do their homework when it involves their health. Many women's centers have put in patient libraries in order to make information more readily available.

Gail Sheehy's book *Passages* is a good illustration of the interest women have in menopause and other subjects that used to be considered taboo. As health care becomes a political pawn, the media clamors to provide coverage on topics once spoken about only in the locker room or at girls' sleepovers. Health care and fitness, better eating, and the environment are all issues that concern women today, especially the baby boomer generation and the younger set. There is more emphasis on heart healthy foods; fitness to increase productivity rather than just produce slimness; and contraception alternatives, not just to avoid unwanted pregnancies but to prevent sexually transmitted diseases, including AIDS.

Women are demanding more from their doctors and more from the medical community in general. The new professional woman is taking charge of her life and her healthcare in a way that her mother and grandmother never dreamed of. The medical community can no longer ignore her voice because, like any other business, if the present providers do not address the needs of the market, someone will come in and fill the void.

Marketers need to know that women tend to postpone healthcare when possible. As professional women's schedules become even more crowded, they resent the time spent in physicians' waiting rooms. More consciousness of a working woman's time restraints is mandatory to building rapport with most women today. Women respond to word-of-mouth advertising more than any other means. Therefore, what occurs in a physician's waiting and examination rooms will very likely affect a number of future appointments. Getting women to implement a sound program of preventive care is very important and again depends on building trust and being sensitive to their time constraints.

Since women are the major consumers of healthcare products and services, marketers need to be sure their companies address women and their needs sufficiently.

TABLE 4-1 Women and Health Care	
Household healthcare decision makers	75%
Prescription drug purchases	59%
Nursing home residents over the age of 65	75%
Physician visits	60%
Source: National Research Corporation and *Healthweek News*	

A Healthy Solution

Women's health services have finally begun to be recognized as an industry separate and apart from men. Obviously, the fields of gynecology and obstetrics have existed for some time. Everyone recognized the physical difference and the medical needs of the pregnant woman. What escaped medical science were the needs of women in other areas. Understanding that women and men are different physically and emotionally, and should be treated accordingly, is the basis for the marketing success of centers dedicated to the needs of female patients. Medical centers focused on women are a growing trend throughout the country. While some are staffed with only female physicians, others enjoy the same gender mix of doctors as other hospitals. The difference is the focus and the kind of care provided. While a large percentage of the patient base is in their child-bearing years, a growing specialty is the care of older women entering menopause.

George Oates, marketing manager at Chicago's Illinois Masonic Medical Center, believes one reason for the success of their program is that primary care for women is provided by female doctors.[6] In addition to normal medical services, they provide mammograms, stress management, and nutrition classes, even a course on midwifery. They also have a patient library. "The reason for our rapid growth is that we are giving both the female patients and the doctors what they want.

"The typical patient is a younger woman who is a 'take charge' person. We don't have as many elderly patients. They often prefer the more traditional setting," said Oates, "but that's changing."

The Women's Health Services Center at the Illinois Masonic Medical Center was started about 15 years ago. It was requested by, designed by, and is run by doctors. According to Nancy Curran, educational coordinator, seminars on physical health, such as the heart, aren't as popular now as the ones on personal growth.[7] "We no longer have classes on dieting, but on healthy eating and exercise. We discourage fad diets in lieu of a more complete program."

"Medical clinics aimed at women can be a profitable venture," according to an article in *Business Week*, August 25, 1986.[8] "Women visit doctors more, have more surgery and decide where their families will go 60 percent of the time." Many women's clinics are offering services not provided in general hospitals, including medical libraries for patients and seminars designed strictly for women. Frequently, if the center is operated as part of a hospital, it increases their revenues by filling more beds, often with more affluent patients.

During the last five years, thousands of programs have been implemented for women in hospitals across the country. Programs range from "stork clubs" that provide pink-and-green birthing rooms and special T-shirts for newborns, to those with more substance. Many have created special women's centers staffed with female doctors who say they can take a more preventive, holistic, and feminist approach to caring for the woman than anywhere else.[9]

In a 1990 study by the American Hospital Association, operations unique to women accounted for 11 of the 20 most frequent surgeries. Women in labor accounted for 13 percent of all hospital admissions, and women are admitted to the hospital 15 percent more often than men. "Hospitals tell me they know women are their most important customers; they know women aren't happy with how hospital services are delivered; but they don't know what to do about it," said Sally Rynne, president of Women's Healthcare Consultants. "Women want substantive things like immediate results on mammography, pain-control options for childbirth, women doctors and more health information."[10]

Veterans Memorial Medical Center in Meriden, Connecticut, created its Women's Health and Wellness Center in neighboring Cheshire to expand its geographic range into a new market. In three years, the center has had 9,000 patient visits, producing $2 million in revenues. The Women's Center is an effective marketing tool, according to Mary Fordiani, vice president of Veterans Memorial.[11] It gives patients and women doctors the ability to create the types of programs they want.

The Women's Hospital of Texas is owned by Hospital Corporation of America and is operated for the benefit of women patients. The hospital was started in 1976 when a group of obstetricians and gynecologists realized that women had very specific healthcare needs that weren't being properly addressed in traditional hospitals, Eilene Ong, director of marketing for the Women's Hospital recounts.[12] "A group of doctors who were then working at a major Houston hospital requested that the hospital board develop a separate department or facility for women. The hospital declined the suggestion. The doctors left and began to build their own hospital to provide the healthcare they believed women needed." It was acquired by HCA during construction.

Its services are geared toward women. "We provide general surgery, face lifts, mastectomies, and maternity care, among other things. We have held mother/daughter seminars on self-esteem and sexually transmitted diseases. We also have workshops on stress, nutrition, and exercise. Frequently, we provide speakers to women's organizations on these subjects, as well as plastic surgery, breast health, and how to juggle home, family, and career.

"We have approximately 4,000 births a year, accounting for about half of our patients," said Ong. The Women's Hospital of Texas has sibling activities in conjunction with the maternity area. A sibling tour provides each child with a paper scrub suit and a doll to diaper. There is a nominal charge to cover the cost of materials. "If parents prepare the child, the sibling can even be in the delivery room," said Ong. They also have a sibling birthday party in the room with the mother and new baby, complete with a cake. The hospital staff encourages family and friends to bring the sibling presents so they feel a part of the process. "As far as I know, our CEO, Judy Novak, developed the idea for the sibling birthday party, although I think it is done in many places now."

The Women's Hospital of Texas also provides on-site programs and health fairs for corporations and the city of Houston. The market is reached through traditional advertising venues as well as relying heavily on word-of-mouth advertising. The outstanding reputation of the doctors in the community also attracts patients. "We do radio, television, and newspaper advertising, including a 12-page, four-color insert that explains many of our services," said Ong. In order to serve all women in the community, the hospital has six satellite offices where they see women prior to delivery. However, all babies are born at the main hospital.

The Baptist Memorial Health Care System specializes in diagnostic imaging. Its collection of services aimed at women includes speakers, an 800 number, a patient library, and a diagnostic center. It has reformulated the labor, delivery, and recovery area into a one-room experience so the patient doesn't have to be moved from place to place. The decor for most rooms is contemporary with Oriental rugs and parquet floors in soft, soothing colors.

"Women are the predominant market. They make the healthcare decisions for themselves and, generally, their husbands. They also experience more continuous care from adolescence through maternity and then menopause," asserts Michael Calhoun who heads Baptist Memorial's marketing services.[13] The Center was started in 1988 as a part of the marketing trend that was taking place in women's healthcare. Calhoun believes so much can be done in this area that the only thing that is not effective is doing nothing. Providing quality products and value are keys to Baptist Memorial's success. The center's advertising budget—about $1 million annually—is targeted to women.

The Profitable Prescription Drug Market

Until recently, although new drugs were mainly tested on men, the larger consumer market was women. With the launch of the Office of Research on Women's Health (ORWH) in 1991, women began to be included in the testing of many medications. Studying the way diseases and treatment affect men and women differently is critical to discovering effective cures for heart disease, AIDS, and cancer. Many pharmaceutical companies, including Pfizer, have established a female healthcare research department. At the end of 1991, the Pharmaceutical Manufacturers Association reported that 263 medicines for women were presently in development (Table 4-2). The incentive is the large number of women anticipated to experience fertility and then menopausal problems.[14]

Pharmaceutical companies, research institutions, and doctors are beginning to realize that the chemical and metabolic differences between the genders affects the way their bodies absorb medication. Companies have argued in the past that they have used only men for testing new drugs because a woman's menstrual cycle would throw tests results off. If the cycle threw the tests off, why would researchers or doctors think that results from the tests would be accurate guides for dispensing medi-

TABLE 4-2 Targeting Women in Drug Research

Diseases & Their Affect on Men and Women	Number of Drugs
Neurologic—migraine headaches and Alzheimers affect more women than men.	16
Cardiovascular/cerebrovascular—atherosclerosis and heart attacks kill women and men equally.	48
Cancer—lung cancer surpasses breast cancer in the number of incidences in women.	58
Kidney/urologic—urinary tract infections are more common in women than men.	15
Obstetric/gynecologic—contraceptive needs and other female disorders are getting more attention.	51
Arthritis/musculoskeletal—25 million women suffer from bone loss caused by osteoporosis, which affects more women than men.	57

Source: Pharmaceutical Manufacturers Association/*Business Week* July 20, 1992

cation to women? After all, female patients were going to be in different phases of their cycle when the need for medication occurred.

In 1991, the National Institutes of Health (NIH) launched a $500 million, 10-year plan to study 150,000 post-menopausal women to determine how diet, exercise, and hormone therapy might prevent cardiovascular disease, cancer, and osteoporosis. In fiscal year 1993, $120 million is projected to be spent on AIDS research in women, up 56 percent since 1990.

Advertising dollars are being generously allocated to secure a marketing position for many of these products. Ten years ago, no one advertised drugs for menopause and birth control on television. In 1987, pharmaceutical companies spent $40 million on direct-to-consumer advertising. By 1991, it had increased to $92 million, nearly two-and-a-half times the amount spent only four years before. By 1992, advertising dollars had more than doubled from the previous year to $200 million, five times the 1987 figure. While much of the growth is related to the woman's market, a large portion is also in other areas. Nicotine patches account for a considerable share of medical advertising dollars. Advertising prescription drugs directly to the consumer is a new concept, but one that is likely to be around awhile. Consumers are taking more control of their health care and the decisions made about their medication. Understanding more about available medication is just part of being an informed consumer of the 1990s.[15]

Women as a Growth Segment by Design

As many companies looked at flat or declining sales, they began to search for new markets to change the slant of the revenue line and brighten the profit picture.

Nike, one of the leaders in the industry of men's athletic shoes, entered the woman's market as a way to increase their market share and profitability. According to Deborah Johnsen, Nike's marketing manager for women's products, you can't hope to appeal to women using the same formula you used for men.[16] Nike's ads were not condescending, sexist, or even sexy. They focused on women as individualists who could obtain empowerment through fitness.

Another key to Nike's success is that they involved women in the marketing and design of the product. The current trend to incorporate women into the decision-making process at the marketing and/or design level has had positive results in a number of companies. Manufacturers have begun to realize that if they want to attract women customers more successfully, they need to ask women what they want prior to designing and producing the product. Women are excellent communicators. They will gladly share their instincts and insights. After all, they do have an innate advantage in understanding the female consumer's needs.

Manufacturers should recognize that there is a distinct difference in designing a product *for women*, and designing a product *with women in mind*. One is patronizing, condescending, and destined to failure most of the time. The other, especially if women have participated in the process, has an excellent chance for success.

To illustrate the difference between designing a product *for women*, rather than a product with *women in mind*: A pink or lavender car with a thin steering wheel is a product designed for women. (Actually it is a product that appeals to no one—male or female—but one manufacturer actually thought it was designing a car for women.) Producing a vehicle with adjustable seat belts, a track high heels won't get caught in, and control buttons and handles that are easy to manipulate with long fingernails is designing a product with women in mind. (The automotive industry is discussed in Chapter 5.)

Women have struggled long and hard to be accepted in the workplace and the marketplace. They want to be treated as intelligent, competent, adult consumers who seek products with sensible features that fit their needs, not products with superficial design elements.

Samsonite's ads point out that their Professional Collection luggage is sleek, stylish, and fashionable. "It's a collection designed by a woman, with features for women . . . and tested by women."

New Balance ads read: "Presenting shoes designed by women, built by women and tested by women. All to ensure one thing: They fit women."

Businessmen who continue to say, "Women don't want anything different; we don't have to change the product design or the language in our ads" don't know what they are talking about. They are losing sales for their company now and for the future. Companies that try to capture women's dollars without considering their thoughts will find a tough road ahead.

The Gun Is Right on Target

The male domain of the automotive showrooms would appear to be the last bastion of masculinity. After all, what could be more manly than the automobile? In America, the love affair between man and machine has gone on for decades. But women are infiltrating an even more sacred arena—the shooting range. In that most macho of fields—hunting and shooting—women are having an undeniable, and to many, even surprising effect. Gun enthusiasts have been staggered by the number of women who have began to appear in firearm stores, on target ranges, and in recreational shooting events.

According to Sue King, executive director of the Women's Shooting Sports Foundation, more and more women are joining the sport of hunting.[17] Last year, in Texas alone, 2,800 women purchased hunting licenses. Approximately 10 percent of all participants hunting with a rifle or shotgun are women. Fifteen percent of all clay shooters, 17 percent of all trap or skeet shooters and 20 percent of target shooters are now female.[18] Seminars, such as "Becoming an Outdoor Woman" by Christine Thomas, are attractive to women and are always sold out.

Christine Thomas, associate professor of resource management, the College of Natural Resources, the University of Wisconsin at Stevens Point, conducts three seminars a year.[19] "Approximately one-third of the weekend is spent shooting and hunting, one-third fishing, and one-third on other camping activities, such as canoeing and map and compass skills," explains Thomas. "The women who participate are a very diverse group. Some are very wealthy; others can hardly raise the fee, which is around $150 for the weekend. Some have high school degrees only; others have multiple degrees. They come for a variety of reasons. Most want to learn the skills and meet other women with the same interests. In 1991, I only had one retreat, but the program grows every year. I'm teaching other groups how to put on weekend retreats as well."

According to Thomas, for years only about 2 percent of hunters were women. Now 8 to 10 percent are. "The Women's Shooting Sports Foundation has been a big supporter of ours."

The Foundation, established to provide hunting and shooting opportunities for women, conducts a Ladies Charity Classic each year in Houston, Texas. "The first year, 1988, we had only 97 women attend and put on only one event. In 1993, we had 18 events all around the country," said King. The proceeds from these events go to local charities, so the advertising is through Public Service Announcements. "We give away more guns, and expensive ones, than any other shooting competition in the country," King proudly proclaimed.

King doesn't believe good shotguns have been designed for women yet. She is working with Browning on specifications for a product that is more suitable to the woman hunter. "So far, all they have are youth/lady models, and an adult woman just isn't built like a child. We need something that fits a woman's build and works for her," King said. Another of her observations is that clothing manufacturers haven't made apparel for women either. "I have to buy men's bush pants and then take them to my alterations person and pay them to cut them down. If the hips fit, the waist is way too big."

King's discoveries aren't unique. Too often manufacturers think that all they have to do is make the product smaller, and it will be perfect for women. Thus far, I am unfamiliar with any items that have been very successful with that approach. Yet, it happens over and over again.

The design of the gun and clothing aren't the only obstacles the industry needs to overcome. Women customers are uncomfortable in sporting/gun stores, and conversely, salesmen are uncomfortable with a woman customer. "Salesmen are used to having a man come in, ask for a specific gun or type of gun, and handing it to him. He pays for it, and the transaction is over. That's not what happens when a woman comes in. She needs more assistance. The salesman must be responsive, patient, informative and not use jargon she has never heard before. Often she doesn't know what type of gun she needs or wants. Taking time to communicate with his customer is a skill most gun salesmen still need to learn," said King. Training seminars are one method that King sees as a way to help salesmen become more sensitive to women customers and learn how to talk to them without being patronizing. More than half the dealers who participated in the American Firearms Industry Dealer Survey said women customers represented 5 percent or less of their business, but 84 percent agreed that women were buying more guns and saw the woman's market as a definite growth segment.

As the male market continued to decline about 10 percent a year, firearms manufacturers looked at ways to maintain or increase their market share and profitability. Chris Killoy, director of products and marketing manager for Smith & Wesson, said the company noticed increased interest by women in firearms for personal protection.[20] This feminine interest motivated many to look seriously at this market niche. When Smith & Wesson decided to manufacture a handgun designed for women, focus groups were conducted to find out what women wanted. As a result of the research, the successful LadySmith was designed. The LadySmith has a rounder handle, easier to pull trigger, and a redesigned thumb notch. "We also added some aesthetic characteristics," remarked Killoy, but was quick to add, "we didn't make it pink." The LadySmith has a glass-bead finish and a rosewood laminated grip.

One interesting thing Killoy said, but one that doesn't surprise me, is that after they introduced the women's line and made some adjustments in it, some of the changes eventually found their way to their other guns. "We found many of the product improvements women wanted would be enhancements all of our customers liked."

The National Rifle Association (NRA) estimates that women own between 15 and 20 million guns. Between 1983 and 1986, the number of women owning guns rose only 3 percent. Forty-one percent of the women who responded to a 1991 Gallup Poll said they had a gun in the house.[21] Obviously, Smith & Wesson's marketing strategies are paying off.

Even though the LadySmith doesn't come in pink, Lorcin manufactures a $79 L-25 handgun with a pink grip. "At first I had trouble getting my wholesalers to stock the guns," Jim Waldorf, president of the California-based company, commented.[22] Waldorf doesn't have any data to document who is buying the pink gun. "It might be women, or it might be a father or boyfriend. We sell to retailers, so I don't have any statistics on the ultimate consumers." While the pink gun is not Lorcin's best seller, according to Waldorf, it does sell very well.

One challenge firearms manufacturers have yet to overcome is the acceptance by women's publication to run the ads. *Ladies Home Journal* recently carried an ad for Colt Manufacturing Co. Inc.; the first time that a general-interest woman's magazine had run an ad for firearms. The ad pictured a young mother tucking her child into bed. Under the photo were two semi-automatic pistols with the headline, "Self-protection is more than your right . . . it is your responsibility." The response was so negative from readers that *Ladies Home Journal* decided against running any other ads.[23] Publications like *Women & Guns*, which started in 1989, has targeted this otherwise neglected niche. Since its inception, the publication has doubled its circulation every year. It reaches more than 25,000 women.

The focus of firearm ads aimed at women is that guns should be part of a total personal safety program. Personal safety, self-defense, and home protection are the themes. In response to critics' charges that firearm manufacturers are using fear to sell to women, Killoy retorted, "Guns are only one part of a woman's personal security. We encourage women who buy guns to learn to handle them properly. In fact, we are sponsoring a promotion with the National Rifle Association that offers women a $50 rebate off the purchase price of a LadySmith handgun if she takes an NRA Basic Pistol or Personal Protection Course." Eighty percent of those who take the NRA's Basics of Personal Protection 12-hour program are women.

Smith & Wesson did a mass mailing on the NRA promotion. They provided counter top cards to gun dealers. Two women's magazines, *Glamour* and *Mirabella*, recently ran a story on women and guns. While they won't print advertising, publications realize that personal safety, including information on guns, is a concern of their readers.

One reason for Smith & Wesson's interest in the woman's market is women's own interest in purchasing a gun. Survey results indicate that interest is growing. It is estimated that in the mid-1980s only 8 million women were thinking of buying a gun; now that figure has grown to 15.6 million.

Marketing News, a publication for marketing professionals, quotes Chris Dolnack, public relations manager and a copywriter for the LadySmith campaign as saying, "It's okay today for a professional woman to own a gun." Smith & Wesson, agreeing with the sentiment, even hired the author of *Armed and Female,* Paxton Quigley, as a consultant on the campaign. She helped clarify what would appeal to women in marketing the LadySmith.[24]

Gun manufacturers, convinced that self-protection is the best way to sell guns to women, have tried to create a product designed for this need. Manufacturers have come to understand that women view a handgun as a lethal weapon, not a fashion accessory and are careful not to "feminize" the product too much. What motivates women to buy are the statistics they hear: "In a 24-hour period, 2,000 women will be violently assaulted . . . 638,000 rapes were committed in 1991 . . . Ten percent of all convicted felons test positive for the AIDS virus."[25] As more and more women become single heads-of-households, responsible for their own well-being and frequently that of their children, they are looking for better ways to protect themselves and their families.

Pistol-packing isn't the only way women are protecting themselves. Self-defense classes are proliferating. Many community colleges' continuing education programs are offering classes, such as "Self Defense for

Women," for a nominal fee. One course is described as "a class where you learn how to defend yourself from armed and unarmed attackers. The techniques covered in this course are designed especially for women or people of small stature." Several expensive self-defense programs have also been developed strictly for women by profit and non-profit groups across the country. These classes are marketed to corporations as well as to individuals.

Mike Hayashi, president and CEO of Mike Hayashi Associates, a Phoenix-based company, began offering seminars to corporations in 1986.[26] As more women were employed, traveling, and working late, and as the crime rate continued to climb, many employers saw this as a benefit they could offer. "Some companies use it as a public relations tool," explains Hayashi. "One travel agency I worked with invited their clients to a seminar. When you travel to unfamiliar areas, you are an easier prey." Hayashi offers a catalog replete with many self-protection products.

When women don't find the products they want and can't get manu-facturers to design for their needs, sometimes they take matters into their own hands. That's exactly why Sarah LePere started her business.[27] "I went to a gun show with my husband and saw a handbag that was used to carry a weapon. I really wanted one, and I wanted to sell the handbags for the exhibitor. But I wanted to make some changes that would make the purses more functional for me and other women. He wasn't interested in making too many changes. When he did make alterations, he might ship me black purses with a blue pocket added. So I just started my own company. A purse should be fashionable and made of quality products," LePere declares. "Our company, Feminine Protection, produces and sells handbags that are designed by women for women."

Feminine Protection has been in business eight years and sells be-tween 1,500 and 2,000 purses annually to fathers, husbands, boyfriends, single women, married women, mothers, and grandmothers. "We sell to everyone from doctors and lawyers to women who work late at the mall to fathers who buy them for their daughters when they go off to college," commented LePere.

Her thriving business uses marketing techniques that work. Her product, designed with fashion and quality in mind, has reinforced straps that deter a purse snatcher from cutting the strap and fleeing with the purse. It also has a Velcro strip for keys so that women don't have to dig for them at the bottom of their purse while standing in a dark, deserted parking lot. When ordering, women specify the gun calibre so the design of the holster fits the weapon. Feminine Protection produces 30 styles in either leather or denim ranging in price from $55 to $200.

LePere markets through gun shows, gun magazines, women's maga-zines, and some public relations efforts. "Eight years ago when I started, not many women were at gun shows. That's changed a lot now," she reminisced.

While many people don't like the name of her company, Feminine Protection, and some are even embarrassed by it, "people remember it," she stated, "and that's really what it's all about."

Feminine Protection isn't the only enterprise that has grown in response to the number of women carrying firearms. Linda Mutchnick, a legal assistant who specializes in litigation and is an NRA instructor, was uncomfortable in a business suit with a firearm tucked away for protection. "It was bulky, heavy and uncomfortable."[28] Mutchnick, founder of PistolERA, a line of custom-designed apparel for the well-dressed, well-armed woman, has a catalog of vests, skirts, jackets, and slacks in many styles and fabrics. Each garment is ordered and custom-made for the recipient. While the clothes are fashionable, high-quality, and can be worn without packing a firearm, the uniqueness of the designer line is the ability to carry a weapon. PistolERA's customers are a cross-section including professionals—attorneys, doctors, advertising executives, FBI special agents, policewomen who do undercover work, homemakers—the entire gamut. PistolERA has gotten a lot of media attention since its inception in 1992. "We have received national and international coverage in newspapers and magazines; we've been in *Playboy*; I've done radio talk shows; *60 Minutes* did a segment; and I've been on the *Home Show*. All the press has been very positive and has helped the business develop," said Mutchnick proudly. One day she hopes that PistolERA will be a full-time job.

Women Infiltrate Once Male Domains

Some industries actively pursued the woman consumer as it became apparent that she was a treasure worth capturing. The rewards of winning her business were obvious to many. However, others just watched as the woman consumer became a dominant force in the marketplace. They did little to gain her confidence or her dollars. Nonetheless, as the percentage of women business travelers climbed, hotels scrambled to accommodate her needs. And financial institutions began clamoring for her business as well.

Meeting the Needs of Women Business Travelers

According to the U.S Travel Data Center, women represented 39 percent, or 13.1 million business travelers in 1990, up from 31 percent in 1988. In 1970, women represented only 1 percent. Women spend approximately $23 billion on business travel annually, $10 billion of that on lodging.

Statistics compiled by the American Hotel and Motel Association (AH&MA) indicate that the number of women business travelers is growing three times faster than the number of men travelers.

The AH&MA notes that hotels interested in attracting women guests need to show professional women in their brochures and ads. They need to be cognizant of women travelers and make sure they are seated in prime locations in restaurants, not at inferior tables, when they are dining alone. Hotels should provide adequate security and lighting in the parking areas and corridors, and should train waiters and clerks not to refer to female guests as "honey" or "dear."[29]

As the travel industry began to switch their marketing strategies to incorporate the female traveler, they experimented with many things. Pink-wallpapered rooms or single-sex floors with extra security and amenities were tried. The Albuquerque Hilton had a "For Women Only Floor." However, most hotels opted for the more discriminating "club" floors that were unisex, rather than a single-sex floor. To enter club floors, guests must have a key or coded card. Club floors frequently provide happy hour snacks and continental breakfasts allowing women who hate to dine alone to share conversation with fellow travelers. The Marriott Corporation contends that women like the club floor so much that they plan to offer it in all their new facilities. The Marriott also developed "solo dining" tables—small tables with a reading lamp, notebook, pens, pencils, and a few current periodicals.[30] Other facilities have trained their staffs to immediately seat women who are alone to avoid awkward standing and waiting. Many have adapted their menus to offer smaller portions and healthier cuisine to satisfy women's tastes and diets.

Room-service hours were extended at several hotels, additional interior and exterior lighting was provided, and many offer to escort women to their cars if they are parked in the garage.

To make women feel safer, long corridors and parking areas should be well-lit and well-patrolled. Women should be given rooms close to the elevator, if possible. Since security is one of the prime concerns of women travelers, most hotels have added deadbolts and peepholes, and have initiated simple procedures, such as not announcing room numbers and having the bellboy check rooms prior to entry.

The Radisson Hotel Corporation unit of Carlson Companies spent $439 million in the last few years building 17 new all-suite hotels. Their research indicated women would rather stay in a facility where they can have business meetings without a bed in the room. Other hotels maintained that women prefer to meet in a restaurant or client's office rather than their room.

"The businesswoman told us what she wanted and now the businessman is benefiting," said Marriott's Farrell in the June 1991 issue of

ASTA Agency Management, "Marketing to Women." Women prompted hotels to create more open lobby bar areas because they wouldn't frequent the dimly lit bars that most hotels had in the 1970s and early 1980s. Men have welcomed the change as well, just as men have enjoyed the additional amenities in the hotel rooms. Some hotels have added luxury items for women, such as complimentary manicures, French-milled soaps, and aerobic fitness centers. Many hotels are offering organized group activities, such as tennis tournaments or educational outings. Women frequently stay at more upscale facilities, and these hotels have an opportunity to win their loyalty by providing extraordinary service. Moderately priced hotels, however, can also provide things important to women travelers: cleanliness, privacy, security, and good service.

The Compri Hotels, a division of Management Associates, which manages the Doubletree Hotels, were developed to compete in the business travelers market. The concept was to construct hotels that would meet the needs of business travelers, and initially they did not differentiate between the genders. They realized that since more women traveled for business, they should be included in the focus groups conducted by the hotel's marketers.

"What we found," explained Marian Gerlich, partner of Placidi & Gerlich Communications, "was that men and women wanted a lot of the same things, but their priorities were different.[31] We literally designed our hotels around what business travelers, both men and women, said they wanted. Women were very concerned about their safety and security. Our facilities have a single, well-lit entry way. Everyone who enters passes a reception desk, and it takes the coded room card to utilize the elevator. All our rooms are entered by a coded card that is changed frequently, not a key. Women feel more secure with this system.

"Our research indicated that women were more comfortable in low-rise buildings, rather than high-rises or single rambling facilities. When color was introduced into the discussion, it was immediately obvious that powder-puff pink rooms were real turn-offs to businesswomen.

"One of our most successful features is the club room. Each hotel has a very large room that is divided into sections, not by immovable walls, but by furniture. It provides the guests with a living room atmosphere that is warm and familiar. The club room has many areas: a library, television viewing section, bar, and restaurant.

Women like the ability to have a drink and not feel that they are inviting unwelcomed advances. They can get a glass of wine at the bar, remain there or take it to the television area to watch the news, or go to the library to do some work. Women can mix and mingle with other travelers, discuss the news or just relax and visit." This arrangement provides women the opportunity to socialize in an acceptable manner that men travelers have always enjoyed. To understand the significance of this feature to a woman, a male architect, developer, or investor must think as she thinks and feel as she feels when she remains in her room, unwilling to venture into the dimly lit bar or hating to sit alone in a restaurant. A comfortable, secure place to talk at the end of the day with other women and men is a noteworthy feature that will attract women travelers.

The Compri facility was all inclusive. At check-in, you received coupons for drinks the first night and a complimentary breakfast—all at competitive rates. The Compri, now called Doubletree Clubs, has expanded from its original hotel in 1984 to 18 facilities. Gerlich attributes much of the hotels' success to the fact that they listened to their customers and involved them, especially women, in the process from the beginning. "Men told us they wouldn't stay at hotels that didn't have workout facilities and a pool. While the workout room is utilized far less than the club, it was an important component to men. Men also commented on the friendly environment of the club room and didn't seem to miss the 'good ol' boy' bars in many hotels. They especially liked the limited services that were offered. We provide a bellhop when needed, but guests feel comfortable carrying their own luggage. Men told us several times they didn't like to spend money on tips to carry one or two bags. We never heard this from women.

"Even though we have limited services, we are very attentive to our guests. Our staff is trained to recognize guests and call them by name. We have internal programs that reward employees who demonstrate superior service," said Gerlich.

Many hotels have recognized the women's market and have added amenities women find appealing—skirt hangers, full-length mirrors, well-lit bathrooms, and counters large enough for make-up and other essentials. Women asked for the larger counter tops, but men acknowledged how much they enjoyed having more space for their shaving paraphernalia. Men also expressed delight in better lighting.

Hyatt Hotels also recognize the impact women business travelers are having on their bottom line. "Twenty percent of our Gold Passport, or frequent stayers, are now women," calculated Carrie Reckert, director of public relations for Hyatt Hotels.[32] "We have found that the changes women have requested, men like as well. They even like having skirt hangers so they can hang their pants without folding them. As a result of the current marketplace, the Hyatt has positioned women in executive situations in their advertising. They train their employees to be more sensitive to their guests' needs, to be aware of where they seat women in the restaurant and to inquire if they would like their rooms close to the elevator." According to *Hotels and Restaurants International*, October 1988,

"How do you please the woman business traveler? The same way you do a male traveler, but with more attention to each effort. The results will be a very satisfied woman business guest and, not surprisingly, an even happier male business traveler."[33]

Women and Finance

Traditionally, money matters were men's business. Men provided the income, women managed the house, the children, and the social activities. But that's all changed. In dual-income families, wives are having a large say in the family's financial management—determining the budget, selecting investments, assessing insurance needs and actively planning for the future. When the single head of the household is a woman, she is forced to take charge of her economic interests. And, when the woman is a business owner, she must handle any number of financial situations—payrolls, profit and loss statements, cost controls, and banking relationships.

Understanding the differences in the way women and men make financial decisions is the key to establishing good financial relationships with women. Often, men make erroneous assumptions about what women want financially and proceed to create marketing and sales tools that are ineffective with their target audience. Developing materials and programs that are appealing to women just makes good business sense.

As lifestyles and family structures changed, women were forced to become more knowledgeable in financial matters. Financial professionals need to recognize some often overlooked statistics:

❖ Women have developed wealth in a number of ways; some inherited it from husbands or other family members.

❖ Women often control large estates. Forty-three percent of all individuals with assets of $500,000 or more are women.

❖ Women make up 35 percent of the country's 51 million shareholders. Many earned the money, rather than inheriting it.

❖ Fifty-seven million women work outside the home, and this provides many with more discretionary income than they have ever had.

❖ Six million women own their own businesses.

❖ Ninety-five percent make family financial decisions jointly with their husbands.[34]

On a less optimistic note, women earned 29 percent less than their male counterparts and received just 36 percent of the national income. Women are more security minded than men. They worry more about their financial future. Yet, 61 percent of working women do not have pension plans (versus 53 percent of men). Financial services should offer peace of mind to women, but many aren't targeting them as valuable clients. Marketers, brokers, planners, and agents need to be more aggressive in developing the female client. Many organizations are beginning to address this issue, some very successfully.

Women want to learn. One trait of their gender is they typically do their homework better in a buying situation. If they feel uncomfortable with their expertise in any domain, they will spend the time to research it and to ask questions. In the first three months of 1992, more than 10,000 women attended educational seminars conducted by the American Association of Retired Persons (AARP).[35] Investment brokers, attorneys, banks, accountants ... all have become educational resources for women. Their seminars are geared for married women, older women, professional women ... the entire gamut of the female population. They serve a dual benefit—educating women and adding new clients to the companies' rosters.

Characteristics of Women Making Smart Financial Decisions

According to *Money* magazine, there are five basic traits that distinguish women from men in regard to money.[36] First, they admit ignorance. Knowing the Dow Jones closing doesn't make you a financial wizard. "Men tend to think they know it all, even when they don't. Women tend to doubt they know it all even when they do," asserts Victor Felton-Collins, author of *Couples and Money*, in the *Money* article. Statistically, nearly four times as many men as women can quote the Dow Jones industrial average within 100 points. Forty percent more men understood why bond prices typically fall when interest rates rise. But men are not necessarily better investors.

Second, women seek help. Whether it is for directions to a specific location or a financial interpretation, men are less likely than women to ask for advice. Women want to make sound, safe, good investments and to understand the process as they go along.

Third, women avoid risks. Women are more conservative investors than men. Yes, men want sound, good investments, too, but they are more willing to take a risk, to speculate, to go for the bigger reward associated with the bigger gamble.

Fourth, women do their homework. Men act first, worry later. Making a quick decision is important. Women ponder, consider, research, calculate, and then act. Men will take a buddy's locker room tip; women tend to invest in products they know and understand.

Fifth, women set goals. Men view money as a competitive edge. It is a game piece, a way to keep score. Money is the measuring stick of success and power. To women, money is the means to a goal. It is security for their future. They define success in business in much more complex terms than just money.

Marketing Financial Services to Women

In the same month that Money ran the article, "The Five Ways Women Are Often Smarter Than Men About Money," *The Wall Street Journal* ran the article, "Wall Street Courts Women With Pitch They Have Different Financial Needs," which stated that, "Shearson Lehman Brothers Inc. recently released a survey concluding that women lack confidence making investment decisions, and Oppenheimer Management Corp. released a study saying that women lack knowledge and experience."[37]

The Wall Street Journal article confirms the fact that brokers and financial planners have in the past targeted primarily men or isolated groups of women, such as wealthy widows or divorcees. But the market for these services is far broader. Working women with IRAs, 401(k) plans, lump sum distributions or retirement funds constitute a new market segment. Female entrepreneurs with capital to invest, pension plans to fund, disability insurance, and buy-out plans to consider provide a customer base for brokers, insurance agents, and accountants to target.

Oppenheimer Funds, recognizing this growing new market, has produced two brochures aimed at capturing the female investor's dollars: *Women & Investing* for consumers; and the *Guide to Women & Investing* for financial advisors. Other companies, banks, insurance agencies, and stock brokers have published similar products. Some have made videos explaining investments and various options available. Women's publications, such as *Lear's*, have hosted seminars. Most address money management on an ongoing basis.

Retirement and investing for the future involves everyone, but women historically have less knowledge and experience in this area. According to Merrill Lynch's Fifth Annual Retirement and Planning Survey, there is a retirement gender gap.[38] If born in 1950, the average woman could plan to live to be 87, the average male, 81. Because women earn less and are usually in the work force a shorter amount of time, they usually receive lower Social Security and pension benefits. In the Merrill Lynch survey, 67 percent of the males, but only 46 percent of the female pre-retirees, began preparing for retirement prior to age 40. In the baby boomer category, 68 percent of the men and 55 percent of the women began before age 30. While women save more for major purchases and vacations, men tend to save more for retirement. Twice as many female (35 percent) as male (17 percent) baby boomers and three times as many female (22 percent) as male (8 percent) pre-retirees say they are uninformed about their retirement benefits.

Another variation between the sexes is the way the money is being managed. Only 17 percent, or half as many women use dollar cost averaging (investing a specific sum on a regular basis) as men (35 percent). Only about one-fourth of all women use diversification (allocating assets among stocks, bonds, and cash), while nearly one-half of all men diversify. More than 40 percent of all women say they would rather have someone else manage their retirement savings and investments, while slightly more than a quarter of the men wanted that.

Katherine and Richard Greene teamed up to see if there were really discrepancies in the treatment of males and females in the financial community.[39] They took on virtually the same identity—age, lifestyle, occupation, and income—the only real difference was gender. "Our experiences suggest the following ways in which many financial advisors treated women and men differently—usually to the detriment of their female clients." Katherine told how one banker stereotyped her as an overly cautious investor, no matter what she said. Investment counselors seemed more concerned about Richard's financial security in retirement than Katherine's. Almost all discussed this area with Richard and made suggestions; only half emphasized it with Katherine, and a quarter never brought it up. This lack of interest in retirement for women perpetuates the thinking that she will have a man to provide for her, so no need to worry her pretty little head with such matters. One advisor didn't even ask her age, a crucial piece of data for proper financial planning; but then, it's impolite to ask a lady her age.

The Greenes' conclusion was that women often are given advice to buy products that are either too risky or too conservative. A specific stock, rather than a category, is recommended much more often to women than to men. "The most troubling question they faced: Are women more likely to receive bad financial advice because they are women?" And the answer is "yes."

Financial institutions that take the time to develop the woman's market, to learn about her needs and to properly advise her on investment, savings, and retirement strategies can reap lucrative dividends. As women continue to be more responsible for their own financial future, as they work and earn more income and as they learn more about finances, they will become premium financial clients.

Targeting women is effective, lucrative, and necessary in today's environment. Many financial institutions have developed speakers who present programs to women's professional organizations. Others join women's organizations to have access to their members and the membership roster. This enables them to send them direct mail pieces or invitations to special seminars or workshops. Some marketers have segmented different categories: divorced women, single women, professional women. Many financial planners and brokers have learned that cold calling is less effective with women than with men, but cold calling is still done by some. Meeting women, gaining their trust, and building relationships are the most effective ways to sell to women. If a woman doesn't know any investment advisors personally, she will select one based on the recommendation of a friend or colleague. Financial planners should always ask for referrals, especially from female clients. It will enhance their client base.

Banking on Women

Banks have begun to realize that customer service and innovative programs are ideas whose time has come. According to *The Wall Street Journal*, NationsBank Corp. in Charlotte, North Carolina, is now testing new personnel for their sales ability. Banc One Corp. in Columbus, Ohio, holds an annual loan and credit card "sidewalk sale" complete with hot dogs. These are just two of many programs that banks are implementing in an attempt to retain their customers. With non-bank competitors, such as brokerage houses infringing on traditional banking services, banks have to be more aggressive in their marketing efforts.

In 1980, bank deposits constituted almost half of all household financial investments. By 1990, this figure had shrunk to 38 percent and is projected to drop to 32 percent by 1995, according to McKinsey & Co., a consulting firm. Meanwhile, per household mutual fund investments grew from 2.6 percent in 1980 to 12 percent in 1990.

What's more, customers are dissatisfied with banks and banking services. According to a study done by the American Bankers Association, consumers are unhappy with lower interest rates and changes to existing services and fees. In response, banks are developing new products and repackaging old ones. Boston-based BayBanks Inc. created a value package that combined checking, savings, and credit services into one package with a flat monthly fee. BayBanks offers different packages for college students, young adults, and more affluent couples.[40] Many banks are also redesigning their facilities to be more customer friendly. Circular desks so loan officers and customers can sit side-by-side, computers placed for easier viewing, and more contemporary colors and decor are just a few cosmetic changes that some banks have installed.

As banks rethink their marketing strategies to more aggressively gain and retain customers, they need to consider where the growth market is. As in most other areas, women are impacting the banking industry. They are opening more small businesses than any other sector of the population, and they are looking for a good banking relationship—one where bankers treat them as competent and valued customers.

Women believe they are required to provide more information when they apply for a car loan than are men. They claim when applying for a business loan, more collateral is asked from them than from a male applicant. They are required more frequently to have a co-signer on the loan. When they approach a bank for business needs that they have patronized for years for their personal financial needs, they are frequently treated as a new customer. Obtaining a line of credit is difficult for most women, even at banks they have used for many years.

Women view the basic services provided by banks as inadequate and impersonal. Banks, they believe, have little, if any, initiative to really service an account. To a woman, "service an account" means that someone at the bank is interested in her and her needs. It means she is building trust and a relationship with a loan officer; she is not just an account number.

Just as other businesses have made the mistake of assuming that price is the only, or at least the most important, factor in a woman's buying decision, so have banks. Many have focused their marketing strategies on the interest they charge on loans or the interest they pay on deposits rather than asking what is really important to their female customer. Interest is not the determining factor in getting or keeping the female customer. The personal relationship is. Yes, women look at interest rates, convenience, and a score of other factors that all play a part in deciding where to bank. Male bankers don't always value the importance of the intangible relationship the way female customers do.

Ann Hall, a marketing specialist in Dallas, has done extensive work in the banking industry on marketing more effectively to women.[41] Hall worked with a group of bankers to determine what women business owners were looking for in a banking situation. By conducting focus groups, mail surveys, and one-on-one interviews with nearly 1,000 women, she discovered that one of the key factors in the selection of a financial institution was not the interest rate but the relationship the woman client had with her banker.

The groups, comprised of women business owners and managers, were asked specific questions. For instance, what are convenient hours? Women business owners preferred banks that remain open late one night versus Saturday. Many banks provide neither, or only limited services on Saturday.

A second question that Hall asked this group was "How often do you use an ATM?" The feedback was women use ATMs less than men because they perceive them as unsafe. They felt they are frequently located in undesirable areas that have very little light to protect them at night.

When asked what services were most appealing to them—a free safety deposit box, unlimited free checks, a half percent discount on car loans, or free printed checks—most business women said none of those were important. The relationship with the banker was the most important ingredient. Most believed that all of the incentives mentioned above could be negotiated if they had a sound banker relationship. What they want is someone who will walk them through the loan process; someone who will stick with them and fight for them; someone on their side.

How women are treated is of premium importance. They want the same respect and consideration as a male client. They want to be able to secure loans when they need money for expansion. They want to be taken seriously as a woman business owner, even when they work from their homes.

Perception is reality. If a woman perceives she is being treated differently or being discriminated against because she is a woman, that is reality to her. Making sure that women have good banking experiences will help build a loyal customer base in a very competitive environment. The attitude of the directors and officers of the bank is crucial. It is imperative that the directors and officers not only verbalize a sense of equality, but convey the underlying attitude that they believe women are equal to men in their ability to repay the loan and manage their money or business successfully.

"Another problem women verbalized is that when they had a business problem with a bank, and a man accompanied them to deal with the loan officer, things went smoother," explained Hall.

Divorce compounds the banking problems of many women. If the husband has bad credit, it often takes as long as five years to separate his and her credit ratings, even if her credit is impeccable. When her husband dies, or she gets divorced, frequently her credit cards are canceled. It is generally easier for a man to get new ones than for her, even with the equal credit laws. These situations can be detrimental to a woman who already is having a tougher time building a business and a bank relationship.

Women value other women's opinions. This is true in a number of industries that have been discussed in this book. Women's networking skills and the way they relate to recommendations from other women cannot, and should not, be minimized by any business in operation today.

When I first started my company and needed financial assistance, I selected a banker who one of my good friends used. She knew him well and recommended that I utilize his bank for my business needs. I did. With her introduction, I began a financial relationship with him that lasted for several years. Today, I use Compass Bank (the name now) because I served on a board with their banking office president, and I liked the way she did business. I knew her, and she knew me. I was more than just a number as she scanned financial statements. We had a relationship. I could call her when I needed advice or help. I wouldn't hesitate to recommend Debbie Hipp or the bank to other women. In fact, I have.

Understanding women's needs and meeting them will guarantee a loyal, appreciative customer. Understanding that women have different thoughts, reactions, and values than men does not imply that women want to be a separate entity and have "women's programs." They have earned the right to be mainstreamed as valued customers, just as men have. Realizing the differences and meeting the needs of women, addressing them in a sensitive, professional manner, is very different from relegating them to a lower status.

Being sensitive to women includes being concerned about the look of and information contained in your brochures, advertising message, and media announcements. Programs, investment opportunities, and banking information need to be fully explained, but not oversimplified. The message should communicate that women customers are important to the bank. Seminars should be on topics of interest to women. If the bank is targeting affluent, more mature women, retirement planning would be appropriate. If they are seeking business owners, access to capital would be pertinent.

Creating successful banking and financial services for women requires the same ingredients for success as any other industry. Women must be involved at various levels in order to convey their opinions, view brochures and advertising, and provide input on various bank products and programs that are of interest to them. Training the staff is important so they fully realize the value that can be gained from a program dedicated to establishing relationships with women.

In Hall's case, she put together an advisory board of influential women in the community to provide this information to the bank. The group met monthly to establish a direction and to make recommendations to the bank. The bank found out that while women wanted more financial education and would attend seminars, that alone was not enough. Offering seminars to existing clients and their network as part of the total package of services was successful. Offering it to generate prospective clients wasn't as successful because women wanted more than just the education, they wanted a relationship with the banker.

Word-of-mouth advertising has more power than paid advertising and costs a lot less. Even though it reaches fewer women, a banker who provides a one-on-one approach will be referred to other women seeking the same type of service. Banks need to build coalitions with influential women leaders in the community who will encourage other women to seek their services. Banks also need to form coalitions with other related businesses that have the ability to enhance their bottom line with more female clients—lawyers, financial planners, brokers, accountants—all make good referral allies for bankers.

Insuring Success

If any industry recognizes the differences in men and women, it should be the insurance industry. After all, many of their prices are based on gender. Women under 25 pay 60 percent of what males the same age pay for auto insurance. Women pay 72 percent of what men pay for term insurance. For annuities (pertaining to age 65), they pay 109 percent, or more than their male counterpart. This is true for major medical and disability income. Women pay 148 percent and 166 percent, respectively.

In addition to the dual pricing structure, there are disparities in the service provided by agents. In the May 1992 issue of *Life Insurance Selling*, Jan Wolfe, a CLU, ChFC with New York Life Insurance Company, wrote an article titled, "The Invisible Prospect." In her article she said, "There is a myth in the marketplace that women don't buy life insurance."[42]

What has happened in the marketplace is not surprising. Men don't seek insurance agents out; men are called, pursued, and sought after. This isn't true of women. Men agents stay primarily in their comfort zones, selling to other males who share the same interests, and with whom they can exchange sports scores and fishing stories. Women have less insurance, not because of less need, but because they aren't sold as hard. Women have less life insurance; therefore, the assumption is that women don't buy life insurance.

Another myth Wolfe addressed is "Women can't make up their minds. They have to shop around." Women shop around more because they do their homework better. They are less familiar with insurance and want to be more knowledgeable before they make a decision. But make no mistake, women are just as capable as men of making a decision. They just arrive at the decision in a different manner than men. As with all products and services, women are value-added consumers in the insurance industry. They understand that price is just one element of the product. They evaluate policies against an entire set of criteria, not just one factor.

For years, men were viewed as the breadwinner, the partner with the economic worth. Today, a woman's income helps provide a standard of living for the family, not frills. As a single parent, she may be the sole source of support for herself and her children. As a single or divorced woman with no dependent children, she may have employees she feels responsible for, or grown children she wants to leave something to. Women today view their economic worth in different terms than their mothers did. Their daughters will never question their role as an important financial contributor to their families.

Women today don't view marriage as financial security as they did in the past. With the number of divorces climbing, many women who think they have a secure future may be shocked to realize just how fragile that future can be. More women are seeking to protect themselves and to provide for their future regardless of their spouse's contribution.

As with investments, women are less risk oriented. They buy whole life insurance because they know how much it costs and what the return will be. But a good agent will explain the benefits of disability insurance, a buy-sell agreement, key-man insurance, coverage for children, and various retirement plans.

Too often, even today, agents are guilty of categorizing women as housewives or "just-a-job" workers rather than career-oriented prospects. They need to realize that women today are better educated, have a higher level of income, and have better jobs than in the past. Many are heads-of-households, making decisions for themselves and their families. Agents should recognize that insurance is a relatively new product for women and make sure they understand the product and the options. They should recognize a woman's decision-making ability.[43]

Agents should realize that the woman's market requires better communication skills, more product information, more patience, and a higher level of service than a male customer might require. They should develop a marketing plan that addresses the needs and desires of the potential customer. Women's insurance needs vary depending on where they are in the life cycle. If they are a single head-of-household or part of a dual-income family, their needs will be different, just as their age, the age of their children, and many more variables affect what products they should purchase.

Establishing rapport is the first criteria to selling to women. Trust is earned over time, and most sales can't be made on the first visit. But developing the relationship will pay big dividends in the future. Having access to a woman's network of contacts can improve an agent's closing ratio.

A *Best's Review* article asked the question: "Does Gender Make a Difference?"[44] Authors William Ghee and Carlos Moore presented findings from their study of 10,000 policyholders of a large midwestern life insurance company. Eighteen percent of the responses were usable. They concluded gender was not a factor in the buyers' perceptions of insurance agents or in the type of insurance they purchased. Some distinct gender differences did emerge: men, on the average more than women, believed the profits of life insurance companies were higher than other industries, but women ranked having only one agent for their insurance needs far more important than men. Again, women verbalized their need to build relationships of trust with the people with whom they do business. Men viewed life insurance as protection. Women more often saw it as an efficient way to save. While men also saw it as a way to save, their feelings were not as strong as women's. Women preferred a visit from the agent rather than visiting his office, while men preferred the reverse. When the agent came to the customer, men preferred a meeting at the office. More men than women had insurance coverage in excess of $100,000. Ghee and Moore surmised, "An awareness of these differences will help the agent be more effective in dealing with both present and future male and female clients."

Just as with their banking and other purchases, when it comes to buying insurance women are better listeners, aren't afraid to ask questions, and are more loyal customers once they are sold.

Women Invest for the Future

Women live longer and earn less than men. Women are more conservative investors. Women admit to a limited understanding of many investment concepts. Women are less familiar with handling large sums of money than are men. Women no longer see marriage as security. Women are becoming independent wage earners. Women's investment strategies differ from men's, and women are the fastest growing market segment for financial planning. Understanding how women approach the financial marketplace will enable the financial planner, broker, or marketer of the products to better meet their needs.

Joy Heckendorf, vice president of retail marketing for Janus Funds, is well aware of the woman's market and the amount of dollars it represents.[45] "Our company serves both genders," Heckendorf advised. "What makes us unique is that we have no minimum investment. We allow people to invest that have only a small amount of money." Janus Funds' ads are designed to appeal to the small investor's market with headlines that read, "Start Small. Think Big."

With this basic strategy, Janus Funds has concentrated on the woman's market as well as the small investor. "We did focus groups and research that indicated that single women and young career women, as well as divorced and widowed women, were all interested in investing."

They created an ad to appeal just to women for *Working Woman* magazine, rather than the financial publications where they usually advertise.

" 'A Woman's Place Is In The Markets.' was immensely successful," exclaimed Heckendorf. "We got many more calls to our 800 number than the more generic ad we first ran in *Working Woman*."

Industries You Wouldn't Have Thought About

Dating services, such as Great Expectations, are becoming more prolific as more women go to work, have less time to socialize, and have more money. Services like Rent-a-Wife assume car pooling, grocery shopping, and other responsibilities traditionally performed by stay-at-home wives.

Country clubs have always catered to the family, but city clubs were primarily frequented by businessmen. Now city clubs want the professional woman member as well. "In the 1960s and 1970s, women were reluctant to join city clubs on their own," recalled Jerry Gelinas, vice president of marketing for Club Corporation of America (CCA).[46] The University Club in Dallas created a "club-within-a-club" for professional women, offering once-a-month luncheon programs for members and guests on current business topics. Twelve club members run the professional women's group with a staff liaison. "While CCA is seeing an increase in city club memberships, those clubs that offer golf are growing the fastest with women. In the late 1980s women began to join for the golf privileges," noted Gelinas.

Along with the rise in women joining golf clubs, there is an increase in sales of golf equipment and apparel for women. Major corporations like Mazda Motors are sponsoring golf clinics for women. The accounting firm of Price Waterhouse and law firms like Jenkens & Gilchrist parlayed their "Women in Finance Forums" into golf clinics.

Innovative marketing is working today in many areas, and many companies are discovering that they need to reinvent the wheel. New ingredients must be added to the marketing mix of the 1970s and 1980s in order to reach women of the 1990s.

Even the toy industry has felt the power of the professional woman. If you doubt this statement, ask Mattel what happened when Barbie said, "Math class is tough." Professional women, particularly the American Association of University Women, were outraged, and for the first time in her successful history, Barbie was recalled. Barbie's wardrobe, while still dominated by the frills and fluff lifestyle she leads, now contains some career-oriented clothes. Barbie can be dressed as an astronaut, business executive, or doctor.

Dolores Richie, a qualified mechanic, was tired of the stereotyping the toy industry portrayed in the dolls they created for little girls. She has developed and is marketing a line of career dolls. Her porcelain dolls come in either a mechanic's uniform, a soldier's camouflage fatigues, or a biker's black vinyl outfit.[47]

Women buyers are impacting the real estate market. Not as an agent selling property, but as the buyer. "Even though home ownership by couples decreased between 1982 and 1990, among women it increased at least 25 percent," according to Dr. James W. Hughes, a housing expert at Rutgers University, in an article in the *Dallas Morning News*. The National Association of Home Builders confirmed this fact. Single women purchased 3.5 percent, or 17,815, of the new single-family homes in 1991. By comparison, single men purchased only 2.3 percent, or 11,707 homes. Consistent with the traits women consumers have shown in other areas, they do their homework in home buying as well. "More than half the people enrolled in the NationsBank Community Home Buyer's Program classes are women," stated Bob Boehm, assistant vice president of NationsBank Mortgage Corp." Such classes are an excellent marketing device to attract women as banking customers. "More than 27 percent of the loans granted by the Enterprise Foundation between November 1 and April 1992, were to female heads of households," said Barbara Cassel.[48]

As more women buy homes, they also are buying electronic equipment, computers, lawn and garden equipment, and tools. "Ace is the place" is a slogan no longer aimed only at men. Ads promoting "Ace Hardware's Unconventional Bridal Registry" run in *Modern Bride* magazine. For those who want to register, Ace displays their dishes and flatware in a special bridal section. "Many showers are for couples now, not just women, so our merchandise offers a variety of options.

"These registries have been very successful in small towns," noted Sheila Peters, houseware and gift buyer for Ace Hardware.[49] "We have written a manual to help our retailers better implement the program." Peters indicated, "Much has changed. Couples are marrying later, or they are on their second or third marriage. They already have all the traditional wedding gift items. Often they are buying a house and need lawn and garden equipment and tools more than crystal and china."

Women have also joined the ranks of do-it-yourselfers. "It's hard to tell how many women are actually doing the work and how many are just the purchasing agent for the project," observed Ellen Hackney, communications director for the National Retail Hardware Association.[50] Women are definitely instrumental in getting the projects started, and they influence the color and quality of the materials purchased. Hackney believes that even single women usually have help on projects with a male neighbor, friend, or relative. A lot of women don't feel particularly at ease in a hardware store. Many stores are trying to organize the displays better, make them more visually appealing to women, and train their sales staff to assist women customers more effectively.

Notes

[1] Patricia Leigh Brown, "New Designs to Keep Tupperware Fresh," *The New York Times* (10 June 1993): B–1.

[2] Dory Owens, "Tupperware Follows Women to Work," *Detroit Free Press* (3 August 1987): D–2.

[3] Brown, "New Designs," B–1.

[4] Patricia Aburdene and John Naisbitt, *Megatrends for Women* (New York: Villard Books, 1992), 134–140.

[5] Ibid, 128–142.

[6] George Oates, marketing manager, Illinois Masonic Medical Center, interview with author, 2 June 1993.

[7] Nancy Curran, education coordinator, Illinois Masonic Medical Center, interview with author, 2 June 1993.

[8] Kathleen Deveny, "The Health Industry Finally Asks: What Do Women Want?" *Business Week* (25 August 1986): 81.

[9] "Women's Services Give Hospitals Shot in the Arm," by New York Times Weekly Business, *Sun Sentinel* (2 November 1992): 7.

[10] Ibid.

[11] Ibid.

[12] Eileen Ong, director of marketing, Women's Hospital of Texas, interview with author, 16 June 1993.

[13] Michael Calhoun, director of marketing services, Baptist Memorial Health Care System, interview with author, 2 June 1993.

[14] Sunita Wadekar Bhargava, "Finally, a Healthy Interest in Women," *Business Week* (20 July 1992): 88–89.

[15] Patricia Winters, "Information-hungry Boomers to Fuel Continued Growth," *Advertising Age* (18 January 1993): 10.

[16] Matthew Grimm, "Nike Realigns for Women's Foot Race," *Brandweek* (18 January 1993): 2.

[17]Sue King, executive director, Women's Shooting Sports Foundation, interview with author, 29 May 1993.

[18]American Sports Analysis as cited by the National Shooting Sports Foundation, "Consumer Products: Arms and the Woman," *Marketing to Women* (March 1993): 12.

[19]Christine Thomas, associate professor of resource management, University of Wisconsin—Stevens Point, interview with author, 1 June 1993.

[20]Chris Killoy, director of production and marketing management, Smith & Wesson, interview with author, 19 May 1993.

[21]"Consumer Products: Arms and the Woman," *Marketing to Women* (March 1993): 12.

[22]Jim Waldorf, president/owner, Lorcin Engineering, interview with author, 29 June 1993.

[23]Carrie Goerne, "Gun Companies Target Women; Foes Call It 'Marketing to Fear,' " *Marketing News* (Vol. 26 no. 18): 1.

[24]Maggie Jones, "Gunmakers Target Women," *Working Woman* (July 1993): 10.

[25]Sonny Jones, "The War on Gun Ownership Still Goes On! Women and Guns—A Matter of Choice," *Guns & Ammo* (August 1992): 31, 83.

[26]Mike Hayashi, president/CEO, Mike Hayashi Associates, interview with author, 3 August 1993.

[27]Sara LePere, president/owner, Feminine Protection, interview with author, 26 May 1993.

[28]Linda Mutchnick, president/owner, PistolERA, interview with author, 3 June 1993.

[29]Regina McGee, "What Do Women Business Travelers Really Want?," *Successful Meetings* (August 1988): 55–57.

[30]Michele Manges, "Hotels Change Pitch to Businesswomen," *The Meeting Manager* (December 1988): 38–39.

[31]Marian Gerlich, partner, Placidi & Gerlich Communications, interview with author, 17 May 1993.

[32]Carrie Reckert, director of public relations, Hyatt Hotels, interview with author, 22 July 1993.

[33]Candy L. Stoner, "Women Are 36% of Stays in Key Markets," *Hotels & Restaurants International* (October, 1988): 84–86.

[35]Ibid, 77.

[36]Ibid, 75–82.

[37]Ellen S. Schultz, "Wall Street Courts Women with Pitch They Have Different Financial Needs," *The Wall Street Journal* (11 June 1992).

[38]Retirement Savings in America, "The Retirement Gender Gap: Women Live Longer and Have More Reasons to be Concerned About Retirement than Men," *Merrill Lynch Fifth Annual Retirement and Planning Survey* (1993): 6–9.

[39]Katherine Greene and Richard Greene, "Is Financial Advice Sexist?" *Working Woman* (September 1993): 54–59/104–105.

[40]Eleena De Lisser, "Banks Court Disenchanted Customers," *The Wall Street Journal* (30 August 1993).

[41]Ann Hall, Ann Eldridge Hall, Inc., interview with author, 27 May 1993.

[42]Jan H. Wolfe, "The Invisible Prospect," *American Council of Life Insurance, National Association of Insurance Commissioner, New York State Department of Insurance—Fortune* (May 1992): 24–31.

[43]Thomas C. Eusebio, *Insurance Sales* (March 1990): 3–37.

[44]William K Ghee, and Carlos W. Moore, "Does Gender Make a Difference?" *Best's Review* (March 1989): 49–54.

[45]Joy Heckendorf, vice president of marketing, Janus Funds, interview with author, 25 May 1993.

[46]Jerry Gelinas, vice president of marketing, Club Corporation of America, interview with author, 3 August 1993.

[47]Norma Adams Wade, "Bus Mechanic Markets 'Career Dolls' in Her Image," *Dallas Morning News* (7 January 1992): A11–13.

[48]Toni Y. Joseph, "Home Alone," *Dallas Morning News* (29 April 1992): C5, 8.

[49]Sheila Peters, houseware and gift buyer, Ace Hardware, interview with author, 23 April 1993.

[50]Ellen Hackney, communication director, National Retail Hardware Association, interview with author, 11 August 1993.

Chapter 5

The Feminization of the Automotive Industry

In 1970, only 23 percent of all cars were sold to women. Women's main role was to select the color. By the early 1990s, a major transformation had occurred: Women were now purchasing nearly 50 percent of all cars. They were becoming the majority consumer! No industry has been more affected by the increase of women consumers than the automotive, and no industry, to my knowledge, has responded as slowly or inappropriately to a market segment that is their future lifeblood.

As women began to buy more cars, light trucks, and minivans, nobody in Detroit noticed. Nothing was happening in the manufacturing, design, advertising, or sales training that said to women, "We respect you as a valued customer and we want your business." Seat belts continued to be designed to fit the larger male frame. Performance won over safety and reliability in the message manufacturers were conveying, and women continued to be the decor, rather than the driver, in advertising.

Fearing that men, now barely 50 percent of the market, would stop buying their cars if they designed, advertised, and marketed cars to women, domestic manufacturers turned a deaf ear to this growing, powerful group. There is no reason to believe that marketing and selling more effectively to women would infringe on the male image of man's beloved automobile. Women will never view this machine with the same eyes men do, but they will buy it with the same kind of dollars. The feminization of the automobile industry won't lead to a mass exodus of males. It will lead to better designed vehicles with more safety features, designed with more concern for the environment and ergonomically better suited to women.

What puzzles me, however, is why this is a problem to Detroit. Why are they concerned with losing men's business, but not women's business? Men are going to buy cars; women are going to buy cars. The two are not mutually exclusive. The smart manufacturer will target and sell to both.

Many predominantly male industries have successfully targeted the woman customer. They can testify to the fact that they haven't lost their male market by properly addressing the needs of women. In fact, they have all reaped bountiful rewards.

"In 1914, Henry Ford, trying to sell his automobiles, had a novel idea—courting the female consumer. As it turns out, Ford was a man ahead of his time. While other industries discovered—and played to—the buying power of women over the years, Detroit—that quintessential town of man and machine—preferred to think that cars were made by men for men," wrote Paul Witteman.[1]

According to Witteman's account, and many others, Detroit, like a boy reaching adolescence, suddenly became aware of the female's presence, and awkwardly tried to court her and win her loyalty. Completely unaware that in order to reach her, you must first take time to understand her, Detroit plowed ahead with a mission, but no sound plan. Reflecting your customer's needs and desires is a basic premise taught in Marketing 101, but somehow Detroit failed to comprehend this lesson. The almost totally male hierarchy that operates, designs, and sells cars to women must begin to consider women's views. Manufacturers must ask women for input before cars are designed, before advertising campaigns are completed, and before marketing strategies are put into place.

The company that makes the paradigm shift most successfully will be the leader into the next century. Companies must begin to think of the female buyer, not as the enemy, but as the friend. A friend that will eagerly share her thoughts in order to improve the automotive buying experience. Manufacturers must begin to hire more women at all levels and move them up the corporate ladder, knowing that this will be a positive step for the company, not a fatal move.

Women are not going to suggest automakers design a "woman's car." They don't want a car designed for women, but a car designed with women in mind. Incorporating features that are important to women won't make a vehicle a "woman's car." It will only make it a car that women will buy, drive and tell their friends about. It is a proven fact that some features are more important to women than men. Horsepower is important to women primarily as a means to assure greater safety. Women want enough horsepower to get on a freeway safely or to pass a car easily. Of course, speed and a sporty look are important to some women, but the majority's prime concerns are safety, reliability, and dependability.

Women want to feel secure in their cars. If a car breaks down, it is a hassle for a man. He doesn't want the aggravation or cost of repairs, either. However, he is not as worried about his personal security as a woman is. A breakdown can be dangerous and traumatic to a woman. That's why reliability ranks so high with women.

"Detroit doesn't have a clue," said Edward Lapham, executive editor of *Automotive News*.[2] "The National Automobile Dealers Association (NADA) can preach the doctrine of equality, but it just isn't happening. Most women's committees in the past have been a token gesture with a very narrow focus. Designers must be more aware of the ergonomics of the car and the woman," advised Lapham. He cites Ford's success after testing the knobs and buttons with long-fingernails, the fabric on the seats, and many other features that Ford incorporated as a result of testing its product with women. He also praises BMW's efforts to recognize and aggressively seek the female consumer by reacting quickly to her needs. Lapham emphasized that the showroom is still a major problem that must be dealt with. "Women are still not being taken seriously as the customer, and many dealerships are losing sales as a result. When women are treated badly, or stupidly, they leave." While men don't like bad treatment either, the truth is they are not as likely to receive it, or to be ignored. "We just did a survey with female new car buyers and asked how important gender was in the salesperson. The majority didn't care as long as the person was knowledgeable and treated them with respect. Those who preferred women said they could communicate better with them; those who preferred men thought they knew more about cars." Lapham encourages manufacturers to continue to provide sensitivity training to the dealers as well as designers, engineers, and marketers. Everyone who affects the customer base is important.

By listening to women, and not just assuming they know what women want, corporate executives will make more educated decisions that will increase their sales to both sexes. It's a proven fact. I challenge you to give me one concrete example of a well-implemented program to women that has lost sales to men. But I have given you several examples in Chapters 3 and 4 of programs and design enhancements recommended by women that were equally popular with men. There are also examples where male sales remained constant, and the development of the woman's market had a remarkably positive effect on the company's profitability.

Women Drive Sales More than
50 Percent of the Time

In 1955, nearly forty years ago, when the Big Three were kings of the industry, the Dodge La Femme was designed as a vehicle for women. Four decades later, the Big Three automakers are still trying to figure out how to sell more successfully to this growing, powerful market, but with minimal results.

The Dodge La Femme, produced only in pink and lavender, with a rosebud interior and a matching purse, umbrella, raincoat, and boots, would seem to be the rock-bottom example of marketing cars to women. Less than 1,000 cars were sold.[3] Thirty years ago, Ford tried to lure women with a pink Mustang appropriately named Ms. Mustang. Pontiac's striped Honey Bees, Bluebirds, and Yellowbirds were other futile attempts to market to women.[4]

Less than five years ago, in 1989, this quote appeared in *The Wall Street Journal:* "General Motors reports that its thin steering wheels and pink-and-white color schemes haven't set well with female buyers. 'Women don't specifically want to be catered to,' says George Angersbach, a GM designer."[5] Having failed to learn from the mistakes of the past, General Motors continued to rely on male designers, marketers, advertisers, and executives who haven't a clue about the marketplace. In 1986, GM's Buick Division advised its dealers to host tea parties to lure women into the showrooms. Its continual decline in market share is no surprise.

According to the July 9, 1992, issue of the *San Francisco Chronicle* referring to the Dodge La Femme of the mid-1950s, "It has been apparent ever since that pastel is not the way to go. But four decades later, when women buy half of all new cars and even drive the contraptions themselves, the auto industry still has not quite figured out how to act around women. Its clumsiness has, by many accounts, left the lucrative women's market up for grabs."

Manufacturers, store owners, and general managers are guilty of failing to provide adequate training and information to their sales force. Most salespeople commit "sins" while selling to women out of ignorance, rather than out of a desire to lose the sale. When I watch mistake after mistake being made in their advertising (see Chapter 6) and sales techniques, I have a hard time understanding the egocentric mentality that would allow a downward sales trend to perpetuate, rather than taking steps to alleviate it and turn it around. Acknowledging the presence of women in the marketplace and asking what is important to them are just two steps that could provide a positive shift in the sales trend for the Big Three.

Manufacturers can no longer keep their heads buried in the sand, but must face reality—women drivers are here to stay. Those who develop a product that is fairly priced, deliver an advertising message that is informative, not sexist, and take the pains to properly train their sales staffs in both product knowledge and the treatment of women in the showroom will gain the upper hand. The market is there for the taking. While many salespeople still think "What color would you like?" is as technical a question as you should ask a woman, most dealerships are finding that if they don't retrain their staff to understand and meet the needs of the new professional woman, they won't need a staff much longer.

Time and time again I hear, "There is no difference between women and men. We treat all our customers equally." But the reality is, there is a difference. A big difference. I am often told, "We can't afford that kind of training." Yet, all it would take to provide meaningful training would be to delete one or two ads from the schedule. Not a noticeable difference in the advertising impact. Yet, there would be a very noticeable difference in sales by properly trained personnel, the number of loyal customers they would generate, and the rate at which they turn over, or leave for another job. Dealers and manufacturers, by refusing to acknowledge the need for help with the women's market, have locked themselves into a losing situation. The key to unlock the trend is so obvious, so easy, and so cost effective. I, like others who work in this market, can't understand why anyone would choose to continue to grasp at pink straws rather than grab real dollars.

Tom Healey, a partner with J.D. Power and Associates in Agoura Hills, California, told a personal story that demonstrates how car salespeople consistently lose sales without even being aware of what they are doing wrong. In the article, "Women and Cars," he described the disappointment his wife felt when *he* received the thank-you note for *her* car purchase.[6] What may seem inconsequential to a car salesperson isn't unimportant to the woman whose husband received the note for her purchase. When this procedure is multiplied hundreds of times annually, what might appear initially to be a minor mistake is losing thousands of future sales and millions of dollars.

Other gestures and language used by the sales staff, holdovers from a different era, are also losing sales. "We'll negotiate the price when you bring your husband in," or talking to the male companion/spouse in lieu of the woman buyer are just two of the many faux pas happening in showrooms across the country daily. When politicians loudly proclaimed 1992 as the "Year of the Woman," no one made sure the automotive industry was listening and got the message. When the woman is ignored, talked down to, or told to bring her husband in, she almost always buys elsewhere.

A survey conducted by *Woman's Day* magazine in January 1993, verifies these facts.[7] Of the 500 males and 500 females surveyed, 83 percent of the women felt purchasing a car was a difficult process. Sixty-two percent of the women believed they were treated worse in the showroom than men. While 50 percent of the men worried about being ripped off by the salesperson, more than 63 percent of women expressed that concern. The disparities are even greater with regard to auto mechanics. Eighty-three percent of the men surveyed said they were comfortable changing a tire, but only 41 percent of the women responded affirmatively.

Amazingly, as the 1990s continue to produce educated, sophisticated women consumers, automotive manufacturers continue to flounder in their search for the right formula. Understanding the woman consumer and how to reach her isn't really all that difficult.

First, most successful product marketing and advertising efforts specifically intended to attract women utilize women in their planning process. Throughout this book, example after example shows how women have impacted the successful design of the product and the effective creation of advertising, and how this success has not only increased sales to women but frequently to men as well. Men have realized the value of air bags, lumbar back supports and illuminated and remote entries in cars—benefits implemented with women in mind.

Manufacturers who believe women are going to buy vehicles anyhow, so there is no need to do anything special, will watch as the female market drives off in the competition's product.

Yes, women are going to buy cars, trucks, and minivans—and in record numbers. They are the purchaser of nearly 50 percent of new cars, and they influence the purchase of nearly 85 percent of all new car and truck sales. Sales to women account for approximately $65 billion. That is a fact. The questions are: Will it be your product or your competitor's? Will it be a domestic or an import? In the past, women have frequently chosen to buy imports rather than domestics because foreign car manufacturers listened to them and responded to their needs. Foreign manufacturers stressed the attributes that women wanted in their cars and in their advertising.

Meanwhile, the Big Three were busy creating a world where only the male was supreme and women knew their place—on the hood of the car, not in the driver's seat. Today, this is changing. But women have good memories.

Unfortunately, many times when manufacturers, dealers, or salespersons recognize the error of their ways, they attempt to rectify this injustice, but inadvertently create another blunder—just as damaging.

While drastically changing their strategies, they continue to be condescending to women. The line is thin, and it's easy to miss the mark if you don't have sufficient insight into what works and what doesn't work with women. Not surprisingly, women are best equipped to provide this information.

Some manufacturers, like Volvo, enjoy a predominantly female following. They continue to stress their outstanding safety records in their advertising and to add features to their vehicles that attract women. The three-point rear seat belt, air bags, anti-lock brakes, and automatic door locks win women buyers. Volvo believes, and has sales to back up their belief, that safety sells. At least, it does to women. Women buy more than 65 percent of all Volvos and 70 percent of its wagons.

The Infiniti J30, positioned as a car that makes a personal statement about your style, has also had great success with women. Women buy 50 percent of all J30s sold, even though they presently buy only 36 percent in the luxury car market. Infiniti's outstanding service, comfort, and styling appeal to women. Infiniti has created direct-mail videos and has used mailing lists from popular women's publications to enhance their existing lists and their visibility with women.[8] The Volkswagen Cabriolet is another example of a car that has sold well to women. Sixty-one percent of its buyers are women.

Many other imports have focused successfully on the main concerns of women—safety and dependability—and, as a result, have captured a large share of the market. While many imports have taken advantage of the lucrative female car buying market, not all have wooed women with zeal. Those that have taken the stance that there is no difference between men and women car buyers should re-evaluate their position. Even though Nissan and Mitsubishi have some models that sell very well to women, their percentage of sales to women is lower than many other foreign manufacturers.

According to Jule Clavadetscher, general marketing manager at Nissan Corporation U.S.A.: "Our strategy is product-focused. If the product has the attributes that will appeal to women buyers, then we'll make sure to mention those attributes. I don't think we need to send out free lipstick samples to get women into our showrooms."[9] The mere fact that the concept of a tube of lipstick was Nissan's idea of how companies market to women says a lot. It is astonishing that they could make such an inane statement knowing the effect women have on an automotive company's bottom line. It demonstrates a lack of understanding of the new professional woman, and, therefore, how can they hope to meet her needs? Ironically, Infiniti is part of the Nissan Corporation. Hopefully, Infiniti will share their insight into successful marketing to women with their parent company, as Lexus has done with Toyota.

Another Japanese carmaker, Mazda, created programs designed to captivate the woman's market. Not surprisingly, Mazda sells a higher percentage of their vehicles to women than does either Nissan or Mitsubishi. Mazda recognized the woman's market, aggressively sought it, and developed programs sensibly tailored to the career women they wanted as customers. Also, not surprising is the fact that Mazda had a woman in charge of the marketing effort and women involved in the advertising campaign.

Jan Thompson, then marketing vice president for the Mazda Division of Mazda Motors of America Inc., along with her staff, created the kind of promotion women wanted from an automobile manufacturer.[10] Mazda began sponsoring Executive Women Golf Clinics, first in six selected cities, later expanded to nine. Mazda selected as its beneficiary a charity that would appeal to women—the Susan G. Komen Foundation for breast cancer. By using mailing lists from businesses such as the National Association of Women Business Owners, it zeroed in on its market. Mazda designed an innovative program that would be of interest to women in business rather than a *feminine* enticement such as a *pink* gimmick. Mazda also sponsors women's sporting events including the Mazda LPGA Championship and the Mazda Tennis Classic. These high-visibility events helped increase Mazda's female buyers from 45 percent in 1989 to more than 52 percent in 1992.

Mazda didn't leave the results from the multiple-city golf clinics to chance. Thompson followed up. Each participant who took a test-drive received an incentive—a $75 gift certificate for golf merchandise. She received a $500 certificate if she bought the car. The recipients were sent a survey to fill out, and their names were entered in a data base so that purchases could be tracked in each market.

Marketing and selling to women starts long before the showroom. Having women involved in design features, advertising campaigns, and marketing efforts helps eliminate costly mistakes. Testing ads with women to ensure they don't find them offensive or condescending is important in formulating advertising messages. What men think is okay may not be okay to women.

Forty years ago, DeSoto designed a brochure with a smiling woman who boasted that the power steering was as "easy as dialing a telephone." Even though times have changed and the demographics of the consumer have changed, many marketing messages today are just as ineffective as this one was forty years ago. Only a few years ago, in 1990, Gloria Steinem wrote in *Ms.* magazine that "Detroit never quite learned the secret of creating intelligent ads that exclude no one, and then placing them in women's magazines."[11]

Good News, Finally

On a more positive note, much is finally being done to capture the woman's market in a sensible, effective way.

Many manufacturers have begun to implement design features that are appealing to women, and by looking at the ergonomics of the car, have made many design elements more attractive to the female. Women are not just smaller versions of men. Their needs are truly different than their male counterparts.

Niki Safron, head of Chrysler's women's committee, emphasized the importance of considering a woman's fingernail length in the design of the knobs, handles, and control buttons. Professional women have well-manicured nails and want a vehicle that works with them, not against them. Manufacturers must realize that enhancing the car to accommodate the female consumer isn't going to lose sales to men. While men don't have long nails, they like the new button design because it fits their larger hands better. Vehicles with practical improvements like these are not considered "women's cars." Safety features originally added for women have become standard on many cars.

The Mercury Villager minivan is an excellent example of how a woman's input can have a positive effect on the product. The minivan was being driven by a woman during its initial testing period when her high heel got caught in one of the seating tracks. While this was a relatively simple problem to solve, without the woman's participation in the testing, the problem would have gone unnoticed until after the vehicles were in production. No male designer, engineer, or marketing executive's heel would have wedged in the track. In sales to women, it's the little things that make the big differences.

After a manufacturer has designed products with features that will appeal to women, it must present this message in clear, concise terms in its advertising and in its sales demonstration. The Crown Victoria's adjustable seat belt is a terrific feature. Most women find seat belts very uncomfortable because they were developed to fit the larger torso of the male driver. Demonstrating the adjustable seat belt in ads and when women are test driving the car will boost sales. Yet when I went for a test drive of the car at a local dealership, the salesman never mentioned the feature to me, and I'm a petite five feet.

When General Motors installed ABS brakes (anti-lock braking system) on nearly all its cars, Cavalier sales plummeted. Prior to the installation of the brakes, Cavalier sales to women had been very strong. The price of the car went up, and women bought elsewhere because General

Motors neglected to relate the value of the brakes to the increased cost. Women simply didn't know what ABS brakes were and, therefore, were reluctant to pay the additional price. The sales line changed dramatically, but sales should have gone off the top of the chart, not the bottom. General Motors had an opportunity no other manufacturer, domestic or import, had to increase sales of the Cavalier simply by properly marketing and advertising this significant feature. Illustrate to women the benefits, show them the long-term cost savings in dollars, injuries, and lives, and visually produce ads that tell that story.

Instead, General Motors chose to let its advantage be the best kept secret in America. While Chrysler blatantly continued to demonstrate the value of the air bag, General Motors remained quiet about the ABS brakes, or discreetly tagged ads: "ABS brakes standard equipment." While Chrysler lobbied the insurance industry to give price reductions for air bags, nothing was immediately happening in the insurance field to convince drivers they needed ABS brakes. Air bags are triggered only when a head-on collision occurs; ABS brakes are part of safe driving on a daily basis.

Developing features that will increase sales to women is only the first step. The second is getting the message out—telling women the benefits of the features in language they relate to. The third is making sure all salespersons are knowledgeable about the features and benefits, and that it is part of their sales presentation.

The Ultimate Team—Sales, Service, and the Customer

When the sales department begins to recognize that it doesn't function in a vacuum, long-term, satisfied customers will result. Far too often, I am told by salespersons, "We don't control what happens in the service area." Owners, general managers, sales managers, and service managers need to understand that the future is going to be based not on their autonomy, but on their collective ability to operate as a single unit, at least as far as the customer is concerned. How the books are kept is irrelevant to the marketing process.

In the automotive industry, the service department holds the key to whether a customer buys there again. It plays a significant role in building loyalty and securing a woman customer's network. Karen Rowan, service and parts director for Pray Infiniti in Greenwich, Connecticut, has taught her staff how to say *yes*.[12] "Too often customers are told, 'No, we can't do that, we don't have that in stock' or 'we can't fix that today,'" said

Rowan. "I want our staff to say *yes* and find a way to accommodate our customers' needs."

Infiniti's service area is designed with the customer in mind. The all-glass walls allow customers to easily watch as the work is performed on their vehicles. In most dealerships, the work areas are off-limits to the customers. "We don't want our customers to think we have anything to hide," explained Rowan. The service department is open, simple, well-lit, and clean.

"Infiniti's Total Ownership Experience (TOE) makes the customer feel comfortable from the first moment they walk into a showroom. The service area is just an extension of that." Rowan believes honesty is the best policy with customers. Any dealership that can make women comfortable, is honest with them, and respects them as valued customers will have an edge on most of the competition.

Obtaining impressive Customer Service Index (CSI) ratings is important, but happy, loyal customers are what most dealers should strive for. The customer must be number one. However, most automobile owners don't feel they are appreciated or well treated in the service area of the dealership. Service and sales can't be separated in the automotive industry. Service will either enhance the sales effort, or it will destroy it.

"Dealers need to be more aware of the service area and the complaints," said Mary Flowers, managing editor of *Dealer Business*.[13] "There is a lack of communication between the customer and the service personnel. They need to spend more time understanding the problem initially so that it can be fixed right the first time. The technicians need to be held more accountable for the work they perform," said Flowers.

Flowers believes that the manufacturers have finally realized the importance of the woman's market, but there are still problems in the showrooms. "Things don't always trickle down to the salespeople," she said. "Some are ignorant of the woman consumer; others are just lazy."

In the July 12, 1993, *Automotive News*, J. Ferron with J. D. Power and Associates listed the cars receiving the best CSI (Table 5-1).

TABLE 5-1   CSI Top 10

1. Lexus LS400	6. Infiniti J30
2. Infiniti Q45	7. Infiniti G20
3. Lexus SC300/400	8. Mercedes-Benz 190E
4. Lexus ES300	9. Saturn sedan
5. Infiniti M30	10. Toyota Corolla

Source: J.D. Power and Associates, *Automotive News*

Research indicates that while the service area is the place of greatest customer dissatisfaction in the dealership, the financing and insurance (F&I) department has the lowest personal ratings in the sales area.

Because it is often more difficult for women to get credit, they fear rejection and the F&I process. According to Janet Eckhoff, director of product and marketing strategy, Cadillac will be introducing a program that will alleviate this anxiety with the female buyer.[14] "Making the transaction more comfortable for women is one of our objectives," declared Eckhoff.

Cadillac is beginning to understand that making women feel like valued customers is as important as the features on the car. While this seems so basic, it is often forgotten in the showroom. When affluent women are ignored, talked down to or angered, they buy elsewhere. Frequently, they even buy a different make.

One-price or no-hassle negotiation is another approach dealerships are experimenting with in hopes of improving the buying experience. This is more complex than just a simple pricing strategy. For some makes, such as Saturn, all cars are one price. Some manufacturers have certain models, such as the Ford Escort, that are one price, but not the entire line. Some dealerships have decided to mark all vehicles with one-price stickers; others have only marked some.

"At the end of 1992, only about 500 dealers had elected to be no-hassle dealerships," said Doris Ehlers, account director at J. D. Power and Associates.[15] "It is a very hard concept to implement in a competitive market. If you post a price, someone can go down the block and get the car for $50 less," explained Ehlers. "To work successfully, the dealer must gain the consumer's trust. Most successful dealers have instituted innovative marketing approaches to gain and retain customers. Another strategy is to get the customer involved in appraising the trade-in. Why they think the car is worth a certain amount. The owner may have to justify any enhancements they made to the car."

Enide Allison is switching her Mazda dealership in California to totally one-price selling.[16] "We are going to focus on the woman's market, and one way is by becoming more service-oriented and less confrontational." Everyone at Oak Tree Mazda underwent extensive training. They all attended a Dale Carnegie course to learn better communication skills and how to be a good listener. They will be on a salary rather than on a commission, and they will receive a bonus based on the number of cars they sell, not the price.

Allison believes that the sales staff must first sell themselves, then make sure the customer knows that the dealership is there for them. "There will be extensive follow-up on every prospect who comes in and a tracking system to see if they buy from us and, if not, why not," promised Allison. Personal service is what the staff will be selling along with the car. Unlike many dealers, Allison understands that the fragile link between the sales and service departments is critical for success. "Our sales staff will work with the customer in the service area to make sure everything is okay." Allison realizes that some people will shop price, and perhaps not buy from her, but she is banking on the fact that the majority don't want the hassle of the old system and will prefer to have everything upfront. Building trust is the cornerstone of one-price selling. The staff has also undergone product training, new dealership procedures and many hours of role-playing exercises in an effort to be ready for their new challenge.

Another method used by some customers to minimize the frustration associated with purchasing a car is the broker or buying club concept. Once buyers decide what they want, they often contact brokers or buying clubs that will locate and negotiate for the car. Therefore, the buyer doesn't have to do the legwork or endure the hassle or frustration. This is particularly attractive to women who prefer to isolate themselves from the buying experience. According to Ehlers, when new car buyers were asked about their buying experiences, 14 percent said they enjoyed negotiating the price; 32 percent said they didn't like negotiating the price but felt it was important to obtain the best price; 26 percent responded that they did not enjoy the process and would consider buying from a non-negotiating dealership; 20 percent said they dreaded the negotiation and would actively try to find an alternative method; and 8 percent had no response to the question. "Basically, it was split pretty evenly. Forty-six percent said they would negotiate, 46 percent said they wouldn't if they could find another means and 8 percent had no response or opinion.

"Of the 45,500 people who bought a car or truck in November and December 1993, 11.3 percent used some type of referral service when shopping for the vehicle," said Ehlers.

Are Women Leasing More?

Retail leasing has grown dramatically the last 10 years. In 1982, less than 3 percent of total retail car sales were leases. According to the National Vehicle Leasing Association, in 1992, 14 percent of light trucks were leased and 22 percent of cars. By 1993, that had increased to 18 percent and 23 percent respectively. It is projected that by 1997, approximately 20 percent of light trucks and 28 percent of cars will be leased. Art Spinella, vice president and general manager of CNW Marketing Research, explained that Ford Motor Company was the first to understand the potential of leasing. "Ford used leasing as a marketing tool," said Spinella.[17] Leasing has changed tremendously. Terms are shorter, giving the consumer the opportunity to trade the car more frequently and, thus, drive a new car more often.

Two advantages of leasing that appeal to women are lower payments and the warranty coverage. Because peace of mind is so important to women, the fact that often the car is under warranty for the duration of the lease is a major selling feature. When women are happy with the product and dealer, they tend to stay there. More than 50 percent of all 24-month lease customers at Ford and Lincoln-Mercury dealerships either buy or lease again from the same dealer. This statistic applies to both male and female lessees. Thus, leasing can be instrumental in developing satisfied, repeat customers of both genders.

Ford is presently testing a new lease program—Ford's Future Lease. The plan is a package of six two-year leases that guarantee the same monthly payments through 2005 if you trade for the same model. The program puts you in a new car every two years for 12 years. At the end of the 12 years, you get to keep the last car, for no additional cost. The innovative program is designed to attract new customers and transform them into loyal, long-term ones.[18]

In 1992, 1,234,100 vehicles were leased. The largest sector, luxury cars, accounted for 32.8 percent. Mid-size cars were 30 percent, but all types of vehicles are being leased today. Ford, General Motors, and Lexus now offer the leasing option to used car buyers.

"Leasing is definitely here to stay," said Tom Healey, a partner with J. D. Power and Associates. "Leasing is a way to have a new car every three years. With luxury cars, people often opt for a five-year pay out. Plus, leasing binds the customer to the manufacturer more than buying."[19]

Who's Buying What?

Many factors go into the car buying process—design, features, advertising, treatment, and price. All manufacturers track their customers, but they don't all use the same standards. Many factors skew the results. For instance, one reason Ford's percentage is so low with women is because of the number of full-size pickup trucks they sell primarily to men. According to recent figures, women account for 32 percent of all Ford Motor Company buyers, compared with 45 percent at General Motors, 50 percent at Chrysler Corporation and 52.3 percent at Mazda Motors of America Inc.[20]

According to J. D. Power and Associates, women are the principal driver of basic domestic small cars 50 percent of the time, and imports, 53 percent. Fifty-four percent of the time they drive domestic lower-middle cars, and imports 49 percent of the time. In the upper-middle segment, women are the principal driver 43 percent of the time for both domestic and import cars. In the small sporty segment, women drive domestics 49 percent of the time and imports 55 percent (Figure 5-1).

Kristine Stiven Breeses, Crain News Service, said, "Some companies track their customers by principal driver, some by buyer and some by primary decision maker, so figures may not be precisely comparable." But the two tables on the following page (Tables 5-2 and 5-3) will give some indication of what women are buying.

J. D. Power and Associates, a California consulting and research firm, listed the top 10 car models preferred by women drivers in 1992–93.

Obviously, in addition to safety features, price is a factor and, while women purchase vehicles in all price ranges, they purchase a greater proportion of the less expensive models.

In 1988, women purchased nearly half of all Honda Accord compacts sold in the United States and more than half the Ford Escorts and Chevrolet Cavaliers. Women bought 43 percent of Ford Mustang convert-

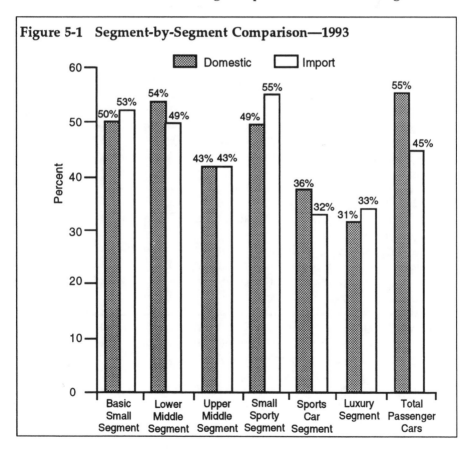

Figure 5-1   Segment-by-Segment Comparison—1993

TABLE 5-2   1992 Manufacturers—Female Buyers

Mazda	52.3	Toyota/Lexus	48.0
Honda/Acura	51.3	General Motors	45.0
Chrysler	50.0	Mitsubishi	43.0
Nissan/Infiniti	49.0	Ford	32.0

Source: Crain News Service, *Automotive News*

TABLE 5-3   Percentages of Models Purchased By Women

Subaru XT	64.3	Volkswagen Cabriolet	61.3
Toyota Celica	64.0	Toyota Tercel	61.2
Mazda MX-6	62.7	Pontiac Sunbird	60.9
Toyota Paseo	62.6	Hyundai Scoupe	59.6
Chevrolet Beretta	61.9	Plymouth Colt Vista	59.0

Source: J. D. Power and Associates

ibles, 70 percent of Volkswagen convertibles, and 76 percent of Nissan Pulsar NX models.[21] In 1990, the plush Ford sports utility four-door Explorer garnered 46 percent of the female market, while the two-door version captured 40 percent. Women liked the more luxurious features on these vehicles, including the smoother ride and softer seats. As a result, the Grand Cherokee has attracted even more women than the Explorer. Other sports utility vehicles have also done very well with the female consumer.[22]

"Of the 81,349 Suzuki Samurai purchased in 1988, 40 percent of them were bought by women. Women also bought 20 percent of the Chevy Blazer and Jeep Wagoneer," according to Jean Pellegrino, an analyst with J. D. Power and Associates.

In addition to purchasing minivans and sports utility vehicles, women are becoming major consumers of light trucks. Women of all ages, all geographic regions, and all income brackets are driving trucks. In the light truck category, women purchased 936,000 vehicles, or 19 percent of the total sales in 1988, according to industry estimates. That figure includes 327,000 compact vans and 214,000 compact sports utility vehicles. By comparing the nearly 20 percent of sales of these specialized vehicles to women in 1990 to the 2 percent in 1970, it is obvious that their purchases cover the full gamut. Analysts project this growth trend to continue and that by the year 2000 sales to women in this category will be around 30 percent. That's a market every truck manufacturer should be aggressively targeting.

Other marketing techniques that have worked well, and that women relate to, are car care clinics. Buick's single-sexed "Know Your Automobile" campaign in the 1980s was so popular that it went co-ed so men could benefit as well. Tailoring the agenda to women only has certain advantages. Women feel less threatened by their lack of knowledge and are able to relax and ask questions more in an all-female environment than in mixed groups. However, if you choose to design a car clinic for women only, don't make the fatal mistake many have made and call them "powder puff clinics"—definitely an antiquated and stereotypical term. It is also crucial that you have a well-planned agenda for the presentation, so that it is informative and a good use of the participant's time.

Successful marketing involves knowing what the customer wants and making whatever paradigm shifts are necessary in the corporate culture to produce the result. JoAnn Muller's article in *The Detroit Free Press* quoted Elizabeth Wetzel, who designs interiors for Cadillac: "Auto companies never went out and asked customers what they wanted. They just said, 'Here's the car. Do you want it?' " This approach just won't work anymore. Manufacturers must gather input before the design and manufacturing of a product, not after.

As Mimi Vandermolen, the highest ranking design executive at Ford, said in reference to the female market, "Any company that sits back and says I'm not concerned with that will lose market share." And in these tough economic times not many companies have that luxury.[23]

Credit General Motors

In September of 1992, General Motors began issuing a credit card good anywhere Mastercard was accepted. The innovative twist leading to its overwhelming success was that users of the card could accumulate rebate dollars toward the purchase of a new GM vehicle. In essence, you designed your own rebate program. The customers could cash in their dollars on a new vehicle at any time or could continue to save them. The card had a ceiling of $500 per year, or $3,500 over a seven-year period. In February, 1993, GM launched the gold card with a ceiling of $1,000 per month or $7,000 over a seven-year period.

"General Motors is in the business of making and selling cars and trucks. They developed the program to strengthen buyer loyalty and to increase conquest sales [a sale made to an owner of another brand]," said Joe St. Henry of DMB&B Public Relations.[24] "It was a marketing tool that provided a strong financial incentive."

The program attracted current GM customers as well as prospective ones.

"From September 1992 to June 1993 the following year, more than 30,000 vehicles were sold using the GM credit card rebate. There are more than 5 million card holders. One of the biggest incentives we built into the program," declared St. Henry, "was that people could transfer their balances from other credit cards to the GM card and earn instant rebate dollars on money they had already spent." Credit card sales made up 1 percent of the 3,258,257 U.S. sales for the first nine-month period.

General Motors is already reaping the rewards of the program that hit the marketplace with all the signs that they were finally thinking of the consumer. They are attracting a younger, more affluent group of buyers through this innovative marketing approach. "General Motors is meeting the needs of today's credit card consumer, and they are providing an extra value," said St. Henry.

Like General Motors, Ford has issued a credit card where a percent of the purchases can add up to rebates on Ford vehicles. Both male and female prospects enjoy the benefits of earning dollars on debt.

Ignorance Isn't Bliss: It's Costly

Watching the automotive industry take notice of the woman's market can be gratifying. While there is still much to do to make the buying experience more pleasant for both genders, recognizing there is a problem is the first step to solving it. Even though the automotive industry hasn't solved all the questions of how to treat women in the showrooms, what designs are more appealing to them, what features they want, and so on, they are at least addressing these issues and beginning to seek help from women.

I was alarmed at my initial encounter with the National Automobile Dealers Association (NADA) as I was writing this book. Since marketing and selling more effectively to women is so crucial to the survival and profitability of the automobile industry, I felt sure that they were diligently working to convey as much information to their dealer-members on the woman's market as possible. That was not what I found.

While Ford, General Motors, Chrysler, BMW, Mazda, and most of the other manufacturers are spending millions of dollars in research to develop programs and products to appeal to professional women, NADA, their trade association, didn't see the woman's market as an issue that needed addressing.

Kathi Brown, workshop coordinator for the NADA national convention, said, "We tell dealers to consider each customer as an individual.[25] We don't believe you should teach them to treat women differently. That would be stereotyping."

How many men customers do the salesmen call *honey*? How often is a male customer ignored or told to get his spouse? I have never had a man tell me he was treated poorly in the showroom *because he was a man*. But many women have drawn the conclusion that their treatment was related to their gender. Teaching salespeople to be professional with all customers is important, but a man's perception of the buying situation is very different than a woman's.

Statistics indicate that women prioritize the product features differently than men, they are more sensitive to their treatment, and they tell their experiences to far more people. Women are more cognizant of the appearance of the facility. A few poorly chosen words or phrases can lose the sale to a woman. These subtleties are critical for salespeople to know if they are to be most effective in selling to women.

Diane Caldwell heads the recently created NADA Certification Program, which has no training module dealing with the woman's market.[26] "We don't get into the women's area. We believe in treating all customers equally and fairly," said Caldwell.

Ford Motor Company has created a 25-member women's committee to work with all areas of the company to achieve the best products and marketing strategies to win this vital consumer. In the late 1980s, Ford created its own training videotape instructing dealers on how to sell more effectively to women. Recently, Ford has worked with *Cosmopolitan* magazine to create a new videotape with selling tips and techniques to help salesmen increase their sales to women. Chrysler has formed a woman's committee, and General Motors, while lagging behind the other two, is trying to refocus and develop a more comprehensive training philosophy that will assist their dealers and staffs in selling to this very important market segment. BMW is sponsoring women's sporting events and business conferences and has hired consultants for the sole purpose of helping develop marketing strategies to increase BMW's visibility and sales to women. Mazda is conducting executive women golf clinics and sponsoring LPGA and tennis events in hopes of strengthening its hold on the woman's market. All know their future is dependent on selling successful to women.

Caldwell continued, "We do provide some statistics that show that women are more influential in the purchase of a car than in the past." But they provide little insight into practical, easy-to-implement ideas. They don't bring in experts to help them implement programs in this critical area.

Women buy approximately 50 percent of all new vehicles and they influence more than 80 percent of new vehicle purchases. Marketing and selling successfully to women isn't a luxury; it is part of staying in business.

A letter I received from Anna Marie Arnone, director of management education, stated: "The National Automobile Dealers Association promotes the professional treatment of the retail automobile customer.[27] This is such a high priority that we spent more than $1 million developing a professional certification training and testing program for salespeople and sales managers. Our training focus is on treating the customer as an individual with unique needs and wants . . . . Several years ago, when women began to emerge as a major segment of the retail buying public, NADA joined many others and offered educational training sessions on selling to the female customer. But we have since recognized that women are no different than men in their desire to be treated professionally when purchasing a new car."

As has been apparent in Chapters 3 and 4, those industries that have recognized the women's market and have put women in charge of developing and marketing the product, or have sought advice from consultants or a women's committee, have all seen dramatic, almost unbelievable results. Only 6 percent of the 170,000 automobile salespeople in the country are women. Only 41 percent of new car dealerships even employ at least one female salesperson. Yet, the sales staff must sell to women if they hope to stay in business. Training is the only solution until the ratio of sales personnel and consumers are more in balance.

Many organizations have gone beyond utilizing the female resources available within the company and have formed women's advisory committees or ad hoc committees to offer advice and disburse information on women and the views they hold. This insight has rescued many a product that may have otherwise been in jeopardy. Input from women is becoming commonplace for many companies.

The next worst thing to doing nothing is believing you are doing something when you really aren't. Ted Orme, director of public relations for NADA, said, "This is a male-dominated industry; that's why we don't have many women who can speak at our meetings."[28] That's exactly the point. Because it is a male-dominated business, the automotive industry needs continual input from women.

He ended with an interesting statement: "Last year at the NADA convention, the dealer of the year was a woman."

I had the feeling I was supposed to connect this woman's success to NADA. The reality is twofold: The award was not an NADA award, but a *Time* Magazine Quality Award; and perhaps she won because she understood how to market and sell effectively to women!

Two-and-a-half months after I conducted these interviews, I was called by NADA. They were doing an article for their publication on marketing to women. I was pleased to know that somewhere along the way, they had been listening. This only reconfirmed my belief that most people don't purposefully do the wrong thing; they just don't have the knowledge or expertise to do any better. If the automotive industry can make changes, I am convinved that other businesses struggling with the issues of how to market and sell successfully to the professional woman can make changes as well. The first step is acknowledging the market exists. Next is creating a strategy that will make you competitive into the twenty-first century. NADA took the first step. Hopefully, now they will reach for the second plateau. They will find it will provide them with bountiful rewards.

Three Approaches that Can Be Taken

We can talk about the marketplace. We can continue to meet and discuss. We can form task forces. We can devise plans. We can implement recommendations. But what it all boils down to are three things: what we *could* do, what we *should* do, and what we *must* do.

Marketers, product managers, general managers, advertisers, and training departments

Could

- ❖ Ignore the woman's market;

- ❖ Wait for it to disappear, in which case, they may disappear first;

- ❖ Create new programs that are just as patronizing or wrong as what they are presently doing;

- ❖ Continue to talk about it, meet about it, and think they are doing something constructive toward capturing the female consumers' loyalty and dollars.

Should

- ❖ Be aware of the impact women are having on all industries;

- ❖ Learn more about how women think, feel, react, network, and buy;

- ❖ Bring in experts for advice, guidance, and information;

- ❖ Pass the information on to everyone in the organization.

Must

- ❖ Recognize the impact of women consumers on their company's bottom line;

❖ Realize how the woman customer has changed in the last 20 years;

❖ Stay in touch with the times and focus on the future;

❖ Understand and meet the needs of today's woman consumer;

❖ Make sure that all areas of the company are in agreement and all personnel are knowledgeable—from the sales manager to the brand manager to the marketing strategist;

❖ Create appropriate and meaningful advertising messages;

❖ Train the sales force to effectively sell to women;

❖ Take action *now*.

Car Care Clinics

There are many ideas that can set you apart from the competition that are not as magnanimous as the credit card program, but will provide value for the customer, and "bang for your bucks."

Women are eager to learn more about cars and car maintenance. In surveys, women repeatedly expressed interest in attending car care clinics. However, a word of caution: Because many women's time is so limited, they often find it difficult to fit a car care clinic into their schedule. I believe they are worth trying but be sure to design a good curriculum for the event.

When developing and presenting a car care clinic:

❖ Make sure that you have a variety of information and hands-on activities available.

❖ Encourage attendees to dress casually, so they can participate in the hands-on portion of the program if they wish.

❖ Plan to provide demonstrations in small groups: how to change the oil, how to change a tire, how to check for antifreeze or water in the battery, etc. Let women be active participants in the program.

❖ Don't embarrass anyone—by asking technical questions she may not understand; by saying she did it wrong, or "like a woman,"etc.

❖ Realize that the composition of any group will contain married women, single women, young women, older women, etc.

❖ Don't refer to her husband. She may not be married. If she is, she is the one there to learn, not her husband. Examples: Your husband will be so proud of you for learning this, or your husband will be able to explain this to you later.

❖ Make sure you have professional technicians to work with the group.

❖ Make it a fun-filled learning experience.

❖ Run the program on time. Today, everyone is very busy, so be sensitive to providing meaningful information in a punctual format.

❖ Decide if the attendees should be customers or if the workshop should be used for business development as well.

❖ Have a token gift for all the attendees, something with your name and telephone number on it.

Small gifts can be very effective in increasing your visibility and business. For instance, many women don't have a tire pressure gauge. Giving them one with your name and address is an inexpensive way to make sure they know how to reach you if they need to. Credit card keys are also a nice gift, especially if they have ever left their keys dangling in the ignition.

Sonny Cesare, a female former formula race car driver and mechanic, is the founder of Autopreneur.[29] The company works with dealers to develop loyal female customers by providing them educational car care clinics. "Making women more comfortable in the dealership, without the pressure of the sale, is an important step to building customer loyalty," advised Cesare. "Women are not usually very well versed in auto lingo. I provide an easy to understand, non-threatening, enjoyable presentation. The women learn a lot, and usually ask for more."

Cesare believes dealers should schedule car care clinics at regular intervals. Summer and holiday seasons are not usually good. Women are so busy then. "Targeting the pre-buying seasons of spring and fall would be ideal. They could coordinate the clinics with new product launches." Cesare is quick to caution that the clinics can't be a buying situation. She has provided clinics for "just women" and for mixed groups. "Women are quieter and more self-conscious in a mixed group than when only women are present. They feel men know more about cars and, therefore, women are less involved in mixed groups," said Cesare.

As more women have the responsibility for the maintenance of their car, car care clinics can be an important marketing tool for dealers.

Regardless of a woman's interest in fixing the car herself, she wants to be able to communicate more effectively with the service advisor or mechanic when her car needs service. It is essential to understand that all women may not attend for the same reason. One might want to change her oil and perform other repairs herself. Another might just want to understand the basics of how a car works, why it's necessary to change the oil at regular intervals, what happens when you don't, and other repair and maintenance information.

Innovative Marketing Ideas that Work

There are other ways besides car care clinics to increase routine maintenance business, especially with women. Setting up the next appointment in advance, sending reminder notices, or calling when it's time to bring the car in will increase profitability in the service area. Explain to women the need for the work—it will make their cars last longer, be more dependable, and bring a higher trade-in allowance. Women will understand the reason for spending the dollars.

Give them something for being loyal customers. Make servicing their cars easy. Relate to women on their own terms and in their own way. Don't stereotype women by giving them a magnet for their refrigerator unless it has some additional value besides promoting your name and number. If the magnet held a card with the date of the next time she needed to service the car, it would have some value. One of the most popular ideas I have suggested for dealers is the "credit card" format.

The card serves multiple functions. It should be small, the size of other credit cards, and easily fit in a purse or wallet. This way she will always have your name and number with her should she have an unexpected problem. Each time her car is serviced, the appropriate space is punched out. Because she will be receiving free items as she utilizes the card, you will tie her to you as a loyal customer. Just getting her to come in for service is not enough. Make sure she is treated as a valued customer when she does.

Offers of free or greatly reduced-price oil changes or car washes have been somewhat successful with both present customers and potential ones. But those items simply are not unique or anything a woman will remember or talk about. Those promotions alone will not build loyal, long-term customers. Try to give your customers something new, different, and interesting. A woman is much more likely to tell her friends about a tire pressure gauge she received than a free oil change. And the cost is probably less to the dealership.

Credit Card Illustration

20% OFF Maintenance/ Service	Oil Change 7,500 ml.	Oil Change 15,000 ml.	Oil Change 22,500 ml.	Oil Change 30,000 ml.	Oil Change 37,500 ml.
Maintenance/ Service 75,000 ml.	**Get a** ***FREE* Oil Change** **and** ***20% OFF*** **Maintenance Service**				Oil Change 45,000 ml.
Maintenance/ Service 67,500 ml.					Oil Change 52,500 ml.
Maintenance/ Service 60,000 ml.					Oil Change 60,000 ml.
Maintenance/ Service 52,500 ml.					Oil Change 67,500 ml.
Maintenance/ Service 45,000 ml.	The Myers Group 6330 LBJ Freeway Suite 136 Dallas, TX 75240 (214)991-4622				Oil Change 75,000 ml.
Maintenance/ Service 37,500 ml.	Maintenance/ Service 30,000 ml.	Maintenance/ Service 22,500 ml.	Maintenance/ Service 15,000 ml.	Maintenance/ Service 7,500 ml.	FREE Oil Change

Women, as well as men, like their cars washed before they are returned. If possible, return customers' cars washed whenever they are in for any type of service.

Stay in touch with your customers. Knowing their opinions is essential to creating successful marketing strategies. One of the best ways to do this is to structure a women's advisory board. The automotive industry must be proactive in soliciting information from their number-one customer. Manufacturers can also benefit from creating a women's advisory board made up of influential businesswomen, homemakers, opinion leaders, and young women. Whoever is the customer target for a particular vehicle, that demographic and psychographic woman should be represented on an advisory committee. Middle-aged male corporate executives who have been in the industry for years aren't representative of the marketplace. They *can't* begin to understand the feelings and thinking of the female customer. Their advertising shows their lack of understanding, their products frequently miss the mark, and their sales training is sadly insufficient. Manufacturers *must* come to grips with the fact that women are, and will continue to be, a major player in the industry.

Women advisors can serve as an ongoing information source to test sales techniques and review service department procedural problems. This type of data can differentiate you from the competition—that is, if you listen to what is said and implement the suggestions that make sense.

Women advisory committees benefit the manufacturer and the store. The women participants will buy from you, service their cars with you, bring their friends to you, and provide necessary feedback in a cost-effective manner.

Aftermarket Products

It would stand to reason that if women are buying more cars, they will also be buying more tires. To capture this emerging market, like any other manufacturer, a tire company needs to know what is important to the woman consumer. Safety is a major consideration in the purchase of a tire. Therefore, women buy more premium tires.

"Tire sales have been flat the last eight years," stated Ron Conlin, manager for market planning and research for Goodyear Tire & Rubber Co.[30] Today, approximately 37 percent of all tires are sold to women. The 37 percent is broken down into two categories—30 percent are to women who make the purchasing decision and 7 percent are to women who are the purchasing agent—that is, they are there physically buying the tire, but on someone else's instruction.

"The new Aqua-Tread is a tire we developed and have aggressively marketed to women because of its safety features. We target our advertising a little differently so that we are on more prime time television, not just sports. Our print buys are more mainstreamed, rather than hot rod magazines." Conlin believes as long as the product has what women want, they will buy it. "Women care less about the performance value and the handling speed ratings than men. It doesn't matter to them if the tires last 80,000 miles." Goodyear believes if their ad messages communicate the ability to stop safely, as well as some other product features, they will appeal to both men and women. "Men want to be able to stop safely, too," added Conlin.

The gasoline industry is also feeling the impact of professional women and is cautiously watching as more women are priming the pumps. Exxon decided to test the water with a two-page spread that ran in the August 1993 issue of *Cosmopolitan* magazine. (See ad in Chapter 6.)

Conoco believes its ads convey important information to women, even though they haven't designed ads strictly for female buyers. "Our research indicates that women are concerned about their security and pay more attention to the cleanliness of the facility. We make a point to show that our facilities are well-lit and clean," said Marshall Cohen, coordinator of advertising for Conoco.[31] "We offer a guarantee. Women really like that. We guarantee that if you use Conoco gasoline exclusively for 60 days and encounter fuel-related engine problems, we will reimburse you for your repair costs." Women like having a guarantee that they perceive will minimize their financial risk.

Texaco echoes Conoco's stance. Their research indicated the same two areas were of prime importance to women. They also have tailored their ad buys to be more generic or female oriented. "We don't buy in just *Road & Track* or *Car and Driver*," said Mark Johnson, manager of gasoline advertising.[32]

Henry Lartigue, vice president of marketing and public affairs with Fina, said Fina is not targeting women as a special audience.[33] "We have enhanced our attraction to women with well-lit, safe stores that are easy to access. Our marketing strategies have been more to tie in with sporting and cultural events on a regional or local level, rather than heavy advertising." State fairs, air shows, auto racing, and civic and cultural events are Fina's marketing programs. "We are a ticket distribution center for many of the events and have other P-O-P [point-of-purchase] materials. We just get more bang for the buck with these promotions," remarked Lartigue.

It's too early to tell what impact the Exxon ad will have on the industry, but an undisputed fact is the oil company that has an edge with the female market will be in a better position than those that wait around to see what happens. Aggressively positioning your product to appeal to women and providing sound reasons why they should patronize your stations should be part of all oil companies' marketing strategies.

Different Manufacturers See Things Differently

BMW

BMW has made a concerted effort to revamp its marketing strategies to include the growing professional woman's market. Events, such as the national Danskin women's triathlon series, popular with advertising executives, attorneys, doctors, entrepreneurs, and financial analysts, sport the BMW logo. BMW sponsors women's business conferences, provides workshops, displays at targeted events, and organizes tennis tournaments for the country club set. As more women climb the corporate ladder and bring home bigger paychecks, BMW realizes that they will use part of the money to purchase a more luxurious car. Today, women make up 36 percent of the luxury car market. By 2000, that figure is projected to be 50 percent.

The powers at BMW know that reaching the woman's market won't be easy. BMW understands it can't just decide women should buy its car, and women will. The manufacturer recognizes it will take time to win this market over, but knows it will be worth it. BMW believes interaction with its target consumers through well-planned programs is the answer. Exposing women to the BMW driving experience, supporting events that are important to women, and making sure women know they are a valued consumer is all part of BMW's marketing strategy.

"Everyone realizes now that just putting women in the ads won't solve the issue," commented Marie Paret, business planning manager at BMW.[34] Paret has recently instituted a BMW Women's Council to stay in tune with women consumers and their opinions and concerns. "The seven-member council is comprised of female managers who will utilize internal professional expertise and personal views of women within the BMW organization to develop appropriate products, marketing/communications strategies, and customer care policies which ultimately will make BMW the 'best motorcar for women,'" said Paret. "Women like the feel of the road that our cars offer. It's dependable, yet fun to drive. Once women experience it, they will want to continually drive it."

BMW has conducted a number of focus groups. Female journalists have been invited to view a videotape. "BMW Asks: What Do Women Want?" profiles women BMW owners and their views on key areas of the ownership experience, including handling/performance, safety, comfort and design. As part of the driving experience program, BMW sponsors driving schools at women's conferences and special events that teach control over the machine in skids and high-speed turning maneuvers. "Our car is built with safety features to avoid accidents. But if the car is in an accident, we have installed features to aid passengers' recovery from the vehicle. The door locks automatically open and lights flash alerting passersby to a problem," stressed Paret.

Sponsoring events such as the triathlon targets active, physically fit women between 25 and 50, BMW's market. BMW has also created promotions with women's publications: 40 new vehicles were driven in an architectural tour of Santa Barbara, California, with subscribers of *House & Garden* and *Martha Stewart's Living* magazine offered an opportunity to receive the video and test drive one of the cars in the 5-series. BMW was also the first automotive company to sponsor the National Museum of Women in the Arts in Washington, D.C., which offers the most important collection of art by women in the world.

One problem BMW faces is overcoming its image as a "yuppie" or male driving machine. Because of its strong emphasis on performance,

BMW has been equated with the male market, rather than being considered a car for women. By taking the car to events and conferences that attract women, the first obstacle is being overcome. BMW has also incorporated sensitivity training at its dealerships. With a new marketing and advertising thrust, BMW is well on its way to making a significant impact on the female luxury car market.

Ford

The Mercury Sable appeals to women because it has an attractive and roomy interior, excellent design and styling and convenient control panels, and it provides value. "Women tend to place much more importance on the interior design then men do," explained Bobbie Koehler-Gaunt, general sales manager for Lincoln-Mercury.[35] Prior to her position at Lincoln-Mercury, Koehler-Gaunt was marketing research director for Ford Motor Company. Part of her job was to convey to the company the power women were generating in the marketplace. "Everyone was completely shocked by the numbers," said Koehler-Gaunt.

Knowing that she would bring a different perspective to a product or marketing effort, she worked to make sure that women's needs were being addressed both in product development and sales. She is active in the company's 25-member women's marketing committee. The committee, made up of male and female employees, represents many operations at Ford, including design, engineering, sales, corporate staffs, and company subsidiaries such as Ford Credit. Within the committee, a women's speaker's bureau was formed to make women more aware of Ford and its products. Since 1987, the bureau has reached more than 10,000 professional women. Ford holds focus groups to gain customer feedback. "We want to know what our customers are thinking and saying," stated Koehler-Gaunt.

As a result of its research, Ford has improved the interior quietness "because a woman's hearing is more sensitive than a man's." Seats have been redesigned to accommodate women's shorter legs, and knobs and control buttons reshaped for women's longer nails. Gas and brake pedals are now designed with high heels in mind. Another feature Ford is working to improve is the seat belt. An adjustable D-ring has been added to make seat belts more comfortable for a woman's smaller frame.

Ford is not designing a woman's car, but is making their cars "female friendly" so that they will appeal to women as well as to men. Forty-three percent of all Sables are bought by women. Women bought approximately 40 percent of the Taurus cars sold in 1992, and Ford anticipates the Mark VIII will capture a large percentage of the luxury car market that is growing among female buyers. Women also buy a substantial number of the Villager minivans and Cougar and Grand Marquis cars.

"Women are more value conscious," said Darryl Hazel, director of marketing research at Ford of North America.[36] "Many of the items that are brought to our attention by women are really issues for everyone. Both men and women like the safety features of power door locks, remote keyless entry and windows placed for greater visibility." Hazel does admit that women are more concerned than men about reliability and durability, as well as the cost and ease of repairs.

Presently only 33 percent of Ford sales are to women, but that figure is up considerably from 10 years ago. With Ford's new programs and sensitivity to the market, it anticipates that figure going much higher.

As women move up the economic ladder, Lincoln-Mercury sees younger professional women enjoying the power of the Mark VIII. "Women appreciate power differently than men. To women, it is more of a safety aspect. They want to know they can pass safely and enter freeways easily. Men enjoy the excitement of the acceleration. Men seldom mention power in terms of safety," said Koehler-Gaunt.

In addition to its luxury vehicles, sports utility, minivan, and smaller cars are popular with female consumers. Ford is working to enhance their pickup truck sales to women. With the number of women buying light trucks increasing, particularly in certain geographic areas like Texas, Ford hopes to be a part of this growth.

Koehler-Gaunt has seen the industry change dramatically in the 21 years she has been in the business. "Today, the marketing and advertising efforts have to be much more focused. The strategies and message have to be more product oriented. Our advertising doesn't have a lot of people in it. We want to reinforce the features of the car."

General Motors

"J. Michael Losh, VP-group executive for North American vehicle sales, service, and marketing, said his goal is for GM to become within five years 'the undisputed industry leader across the board . . . in terms of being responsive to the customer' when it comes to product, sales, service and the total ownership experience."[37] This will mean turning around a declining sales trend. In 1980, General Motors had a 45 percent share of the market. In 1992, General Motors' new car and light truck market had dropped to 34.1 percent.

In May of 1993, *Automotive News* ran the following quote: "Before the 1991 Chevrolet Caprice was introduced, customers in clinics told designers they didn't like closed wheel wells, which accentuated the car's whale-like shape. Yet GM stayed with the design, and the car flopped . . .

'Sometimes we have to tell the customer what he should like,' Chuck Jordan, former design staff vice president, was fond of saying."

General Motors chose to make what they thought their customers should buy. They are not alone in this stance. Many other industries have subscribed to this philosophy. They watched as their market share continued to erode, unwilling to change. It is always easier to blame problems on outside factors than to look internally and accept responsibility.

As a result of the declining revenue, GM is undergoing some dramatic changes. The Chevrolet Division, affectionately thought of for years as the "Heartbeat of America," wants to be thought of as "America's automotive leader . . . producing Total Customer Enthusiasm through: Empowered People, Exceptional Products, Excellent Purchase and Ownership Experience, providing Outstanding Value and a superior return on investment for the Stakeholders." That statement is the essence of the Chevrolet Geo's division's new "Vision Statement." To accomplish its goal, Chevrolet will have to make some dramatic paradigm shifts in its thinking.

Jim Chrz, director of Total Customer Enthusiasm, said General Motors, and Chevrolet in particular, is reassessing how they do business.[38] "Our new direction has an experiential focus and is a total mindset. We aren't providing isolated training programs that have a distinct beginning and end, but an ongoing process that is no longer interested in just improving the customer's experience but in also providing an exceptional customer purchase and ownership experience." Chrz continued, "We have begun to realize that the hard-line items, the products, aren't the only variables. The 'soft-side' issues of our image have become top priorities: how we treat customers, our interest in understanding and meeting their needs and our concern for exceeding their expectations."

Chevrolet's new strategy recognizes three distinct markets: the dealers, their employees, and retail customers. "We need to address the needs of each of our customers in order to better serve all three. In the past, we assumed we knew what our customers wanted and never bothered to ask," commented Chrz.

Service Supremacy II (SSII) is part of the Chevrolet's Dealer Operating System (DOS). "In the past, we strove for better. Now, we believe, better isn't good enough. We are recognizing dealers in a monetary way for providing their customers with exemplary service. We are no longer spending the majority of our money on trying to retrain those who are doing it wrong, but on those who are doing it good, but with help, could be exceptional."

Chevrolet has spent a good deal of time researching what other successful companies are doing and is learning from them. This is a departure from General Motors' corporate culture of the past. "You don't change a corporate culture overnight, and you don't change it by writing up your mission statement and sending it out in the mail," said Chrz. "We are providing an integrated learning system that encompasses all levels, from senior managers to salespeople. It is a partnering effort. We are focusing less on policies and procedures and more on values. We are working to establish benchmarks to measure our success. Our present system has too many lag indicators. The information is too old before we get it."

Chrz is right. By the time GM gets the information, the customer has already decided not to go back, has told a lot of people about his or her experiences, or has forgotten the whole thing. Receiving timely information from customers and acting on it is imperative to customer satisfaction. (See Chapter 10 for more information on customer service.)

Chevrolet's new focus is much more on target than its past philosophy. But, like many others, Chevrolet must realize not only the significance of the woman consumer, but how to treat her and make her a part of the partnership they are building. Acknowledging that women are playing a major role in the automotive industry and that they are no longer an insignificant market is not the only issue. Being sensitive to the situation, but ignorant of the most effective methods to market and sell to the new professional woman only leaves the management and sales staffs frustrated. Corporations must understand that significant differences exist between the sexes, not just in how to address them properly, but in a multitude of other areas.

General Motors is underwriting a new publication called *Know-How.* It is targeted to women and will cover a range of topics from investments to vehicle maintenance. The publication is scheduled to debut in October 1993. It is an important step to recognizing that women and men read different publications, are interested in different things, and need products that address their individual needs. Whether the publication is properly written for women and what impact it will have on the market has yet to be determined. However, the concept is good.[39]

Diversity is one of the buzzwords of the 1990s, but it generally doesn't pinpoint women's issues in the same depth as ethnic minorities, the elderly, or any number of other segments that are part of the workplace and the marketplace. Corporations that are spending millions of dollars creating a cultural environment that is different from the past need to be cognizant of a very precious commodity—the woman buyer. Not to incorporate a program or add a module to an existing program specifically created to address the needs of this market is short-sighted and will not produce a total vision for the future. Women should not be segmented into their own special category, with special products, incentives, and whatnots. But they should be understood, and their needs professionally addressed.

American women are waiting for a transformation in the type of behavior they experience in the sales and service departments of dealerships. Once the sales staff has been properly trained so that women who walk in to buy, *do* buy, then effective advertising that appeals to women should be created. Advertising can only get women into the showroom; it can't sell the product. Selling takes place in the showroom in a one-on-one encounter. Most sales are dependent on just how successful that encounter is—is it confrontational, condescending, or pleasant? Exceptional salespersons with excellent product knowledge and superior customer service skills are a vital part of the team. Manufacturers must insist that the people who represent them are the best.

Another brand under the GM umbrella is Pontiac. To understand the positioning of Pontiac, one needs to reminisce about youthful cars of the 1950s and 1960s. The "muscle car," the GTO, Bonneville, and Firebird—all conjure up memories. Pontiac had a strong brand identity and everyone knew what it was.

"In the 1970s, Pontiac lost sight of their brand equity. It tried to be all things to all people. It lost touch with whom its buyer was," said Lynn Myers, general marketing manager for Pontiac.[40]

In 1981, as market share continued to decline, Pontiac held a major image conference. From it came a new commitment and an understanding of what had made Pontiac strong in the 1950s and 1960s. The "Pontiac Excitement" slogan was developed. The conference wanted Pontiac to be known for its innovative design and engineering that resulted in exciting products and outstanding roadability.

"It was a typical marketing textbook case study," said Myers. "We had lost sight of who we were and our most valuable commodity, the customer. We had to rebuild our identity. We developed the STE, Pontiac Fiera and, in 1985, the Grand Am." Pontiac's tagline became, "We build excitement." This lasted through 1991.

"We then began to look at how to define excitement in the 1990s," explained Myers. "We went out and talked to customers and asked what excitement meant to them. They still wanted performance and a sporty look, but they wanted more. With the recession, value became a major component. We chose four words to personify our cars and defined them: (1) Bold—daring, innovative, dramatic; (2) Purposeful—focused, reliable, confident; (3) Athletic—energetic, youthful, agile; and (4) Personal—caring, satisfying, driver-oriented."

According to Myers, the main difference between what women and men want when they look at a sporty car is that women are more safety

It's Still a Man's World

Some brands are more appealing to men than women, and vice versa. Ferrari will always sell mainly to men, unless the car and the concept are totally restructured. Performance, speed, reputation, and the dollars involved just don't appeal to women in the same way they do to a male automotive enthusiast with the income to afford such a luxury.

True performance cars appeal to some women, but the attraction is much less than for other vehicles. Women buy only 11 percent of Porsche 911 and 19 percent of Chevrolet Corvettes. Women do like convertibles, however. They buy 43 percent of the Ford Mustang and 70 percent of Volkswagen convertibles.[42]

Women will buy more cars than men. They will lease and service cars, and they will become more involved in caring for them. But women, as a whole, won't ever have the love affair with the automobile that men have had in the past and will probably continue to have.

While the automotive industry had better pay attention to her needs and design and market products that appeal to her, this in no way will make the car less attractive to men. In fact, the opposite is probably true.

Twenty Marketing Tips for the Automotive Industry

The 20 marketing ideas listed below are just the beginning. By implementing even a few of these concepts, others will surface that will make car manufacturers and dealers wonder why it took so long to recognize the woman as a buying entity, and why they settled for "marketing without a clue," when it is so much more profitable to market effectively to women.

1. Provide new car orientation programs.

2. Conduct well-structured car care clinics for current and potential customers.

3. Realize that how a woman is treated in the dealership will have the most impact on the final outcome of the sale. Training your sales staff to be sensitive to women prospects is essential to the bottom line. To be most effective, these training programs *must* have women—preferably, not employees—advising management or physically conducting the training.

15. Display a car at women's conventions, major shopping malls, financial seminars aimed at women, or other events heavily attended by women.

16. Organize a program that is of interest to women in your community. Bring in an author, newspaper editor, or local television personality that has a message women will come to the dealership to hear.

17. Conduct seminars and workshops on how to buy a car, or on the difference between buying and leasing.

18. Understand that safety is number one with most women—not color and not price, although both are factors that figure into the total buying process.

19. Realize that while women share many similarities, each woman has her own uniqueness. They don't all need or want the same things. Young families might find cars with built-in car seats a real bonus. Single women, or those without children, may find a sports car fits their lifestyle best. Recognize that even though a feature may have been developed for a woman, such as the adjustment of the lumbar support, many men will enjoy the benefits provided as well. No one feature is a "woman's feature" entirely. Women are not clones of each other, and they have different needs and wants.

20. Don't produce a car *to market* to women. Make the cars you produce *marketable* to women.

Notes

[1] Paul Witteman, "Carmakers Shifting Gears to Appeal to Women Buyers," *Sun Sentinel* (3 February 1988) in *Savvy* magazine.

[2] Ed Lapham, executive editor, *Automotive News*, interview with author, 31 August 1993.

[3] "Detroit Not Sure How To Lure Women Buyers," *San Francisco Chronicle* (9 July 1992): D–7.

[4] Paul Dean, "Sports Car Market Gearing For Women," *Los Angeles Times* (11 January 1989): View–1.

[5] *The Wall Street Journal* (23 August 1989).

[6] Eric Hollreiser, "Women and Cars," *Adweek's Marketing Week* (10 February 1992): 14.

[7]"Woman at the Wheel," *Woman's Day* (17 August 1992) commissioned by Yankelovich Clancy Shulman, results released.

[8]Mary Beth Lewis, "Carmakers Creating 'Mommymobiles:' Women's Desires Are Taken More Seriously," *San Francisco Chronicle* (6 January 1992): D–3.

[9]Kristin Stiven Breese, Crain News Service, "Mazda Taps Key Market—Women, Mazda Says Its Sales Strategy is Simple: Offer Information, Not Gimmicks, and Women Buyers Will Respond with Their Checkbooks," *Orlando Sentinel* (9 July 1992): PG–1.

[10]Jan Thompson, vice president of corporate sales operation, Mazda, interview with author, 2 July 1993.

[11]Lisa Holewa, "Women Are Winning Attention From Automobile Designers," *Philadelphia Inquirer* (8 November 1992): F–20.

[12]Mary Flowers, managing editor, *Dealer Business,* interview with author, 22 September 1993.

[13]Mark Rechtin, "Lexus Remains Customer Satisfaction Leader: domestics gain in power survey," *Automotive News* (12 July 1993): 16.

[14]Janet Eckhoff, director of product and marketing strategy, Cadillac, interview with author, 26 August 1993.

[15]Doris Ehlers, account director, J. D. Power and Associates, interview with author, 27 July 1993.

[16]Enide Allison, president/owner, Oak Tree Mazda, interview with author, 3 September 1993.

[17]Mary Connelly, Thomas Connelly, Charles M. Connelly, "New Lease On Life: Retail Leasing Is Emerging as the Latest Savior of Sales in Turbulent Times," *Automotive News* (23 August 1993): 4i.

[18]Michael Clements, "Ford's 12-year Lease Offers 6th Car 'Free,'" *USA Today* (24 August 1993).

[19]Tom Healey, partner, J. D. Power and Associates, interview with author, 27 July 1993.

[20]Arlena Sawyers, "Women Speak Mind About Cars," *Orlando Sentinel* (27 August 1992): G–12. Picked up from *Automotive News.*

[21]Micheline Maynard, "Car Sales to Women Near Half the Total," *Detroit Free Press* (28 November 1993): C–7, and S. J. Diamond, "Vehicles That Offer Women a Macho Trip," *Los Angeles Times* (5 July 1991): D–1

[22]Kathy Jackson, "Ford Hopes Luxury, Comfort Will Attract Women To Explorer," *Orlando Sentinel* (3 December 1992): G–4.

[23]JoAnn Muller, "Women's Wheels: automotive world finally catching on to the purchasing power of women," *Detroit Free Press* (13 July 1992): F–10 –14.

[24]Joe St. Henry, account supervisor/GM Credit Cards, DMB&B, interview with author, 1 July 1993.

[25]Kathi Brown, workshop coordinator, NADA, interview with author, 7 July 1993.

[26]Diane Caldwell, certification program coordinator, NADA, interview with author, 2 July 1993.

[27]Anna Marie Arnone, director of management education, NADA, interview with author, 23 July 1993.

[28]Ted Orme, director of public affairs, NADA, interview with author, 7 July 1993.

[29]Sonny Cesare, founder/owner, Autopreneur, interview with author, 3 August 1993.

[30]Ron Conlin, manager of marketing planning and research, Goodyear Tire & Rubber Company, interview with author, 23 June 1993.

[31]Marshall Cohen, coordinator of advertising, Conoco, Inc., interview with author, 4 August 1993.

[32]Mark Johnson, manager of gasoline advertising, Texaco Corp., interview with author, 4 August 1993.

[33]Henry Lartigue, vice president of marketing and public affairs, Fina, Inc., interview with author, 20 August 1993.

[34]Marie Paret, business planning manager, BMW of North America, Inc., interview with author, 13 September 1993.

[35]Bobbie Koehler-Gaunt, general sales manager, Lincoln-Mercury Sales, interview with author, 22 July 1993.

[36]Darryl Hazel, director of marketing research, Ford of North America, interview with author, 6 July 1993.

[37]*Advertising Age* (23 August 1992): 2.

[38]Jim Chrz, director of Total Customer Enthusiasm, Chevrolet Motor Division, interview with author, 14 July 1993.

[39]*Automotive News* (23 August 1992): 2.

[40]Lynn Myers, general marketing manager, Pontiac Motor Division, interview with author, 19 September 1993.

[41]Don Hudler, vice president of sales—service and marketing, Saturn Corporation, interview with author, 1 July 1993.

[42]Micheline Maynard, Reuters, "Car Sales to Women Near Half the Total," *Detroit Free Press* (28 November 1988): C–7.

Chapter 6

Is Your Advertising Designed to Win or Lose Sales?

For the better part of the century, most advertising executives and creative directors have been men. For decades, men have created ads depicting women as they see them, or as they want them to be. Women were categorized as two types—sex objects/glamour girls or housewives dedicated to cleanliness and providing wholesome meals to their families. Even the verbiage, while obviously written to entice women, was filled with overtones that appealed more to the men writing the copy than to the women reading it.

For years, this type of advertising prevailed and worked relatively well. Today, however, there is a different woman seeing and reading advertisements. Women want ads that depict them as they are and that speak to them as intelligent beings, not brainless robots needing a man to show them the way. Today, market research indicates ads depicting *real* women score higher with women than ads of the past that portrayed them as superwomen, dependent housewives consumed with cleaning, or sexy, twenty-year-olds strutting around as decoration.

Realizing the economic impact of the women's market, advertisers are changing their strategies. But what often happens in their attempt to reach the market by avoiding negative stereotypes is that they go too far to the other extreme, producing ads that are equally condescending or offensive to the very people they are trying to please.

Curiously enough, one strategy that has recently surfaced is "male-bashing." Since degrading woman and minorities is now a dangerous ploy, creative directors and copywriters have rationalized that women want to see ads that "put men in their place." The fact is that only a few women, mostly younger, like this concept. The majority find male-bashing ads uncomfortable and often even offensive. Women don't have the need to put men down in ads—it doesn't enhance the product or a woman's desire to purchase it. Women prefer ads that portray a positive self-image and that demonstrate self-esteem.

As has been discussed in previous chapters, men frequently view things differently from women. They create products and advertising that they think women will find appealing. Sometimes they hit their objective, but often they miss the mark. Men's fantasies about women and their fears about women's power or control over them surface in the types of advertising that have been created throughout the decades.

As in other aspects, from the design to the manufacturing, women should be consulted on the advertising message. Women account for approximately 80 percent of all consumer spending. Yet, advertising has traditionally been created in man's image.

The Advertising Revolution

From its early beginning and in its own unique style, advertising has tried to depict the lifestyle of the times. Throughout the decades, advertising has reflected women—wealthy socialites of refined taste; humble home-makers whose only concern in life was to please their husbands and children, and superwomen capable of doing more than leaping tall build-ings in a single bound. She was an executive by day and a sensuous lover to her husband at night. In between she cooked, cleaned, and car pooled children.

Advertising has scorned, teased, tempted, and cajoled women to buy their products, insinuating that it was their only hope for happiness. Happiness was portrayed as catching or seducing a man, making sure that his shirts didn't have "ring around the collar," or buying nutritious products for their children.

Looking at advertising by decades shows how women's roles have changed throughout this century. In the early 1920s, prosperity abounded. The automobile industry began targeting women in the mid-1920s. Ac-cording to the article, "You've come a long way, Madison Avenue" in the March 1993 issue of *Lear's*, "Cars were, in essence, fashion accessories. Artist McClelland Barclay created the Fisher Body girls for the classic Body by Fisher campaign promoting chassis for General Motors. With their elegant-looking models, often on the arm of a man, the ads walked a visual tightrope—selling sex to men and style to women," noted Betsy Sharkey, author of the article and editor-at-large for *Adweek*.[1]

Women in the 1920s had money, education, were independent, worked outside the home, and smoked. "The 1920s rendered two dominant images for women," advised Kimberly Barta, curator for the American Advertising Museum.[2] "Those women with money to spend were illustrated as either a housewife or a single, independent 'flapper girl.' These ads were provocative for the times. Advertising cigarettes to women was also prevalent, and smoking was seen as glamorous. Because most of the ads used illustration rather than photography, women were idealized with long legs and lean bodies," explained Barta.

Then came the Depression, and advertising reflected women as homebodies, working to stay within the family budget. "During times of prosperity, thinness is in, but during a recession, women took a different look in advertisements," commented Barta. Women were much rounder, more voluptuous. The glamorous flapper girl was no longer seen. As photography began to be used in advertising, it allowed for more technological possibilities at a lesser expense. Woodbury soap produced the first ad with a nude. During this same era, men's magazines such as *Esquire* appeared on the scene.[3]

The Depression was followed by the outbreak of World War II, and women began to hold down jobs while the men went to war. The first magazine for women, *Charm*, was introduced in 1944. The publication solicited advertising aimed at working women. "Rosie the Riveter" portrayed the image of American women, both in the jobs they held and in advertising. Women left home to fill in for men as part of the all-American sport—baseball. As women began to excel in sports and gain recognition, female stars were used to endorse products much the same way male athletes were.

That is, until the war ended. Men returned home, replacing women in the workplace and on the baseball fields, and advertising again shifted its focus. As women retreated to the homefront, more advertising began to appear for appliances to make a woman's life easier. Washing machines, vacuum cleaners, toasters, and electric coffee pots would free a woman from the drudgery of her household chores, so she could devote her time to taking care of her husband and children.[4]

By the 1950s, women in advertisements were portrayed as being obsessed with cleaning and cooking for their husbands and children. Their whole life revolved around a single focus—their family. The June Cleaver-style mother image portrayed by advertisers and TV programming was pitted against men's fantasies for the sexy blonde they longed to have. "Beauty became a Jayne Mansfield, Marilyn Monroe look— blonde and busty," Sharkey pointed out.

"A woman's self-esteem was dominated by her ability to get a black heel mark off the floor or to serve guests with spot-free glasses," said Bob Garfield, editor-at-large for *Advertising Age*.[5] "Women were portrayed in subservient roles. Whether advertising created the woman or just reflected the times, the messages were clear. The American woman cared far too deeply about cleanliness and earning her spouse's approval. Her entire worthiness as a person hinged on other people, usually her husband," noted Garfield, who is a columnist and critic for the magazine.

In the 1950s, prosperity returned and parents had discretionary income to spend on children. Toys for little girls included the pink "Pretty Maid" washing machine and the "Sunny Suzy" iron that identified the roles little girls had as they trained to become wives.

"One of the most successful, yet controversial, ads was created by Clairol. 'Does She or Doesn't She?' was the original headline," recalled Barta, "but *Life* magazine turned it down. While the men at *Life* said no to the ad, the women at the publication loved it. The ad ran, but with the addition of 'Only her hair dresser knows for sure.' " After the ad ran a couple of times, they softened it by showing a mother and child in the visual, not a single, independent woman. The campaign ran for approximately six years and was an overwhelming success.

In the workplace, marketers were targeting working women, primarily secretaries and office workers. Manufacturers of office equipment were creating ads they thought women would find appealing. A pink-cased Royal typewriter with a flower coming out of it was boldly featured in one ad. The ad ran in 1959 in *Fortune* magazine. Obviously, the ad was to appeal to the employer as something that his female employees would like and, therefore, would make them more productive.[6]

"Earlier in the century, women were discouraged from chatting on telephones, a piece of serious equipment," wrote Ann Armbruster as she described the exhibit, "Mechanical Brides: Women and Machines From Home to Office" at the Cooper-Hewett Museum in New York.[7] By the 1950s and 1960s, marketers realized that this product could have great appeal to women. Telephones were designed and positioned for women at home. They came in various shapes and colors, including the feminine princess phone. Ads showed women in the kitchen connecting with other women in the kitchen via the phone. Recognizing and marketing to a woman's innate interest in communication and interaction with other women, AT&T sales soared in the residential market.

"The 60s saw the emergence of the woman's movement. *The Feminine Mystique* by Betty Friedan, which among other things, took the male-dominated media to task for the demeaning way in which they portrayed women," wrote Sharkey. Cigarette companies changed their tactics from enticing women "to smoke rather than eat in order to remain curvaceous," to the theme of the day. Virginia Slims introduced their famous "You've come a long way baby" slogan, helping catapult them into one of the best selling cigarettes for women in the country.

While some advertisers were joining this new feminine movement, most still didn't get it. "The Man from Glad, advertising's caped crusader, was swooping down to rescue helpless homemakers," observed Betsy Sharkey in the *Lear's* article on advertising and women. The opposite extreme showed men as incompetents. One ad asked what would happen if a husband and wife changed jobs. It showed her efficient and in charge at the office, while he was a bumbling mess trying to take care of the baby and dropping things as he straightened up.

Other companies' ads also reached their targeted market by diverging from their previous strategies. "Revlon created one of the most successful advertising campaigns of the day by capturing that sense of style," wrote Sharkey. One ad for Charlie perfume featured a man and a woman, both carrying briefcases. It was a back shot that showed *her* patting his rear. Charlie gave the woman the right to be her unique self.[8] During the same era, women began to be seen as authorities who didn't need a man's approval or advice on products.

In the 1970s and 1980s, women went to work en mass, and the image of the successful business executive was that of a "female-male." Pantsuits or pin-striped suits with cotton shirts and bow ties populated the workplace. Women were aggressive beings, and advertising jumped on the trend. However, others kept the man as the "power" figure. Men carried the attache cases, got off the plane and sat in the boardroom, while women were the stewardesses and clerks for rental car agencies.

By the mid-1970s, women wanted self-gratification and independence. Young, single women were buying designer apparel, planning exciting vacations and flashing their newly acquired credit cards. Educated "superwomen" were the stars of many ad campaigns. In sharp contrast to the liberated woman were the ads of the airline industry with sexist headlines including National Airlines' "Fly Me" and Continental's "We really move our tail for you."

During the 1980s, the country was faced with Reaganomics. Elaborate consumption was commonplace and, "yuppies" enjoyed materialism and luxuries. Then, the recession took hold, and more women were forced into the workplace in order to provide the necessities for the family. Dual incomes became prevalent. Women who had been branded as superwomen began to tire. Being perfect at everything was exhausting, and having it all was being questioned. Advertisers were beginning to pay close attention to emerging women's publications and were seriously considering placing ads in them for automobiles, travel, financial and liquor—categories that were once considered "for men only."[9]

As more women entered the labor force, American Express began to see them as a viable target market. However, professional women weren't requesting cards. "In 1984, we conducted focus groups to determine why women weren't applying for membership," said Rochelle Lazarus, president of Ogilvy & Mather, the agency of record for American Express.[10] "What we found out was that women all said the card was great. When we asked them why they didn't have one, they replied, 'it's not for people like me.' " American Express was perceived as a man's card, not for women. "Women feared they would be rejected if they applied. They didn't think American Express wanted them," observed Lazarus. "It was so obvious. All we had to do to capture this very lucrative market was to say 'We want you to be a part of the club.' "

American Express created a series of ads that celebrated all the things a woman can be. They didn't just position her as a business executive or as a superwoman, but showed various phases of her life. "The women were proud of who they were. The tone was right," noted Lazarus. One television ad showed the wife playfully telling her husband she was going to take him out to dinner on her new American Express Card®. Another showed two businesswomen at lunch. A third ad had the male saying, "You've gone back to school, got a job and now an American Express Card®. What's next?" She replies, "You're cute when you're worried." A print ad showed a mother in a business suit at a baseball game with her two daughters. Each ad ended with "Part of a lot of interesting lives." The response to the campaign was tremendous. "The purpose was to get women to respond, and they did," commented Lazarus. "The interesting thing is the campaign also generated a lot more young men applying, as well. I guess they figured if we were giving the Card to women, they could qualify."

The ad on the following page depicts women in a different light. Active and athletic, she skillfully maneuvers the terrain with a baby strapped to her chest.

One reason the American Express campaign worked so well was because it spoke to women in language they related to. Another reason American Express experienced success was that they didn't try to attract women by making a pink card for them. Instead, they recognized what was important to women. They understood the market and what motivated them to action. Having Ms. Lazarus in charge of the creative was definitely an asset.

The American Express Card.
It's part of a lot of interesting lives.

Call 800-528-4800 for an application.

While it is easily recognized that prime time television has made many changes to accommodate its new viewing audience, many feel that daytime TV has remained fairly consistent. That's not the case.

"As in all advertising, daytime television has changed dramatically since the 1960s," declared Garfield. "The typical housewife portrayed then is a vanishing breed today. Daytime television advertising is a mixture aimed at multiple audiences." The commercials are targeted to a diverse group from men to women, and from children to the elderly. Some are stay-at-home homemakers; others may be on accident leave, as personal injury lawyers' ads are rampant. Few ads today address the homemaker assuming that her whole reason-for-being is to serve her family. Today, she does things for herself, whether it is cleaning or buying fitness apparel. She wants to feel good about herself, not necessarily devote her life to pleasing others.

While these ads are better, marketers and advertisers still miss the mark much of the time. "In an effort to reach women without stereotyping them, they often produce condescending ads. Their trials are so transparent that its almost embarrassing," stated Garfield. "However, many packaged good and household products that advertise to women now are using kids as the focus. Women aren't even in the commercials. For instance, Sunny Delight Drink, Honey Graham Crackers, Duncan Hines, Pampers, and Clorox 2 all use children to sell the products. When you do see women, they are solving problems that affect them, not their husbands."

The late 1980s and early 1990s gave some relief to women tired from being the perfect corporate executive, perfect wife, and perfect mother. Daddies became a part of the family and took care of the children. Motrin IB produced a tender ad with the opening scene showing the dad with a headache. He takes the medication because he has an important appointment he can't miss. He must get rid of his headache for the very special tea party with his little girl.

"We had a very strong response to our new Motrin IB series," responded William Sever, director of marketing for Upjohn's Motrin IB.[11] "Our strategy with the commercials, and all our advertising, is to communicate that Motrin IB is a good medicine that will help your headache and arthritis. Women were very wrapped up in the tea party ad. They liked seeing the father make the little girl happy."

The Motrin IB ads are excellent examples of successful advertising to women, in spite of the fact that no women were ever pictured in the ads. In the tea party commercial, the viewer sees only the father and little girl. In another ad in that series, you see the father as he speaks to his

Motrin® IB

THE UPJOHN COMPANY

- **THE RELIEF OF MOTRIN IN NON-PRESCRIPTION STRENGTH**
- **GREAT FOR HEADACHES**

"TEA PARTY"   TV :30

BECKY: More tea, Daddy?
DADDY: Sure honey, fill'er up.

ANNCR (V/O): A short while ago, Mike Ward had a headache.

But he couldn't postpone his tea party

with one of the town's best hostesses.

So he took a Motrin IB. The same medicine as in the Motrin doctors have prescribed for years...but in non-prescription strength.

And now that his headache's gone...

he can concentrate on

the things that really matter.

BECKY: Good tea, huh Daddy?

DADDY: It's excellent tea, Becky.

Excellent!

ANNCR (V/O): Motrin IB. The Relief of Motrin in non-prescription strength.

wife who has a headache, but you never see the wife. He has just come home from work and he offers to finish bathing the baby while she lies down. Very warm, very caring, emotionally moving ads. Women don't have to be the spokesperson in the ad to sell to women, but ads do have to speak to women in language and emotions that reach them. Motrin IB's target market is females 25 to 49. According to Sever, sales for the product increased when this ad ran, but he quickly mentioned, "It was run in conjunction with arthritis advertising, not as a solo flight."

Johnson & Johnson also learned daddies could bathe the baby. Women like seeing the father involved with the family, especially with young children. "Advertising is more reality-oriented. I like seeing men in ads as fathers. That says a lot for the way advertisers are looking at women. Ads are also more diversified in their family situations with single mothers and single fathers, as well as the traditional family unit," noted Sharkey. [12]

Advertising has always positioned stereotypes in the context of cultural trends. When the superwoman image took hold, every ad reflected this dynamic, do-it-all woman. When women reacted and said, "I can't do it all any more," advertising shifted the woman's image to accommodate her lifestyle. The problem comes when advertisers misread what women want. Little nuances that slip into even well-crafted messages can turn a woman off.

Advertising to Women in the Nineties— Who's on Target

Why has the focus changed in the 1990s? For one thing, women have more discretionary income of their own, and Madison Avenue has always recognized the power of the dollar. As more women continue to move into executive positions, advertising must recognize them as more educated, more sophisticated, and more accomplished than in the past. In addition, many have chosen advertising as their careers and are beginning to help shape the messages that are being sent to their gender.

Another change that Sharkey noticed is that beauty is defined differently than it was 10 or 15 years ago. Beauty was young, attractive, tall, thin, and sensuous. Now the total women is considered more in the definition of beauty. Being in better shape is important. Women can sweat and still be beautiful. Independence and self-esteem are positive traits. "Nike's ads were some of the best. An almost perfect ad. The imagery, the positive message, they made me want to buy the product," praised Sharkey.

Advertising Messages Designed to Win Sales

Using the message of empowerment to, *be all you can be,* Nike chose not to preach the virtues of exercise and trimness, but to instead extol the value of feeling good—about yourself. Nike's sales to women jumped 25 percent in 1990 following the introduction of the ad campaign. The ads were bold, creative and a departure from the norm. Women loved the ads. (See Chapter 3 for more details on the campaign and its development.)

The Nike ads departed from tradition in many ways. The print ads are not single-page ads, or usually even double-truck (two-page ads). The "Dialogue" campaign is an insert of four, eight, or twelve pages. It gives women time to get involved, to be part of the story, to relate to the copy. They deal with love, with emotions, with the feelings women experience. They convey a sense of self, of being. Nike ads acknowledge there is no right or wrong sensation, just a complex mixture of emotions women embrace as they experience life.

The success of the campaign was based on Nike's ability to communicate to the women they were targeting. They spoke of hard issues and dealt with them, and of soft memories filled with nostalgia. Nike captured a side of women that other advertising executives have never achieved. Nike portrayed women not just in real-life situations, but with real-life feelings.

Jeffrey Scott said in an article picked up by the *Dallas Morning News* that advertising is finally portraying women as real people in real-life situations.[13] "A Saturn automobile campaign casts women in the role of decision maker," explained Scott. "The stereotypes—woman as sex object; woman as housewife; woman as spinster-in-the-making if she doesn't wear the right make-up, dye her hair properly, use the right deodorants, splash on the right fragrance and keep her floors spick-and-span—still exist in ads, but are increasingly scarce."

Scott continues by mentioning other ads that depict women in professional situations. A futurist AT&T ad shows a mother, away from home on business, saying good night on a videophone. Another ad shows women, rather than men, running their own companies. Marketers hope this will convey the idea that they understand women are making the purchasing decisions for products.

Women have changed, and their roles in society have changed. The biggest mistake most advertisers and marketers make is to underestimate women's intelligence. Women today are sophisticated shoppers who resent being talked down to.

Did you ever wish you were a boy?

Did you? Did you for one moment or one breath or one heartbeat beating over all the years of your life, wish, even a little, that you could spend it as a boy? Honest. Really. Even if you got over it.

Did you ever wish that you could be a boy just so you could do *boy things* and not hear them called *boy things*, did you want to climb trees and skin knees and be third base and not hear the boys say, Sure, play, but that means you have to *be* third base.

Oh *ha ha ha*.

But did you ever wish you were a boy just because there were *boys*, and there were *girls* and they were *them*, and we were, well. *we weren't them*, and we knew there must be a difference because everybody kept telling us there was. But what was it?

You never knew. Like you *knew* that you were a girl *(you run like a girl you throw like a girl you girl you)* and that was great, that was swell, but you

(continued)

couldn't help wondering what it would be like if you... had been...a *boy.*

And if you could have been a boy, what difference would it have made? Would it have made you faster, cuter, cleaner? And if you *were* a boy, this incredibly bouncing boy, what boy would you have been? All the time knowing no two boys are alike any more than all girls are.

So you wake up. And you learn we all have differences (Yes!) You learn we all have similarities (Right!) You learn to stop lumping everybody in the world into two separate categories, or three, or four, or any at all (Finally!) And you learn to stop beating yourself over the head for things that weren't

wrong in the first place.

And one day when you're out in the world running, feet flying dogs barking smiles grinning, you'll hear those immortal words calling, calling inside your head *Oh you run like a girl*

and you will say shout scream whisper call back *Yes. What exactly did you think I was?*

Just do it.

For more information about Nike Women's Products, call 1-800-284-4184.

Reprinted with permission for Wieden & Kennedy for Nike

New Balance had a hard-hitting message for women. "Presenting shoes designed by women, built by women, and tested by women. All to ensure one thing: They fit women." Hard to misinterpret that message.

Advertising shouldn't portray women as dizzy blondes, air heads, or sex objects nor should they so blatantly structure their visuals and copy as to patronize women.

The August 16, 1993, *The Wall Street Journal's* article "Sex Sells Pool Products That Women Buy" reinforces the belief that sexist advertising is alive and well in many industries, even in the 1990s.[14] The article points out that most packaging for swimming pool products show well-endowed women scantily clad in bikinis. "The problem is, women—not men—are the primary purchasers of pool products, a fact that has been slow to filter down to all levels of marketing in the male-dominated, $7 billion pool and spa industry," writes Jack Reitman. According to Reitman's article, Fountainhead Technologies Inc. directly targeted women when it introduced its water purifier. Their trade ad focuses on the benefits of the product, and instead of bikinis, shows a woman and a child wrapped in a large towel. The simple slogan, "For the health of your family. For the life of your pool," was the theme of the less than $1 million point-of-purchase and print campaign.

One ad I liked simply said, "Diamond: What a rock should be." It was followed by informative copy; then, ended with: "Lincoln. What a luxury car should be." Another automotive ad that had attention-grabbing copy said, "Some people think a Mercedes S-Class is nothing more than a symbol of how much you're worth." Then, you turn the page and the copy continues with your focus on the center that says, "They couldn't be more right." The smaller copy was pictorial and talked about the various features of the car. It ends with a crashed car and the copy, "It seems owning a Mercedes-Benz S-Class is not so much a barometer of your net worth as it is your self-worth." The message: the car is safe, well constructed—a big selling feature to women. Volvo discovered that a long time ago.

An ad I thought was appealing, in-tune with the times, and likely to catch women's attention was written for two Audi dealers in Dallas. The headline read, "We'd like you to meet two men who aren't afraid of a commitment." The ad introduced the owners of the two dealerships and went on to emphasize the features of the car and the dealers' commitment to the same quality standards and excellence in service as the manufacturer's.

Chevrolet has struggled with various concepts, trying to create ads that women would find appealing. Contrasting their early ads with some relatively recent ones will demonstrate why some ads work with women, and others don't. Chuck Hipp, assistant manager of passenger car advertising for Chevrolet, admitted, "How we create advertising has changed as a result of the importance of this segment.[15] Some cars, for instance the Cavaliar and Geo, are more gender-specific and attract more women. We want our ads to speak to this market."

On the following pages are an excellent series.

Chevrolet's ad with the headline "Make a statement" does exactly that. And it makes a very good statement. The copy is concise and would appeal to a young woman just out of school, the target market for this ad. With copy stating, "They're proud that I chose a car that makes a lot of sense," the young woman is acknowledging that it was her decision, and it was a good one. Dorthy Miller, president of the Miller Agency, an advertising firm that specializes in automotive advertising, believes that the look of the woman is right on target for the 1990s.[16] "The copy is believable and hits the interest of women in that age group," affirmed Miller.

"I particularly like the copy that reads, 'It's not enough to be smart; you got to look smart, too.' Each ad in the series is right. The look, the copy, the direction are great for the female market the ads are targeting," noted Miller.

By contrasting this series of ads with an earlier series, it will become apparent how the other copy was written more from a man's perceptive than a women's. "For instance," Miller indicated, "the headline read, 'Because the one who gets there first wins' shows the male spirit of competitiveness. It was written for aggressive women. The copy is way off base. 'With cars, there are two measures of engine power potential: horsepower and torque. Essentially, horsepower measures speed potential, and torque measures acceleration potential. When evaluating a car's performance, look at both figures. . . . It continues with 'you'll get the all-systems-are-go-combination of 130 horsepower and 165 ft-lbs of torque. . . .' "

The difference between the two sets of ads is obvious. "Women just don't identify with the headlines or the copy in the second set. They don't care about torque. The copywriter is assuming that women have the same love affair with cars that men do, and that just doesn't exist," said Miller. According to the *Sports Illustrated* "The American Male '91" study, "The biggest interest differential between men and women is cars. Men are more than twice as likely as women (52 percent versus 22 percent) to be interested in cars."[17]

Women wouldn't identify in a positive way with the headlines in the rest of the series either. "Don't spend the next few years wondering if you did the right thing" doesn't inspire self-esteem and confidence the

"What's the rush?"

"Sure, I'd like to get married. But what's the rush? I love my work. And I don't have to answer to anybody. Anytime I want to I can just get into my Chevy Beretta GT and take off, you know? No place in particular. Just go. That's a feeling I'm not ready to give up.

When it comes to going your own way, nobody's winning like The Heartbeat of America.

THE *Heartbeat*
OF AMERICA IS WINNING.
TODAY'S CHEVROLET

Beretta GT is sleek, affordable sport coupe. ■ New, more powerful 3.1 Liter Multi-Port Fuel-Injected V6. ■ Special Sport Suspension for sophisticated handling. ■ Standard Getrag-licensed 5-speed manual overdrive trans. ■ Standard AM/FM stereo radio with Seek and Scan and digital clock. ■ 3-year/ 50,000-mile Bumper to Bumper Plus Warranty*

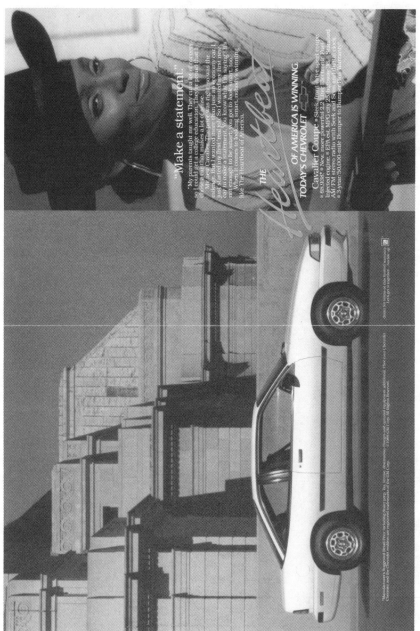

"Make a statement."

"My parents taught me well. They cut a lot of corners so I could get a college education. They're proud that I did. But that makes a lot of sense.

My first Cavalier. The price was right — so was the mileage. Still, I wanted more than just an economy car. I just got started in the working world. So I wanted my first car to make a statement. You know what I'm saying? To be smart enough to be smart, you got to look smart, too.

When it comes to looking smart, nobody's winning like The Heartbeat of America.

THE *Heartbeat*

OF AMERICA IS WINNING.
TODAY'S CHEVROLET

Cavalier Coupe ■ Sticker price starts at just $8,938* ■ New more powerful 2.2 liter 5-Speed or Fuel Injected engine ■ EPA est. MPG city 25* ■ Standard AM-FM stereo, radio with Seek and Scan and Clock ■ 3-year/50,000-mile Bumper to Bumper Plus Warranty.

same way the Nike ads did. But Chevrolet has learned from the past and produced a terrific series in the early 1990s.

Advertisers and marketers who hope to succeed with the women's market should take more time to understand women or to consult with specialists who can help produce meaningful ads. Companies must realize that acknowledging the existence of the market segment is just the first step. It in no way guarantees that women will identify with the products or the ads. Good advertising understands the customers' thinking and speaks to them in terms they relate to and understand. Knowing the market exists is very different from reaching it. Marketers must be able to break that "glass wall" if they are to reach the woman consumer.

One of the best promotional pieces I have ever received was for the Mark VIII, shown below. The mailing tube contained a poster and a smaller piece with the same wonderful image on the front and the information about the car on the inside. The piece was not specifically designed to be marketed to women, nor was it sexist or offensive. It was classy, creative, and did what advertising and direct-mail pieces are suppose to do first. It caught my attention.

Marketing to women doesn't mean that every piece has to be tailored to women. Not every ad needs to have a woman spokesperson. Not every ad has to run in women's magazines. There are numerous ways to market

RESERVED - GERRY MYERS

1993 LINCOLN MARK VIII

Reprinted with permission from Lincoln-Mercury

to women successfully. Unfortunately, sexist ads that portray women as sex objects or as decor in the ad isn't one way. It's so simple—good taste, good informational copy, good visuals—you wonder why so many businesses are still struggling.

Advertising Designed to Lose Sales

You couldn't get much worse than this headline: "Handles the groceries. Carpools the kids. And cooks." This ad with the tagline: "The New Generation of Oldsmobile" is a paradox. The new generation of Oldsmobile certainly wasn't appealing to the new generation of women. The copy had "cute" phrases like the "sedan is just the recipe" or "the laundry list of standard equipment." To make matters worse, the ad ran in *Working Woman* magazine. This ad has to be the epitome of "not getting it." Oldsmobile sales continue to decline. As far as their new campaign, "Demand Better." I think Oldsmobile should take their own advice and "Demand Better." After Oldsmobile's recent agency review, I was very disappointed to see that they had nothing creative, innovative, or even very good.

When Infiniti broke their first series of ads, I wouldn't say the ads were designed to lose sales, they just weren't designed to make sales either. In an attempt to break from the crowd, Infiniti went with trees and rocks and a serene setting rather than a car. No one knew what the car looked like or the features it had. They quickly corrected this mistake. While Infiniti's advertising is not specifically targeted to women, they are capturing a large share of the market. Women buying luxury cars are selecting Infiniti for its styling and the superior customer service it provides.

Family Circle publisher Valerie Salembier stated, "Advertisers have to know the difference between sexy and sexist. When the message is sexy, it can be appealing. When it's sexist, it's a turnoff."[18] Salembier cites examples of Calvin Klein ads that went too far. They resulted in not only a loss of revenue, but also in a new marketing direction. The new ads feature fortysomething model Lisa Taylor, not just a tantalizing young woman purring that nothing comes between her and her Calvins.

"There are marketers using good, clean sex, instead of sexism in their ads," confirmed Salembier, citing Donna Karan's new perfume ad.

"Sex in advertising is okay. It is a legitimate human drive and a way to get a message across," indicated Garfield. But Garfield draws the line on when sex is okay. "There is no excuse for the way it is used in beer advertising. While the beer industry is targeting men, there is no other industry that so objectifies women as beer," he said.

Using women as sex objects in beer commercials isn't new. In the 1950s, a New York beer maker dreamed up the Miss Rheingold beauty pageant.[19] From there, a multitude of buxom blondes have burst across television screens. Fun frolicking females on beaches push beer. Bikini-clad girls bounce beach balls as the beer industry continues to promote the most sexist of advertising. Like other industries, they took it just one step too far. Outrage prevailed when the Stroh's Swedish Bikini team bared so much.

After Stroh's Old Milwaukee took offensive to new heights, things began to change. New ads for Budweiser don't portray women as sex objects. And Miller Lite, 40 percent of whose consumers are women, definitely is revamping their spots. In an article by Martha Moore in *USA Today*, she quoted Bob Gougenour, Michelob brand director, who said, "A good percentage of beer volume that is consumed is consumed by women. You can't ignore it."[20] Greg Clements, an advertising salesman for *Glamour* magazine, said he sold 15 pages of ads to Miller and Michelob in 1991, up from none in 1990.[21]

Miller's print campaign features women who are professional rodeo riders, aerobics instructors and even surfers. Adolph Coors Co., perhaps the first to target women, has designed ads that feature them relaxing after a bike race.[22]

Michelob's print and TV spots feature women in professional roles—not swim suits. Carol Christie, senior vice president and group creative director articulated, "Our ads are designed to target adults.[23] We are not specifically speaking to women, but we don't want to victimize or ridicule anyone. Our work is based on respect and wit, but that doesn't mean humor at someone's expense." One TV ad for Michelob that has been very popular shows a dart board. You see a dart land almost dead center, and the crowd cheers. Then a second and a third, all with the same accuracy. The ending is a woman saying, "Honest, I never played this game before." "Both men and women love the twist at the end," said Christie.

"Sex in advertising definitely catches people's attention," commented Daniel Howard, Ph.D., who teaches consumer behavior at Southern Methodist University.[24] "But sex only works in selling a product when it is relevant. In fact, it can have a negative effect. Catching the consumer's attention doesn't always translate into a sale." Howard tells about an Illinois businessman who created packaging for computer disks with a bikini-clad woman and the slogan "We Satisfy Your Drive." The product quickly failed. "They got people's attention, but people didn't buy them. They thought it was a cheap product," emphasized Howard.

"Women have a more predominant role today. Only 19 percent of all families are the traditional working husband with a stay-at-home wife who takes care of the house and children. Today, women are educated, are more independent, and have greater economic power. Both business and academia are increasingly seeing women as a critical and separate entity," reiterated Howard.

That is, most businesses. Another ad, designed to increase Crain's business subscribers really missed the mark. The background for the ad was rows of premium cigars. The copy read: "67% of all Crain's subscribers are in top management. Who do you think signs off on computer buys? The guy in the mail room?" Obviously, they don't think women head data processing divisions either. The ad was degrading and showed a total lack of sensitivity to many, including honest, hard-working men in the mail room. It totally ignored businesswomen and the clout they carry, particularly in the data processing area of many major corporations. This ad ran in *Advertising Age* September 14, 1992.

Two ads I really disliked were Toyota's "You Could Always Lie and Tell Them It Was Expensive" and an Eclipse ad that ran in local theaters showing the car being used as a getaway car in a robbery. Both ad messages are obvious. The Toyota ad's message was that the buyer received good value for the money. The car looked more expensive than it was. The Eclipse's message was the speed of the car. However, in today's world the last thing I think advertising needs to do is promote unacceptable social values. Yes, movies have plots like *Thelma and Louise* and *Bonnie and Clyde*, which certainly don't portray how you want your kids to turn out. But why would an advertiser want to attach their name to such unacceptable behavior? Most women, being the nurturers of the family, do not relate to these ads in a positive way. As I said before, advertising shouldn't offend one market in order to sell to another. Tastefully done advertising can be effective.

A recent full-page ad for Mercedes-Benz that ran in *U.S. Open* magazine promoting the championship tournament simply pictured a Mercedes and read "Haul Derriere." Did it get my attention? Yes. Will it sell cars? That's another story. The creators, I assume, are positioning the car to the younger, more active audience as fast and fun, rather than a car for the more mature person. But "Haul Ass" is haul ass in any language and doesn't really speak to the Mercedes market.

Sony recently received numerous complaints from a group of professional women on a 30-second commercial for its MiniDisc player. "The commercial shows a young, muscular man wearing jeans, a T-shirt, and sunglasses pushing buttons on his Sony stereo. Each button is programmed to display a woman's name; when the man presses a button, a woman appears. The tag line is 'If you play it, they will come.' "[25] Women are very angry over the double-entendre slogan. While Sony's ad agency is changing the tag, the commercial is supposed to remain the same. For a major manufacturer to continue to run a commercial that angers a large segment of the marketplace seems a questionable strategy. Even if young males are the target for the product, women influence the purchases of entertainment products even when they aren't the primary buyer. Good advertising is effective, not offensive.

Women buy the majority of household products, even soaps aimed at men. Lever Bros. 2000 soap ran an ad that said, "The deodorant soap that's better for your skin." The copy would have worked better if the visual wasn't a man's foot thrust in a woman's face. Attention grabbing, yes. Motivation for women to buy, no.

"Prudential Bache ran an ad with a very professionally dressed women who had just been made a partner in the law firm. Her boss handed her a card and said something to the effect of 'Now that you will be making more money, talk to my broker,' " recalled Garfield. "The message was that while she had just been promoted to partner, she was incapable of understanding finances and needed his broker to take her by the hand. There were definitely undertones of 'little lady.' "

Advertisers constantly think they are on-target, because they don't see the subtle nuances that women read into ads. It's almost like creating ads for another culture. Marketers have to be sensitive to their target's interpretation of the copy. Advertising to women without having women involved in the process, either at the creative end, the pre-testing phase, or as the client, can produce what appears to be good copy, but isn't.

Innovative Advertising Addressing New Markets

"When you really want to treat yourself, nothing makes you feel as good as gold," is a great headline that fits the visual. Understanding that women with discretionary income no longer are dependent on men to buy them gold jewelry, these manufacturers targeted and reached the woman's market. While ad copy that says, "Show her how much you love her" is great for convincing a man to buy gold jewelry for the woman in his life, sophisticated marketers have not limited themselves to just one market. They understand they can capture much more. Ads for Keepsake diamond rings and House of Faberge, a division of The Franklin Mint, also target women. They frequently place ads in magazines such as *Working Woman* and *New Woman*.

Reprinted with permission from the Janus Fund

Diamonds no longer are strictly a man's gift to a woman. Besides her ability to buy them for herself, she has the ability to buy them for him. Creative marketers take advantage of changing trends and add dollars to their bottom line. One ad shows a woman who has her arms lovingly around her husband's shoulders with the caption, "The average guy can't remember the gifts his wife gives him. Then again, the average guy doesn't get a diamond." It ends with "The Man's Diamond: The Gift He'll Never Forget."

Gold and diamonds aren't the only areas where marketers are recognizing the increasing numbers of women consumers. Financial institutions have begun to focus on the working woman. "A Woman's Place is in the Markets," is one headline that caught professional women's attention. The Janus Fund doesn't specialize in investments for women; they just wanted to take advantage of the opportunities available in the marketplace.

The most recent ad I've seen that is aggressively targeting the female consumer is Exxon. And why shouldn't they? Women buy approximately 50 percent of all automobiles, and most of them fill them up themselves. I wonder why the other oil companies aren't doing something to capture this market. The double truck spread headline reads, "Taking Care Of

Your Car Isn't Nearly As Hard As Men Make It Out To Be." While the ad isn't offensive, it isn't great either. Playing on what the creators perceive as the new popularity of male-bashing, the ad gently, or maybe not so gently, puts men in their place.

Bob Garfield believes one way to pander to women is to ridicule men. In observing our social truism that a male is knowledgeable about cars, which then increases his image as a man, an advertiser targeting women can poke fun at his preoccupation with cars and his pride in his superior knowledge of the subject. "If advertisers want to show someone as pompous, or silly, it has to be the white male. It's too risky to portray a woman or an ethnic minority as the fool or the brunt of the joke," advised Garfield.

In the Exxon ad, the visual doesn't particularly match the copy. After all, most teenagers, girls as well as boys, can fill their own cars. And most guys would agree. This woman looks like she can handle just about anything that comes her way. I doubt if filling her tank even caused her a moment's concern. As has been mentioned previously, most women don't relate to male-bashing ads the way men think they do. The ad was obviously created by men. Women wouldn't have written it the same way. There are a number of magazines appealing to businesswomen in which the ad could have run. But, regardless of where it ran, it needed to have a stronger message.

One way the visual could have been used effectively with the same basic message conveyed—"Exxon Supreme is a superior product"—was to write the copy more to women. For instance, a headline that read, "You're careful what you put into your body. Why not be just as careful what you put into your car?" would have talked to women. The copy could have addressed the fact that women exercise so they can perform at their best, they watch what they eat, or they take preventive measures to ensure their continued good health with routine check-ups. Then, it could have concluded with the statement that her car needs good maintenance for top performance, too. And Exxon Supreme will provide the ingredients the car needs to run at its best and remain trouble-free. The copy would appeal to women, and the visual fits. There's no doubt in your mind when you look at the woman in the ad that she takes good care of herself.

According to Daymon Muehl, media and advertising specialist for Exxon, Exxon has targeted women in its television advertising by running ads on programs that are skewed to women.[26] Even though the print ad could have been more effective, I do applaud Exxon for its recognition of the market and its attempt to reach the woman consumer.

Taking Care Of Your Car Isn't Nearly As Hard As Men Make It Out To Be.

EXXON 93 SUPREME

With my schedule, the last thing I need is trouble with my car.

But c'mon guys, we're not talking nuclear physics here. I check my tires, have my oil changed every 3000 miles and use a really good gasoline like Exxon Supreme.

It has 93 octane and it keeps my engine clean, so my car runs great. And that's it. It's as simple as that.

But hey, if guys want to make it more complicated, well, that's guys for you.

Rely on the Tiger

How Women Have Affected Media and Advertising Trends

As women flocked to the workplace, advertisers not only had to adapt their message to this new breed of woman, but find the means to reach her. One method was outdoor advertising, as more woman sat on crowded freeways during rush hour traffic. In some geographic locations, subway advertising is growing as well. Because of the limited message that can be conveyed, outdoor advertising tends to be less condescending than other media to women.[27]

In the 1980s, circulation of traditional women's publications was down, and ad lineage was falling. *Working Woman,* however, was gaining strength. Advertisers of business products and financial services began to select it for their advertising dollars, more than $25 million worth. Between 1980 and 1989, *Working Woman*'s circulation topped one million, making it the most widely read business publication in the country, passing both *Business Week* and *Fortune.*[28]

While the demographics are slightly different, *Savvy* competes with *Working Woman* for the more than 11 million women in management and professional careers. Even traditional publications have modified their format to include topics of interest to busy working woman. *Woman's Day* now includes 30-minute dinner recipes and career-oriented articles.[29]

Katherine Bell, publisher of *Lear's* magazine, believes *Lear's* is in an enviable position.[30] With the population aging, *Lear's* market is expanding, while many other niche magazines are shrinking. "Marketers have a perfect venue available to them to reach this growing, affluent segment of the population," stated Bell. "We have grown from a rate base of 200,000 to 500,000, with a readership of 1.2 million. The marketplace is growing toward us. Baby boomers are the first generation of women to have gone to college in record numbers. Many are now in high-paying careers."

One thing Bell pointed out is magazines that have been around for a long time have a harder time changing their format and adjusting to a new environment because they already have a customer base that expects certain things. *Lear's,* however, had the opportunity to start with just the right formula at the right time. *Lear's* recently conducted a marketing survey to determine how their readers felt about shopping, magazine advertisements, and the products they purchased. They found out that women would like to see more advertisements with the benefits of the product clearly given. They would like believable people to be pictured with the products. Their main complaint was when the product advertised didn't deliver what it promised.

Another vehicle that has reached working women successfully is radio. More than 85 percent of working women spend at least three hours each day listening to the radio. Companies, especially those with packaged goods products, are changing schedules in order to reach women during afternoon drive time, when they are most likely to stop on the way home to shop. In the 1980s, L'eggs Products began sponsoring a 90-second syndicated program featuring news and information for women on the job and at home. Popular radio on-site remote broadcasts from shopping malls no longer reach the number of women they did in the past. Some radio stations are opting to do remotes from companies instead of malls.

A survey conducted in the mid-1980s showed that working women spend 44 percent of their media time listening to the radio, only 41 percent watching television, 9 percent reading newspapers and 6 percent with magazines. These statistics have changed dramatically from 20 years ago when fewer women worked, and television had the largest percentage of the female's media attention. During the daytime, when most purchases are made, working women spend 60 percent of their media time with radio.[31] The advent and popularity of the home shopping channels may skew these figures.

Newspapers, however, have seen a steady decline in female readership during the last 20 years as more women entered the work force. One reason is that most papers feature topics that are of more interest to men than women. Business sections have a disproportionally small amount of news about women entrepreneurs and women in corporate America. Most business reporters are men, and the news about women is relegated to the women's section along with recipes and coupons. Women spend about three hours a week reading printed matter versus three hours a day listening to the radio.[32]

Automotive advertising has seen an increase in ad dollars, but are they targeted to the growing market? According to NADA, in 1970 about $50 was spent on advertising per vehicle. Today, it has risen to nearly $300. Between 1981 and 1991, dealers increased newspaper advertising from 56.1 percent of their advertising budget to 58.6 percent. They increased television ad dollars from 7.5 percent to 14.4 percent and cut radio from 25.3 percent to 16.5 percent. Advertising in all other media declined from 11.1 percent to 10.5 percent of the budget.

A typical dealer spends $86,000 for newspaper advertising, $24,500 for radio and $21,000 for TV ads. The advertising budget equals approximately 1.15 percent of total sales dollars for a dealership.[33] Like other types of advertising, automotive commercials need a strong, single message that isn't flawed with women in tight fitting leather outfits or draped across the hood of the car. The ads don't need to be male bashing to be

When JUDITH REUSSWIG wrote us about the Saturn we were building for her, she didn't expect our reply to have a car attached.

Every year, Miss Reusswig's third-graders learn how to write a proper letter. And they find it is a useful skill, what with their regular field trips into nearby Washington, D.C. (Nor long ago, twenty-three thank-you notes arrived at the Ghanaian Embassy.)

As for Miss Reusswig, she's a pretty good letter writer herself. And she wrote to us. About the car we were building for her.

She wanted us to know *for whom* we were building that SL2. That blue-green one with

The Saturn SL2

How, if you're buying a Saturn, please don't feel you have to write us in order to get a car built with lots of personal attention. We build them all that way. (Really.)

the grey interior. Not just any car. *Her* car. She even sent us a picture of herself.

Well, we liked that. We read her letter and sent it down the line, so everyone who built her car could see who she was.

We liked her idea so much, in fact, that we placed her picture in her new SL2's glove box so she'd know we'd gotten it. Then we all signed a poster in reply, thanking her for buying a Saturn, and we sent that along as well.

Because, you see, we've held on to some of what we learned in the third grade, too.

A DIFFERENT KIND *of* COMPANY. A DIFFERENT KIND *of* CAR.

166 ❖ Successful Marketing Strategies

effective, but they do need to communicate the benefits and features of the car in intelligent, sophisticated language. Little girls don't buy cars. Educated, savvy women do.

Saturn's print ads are positioned to the diverse demographics they are targeting. One ad shows an African-American couple; in another a sheriff says he put 100,000 miles on his car in just one year. This real-life advertising appeals to women. Another shows a single women in a sky-diving outfit, while one features a woman who white-water canoes. When third-grade teacher Judith Reusswig wrote Saturn about the car they were building for her, she didn't know she would become a television and print celebrity.

The media's influence on women has been as profound on the editorial side as in its advertising. In her book *Backlash*, Susan Faludi wrote: "The absence of real women in a news account that is allegedly about real women is a hallmark of '80s backlash journalism. Fear was also driving the media's need to dictate trends and determine social attitudes in the '80s, as print and broadcast audiences, especially female audiences, turned to other news sources and advertising plunged—eventually falling to its lowest level in twenty years," wrote Fauldi. In the 1980s, the media focused on females' failures to find husbands.

The irony of the situation was confusing and frustrating to women. On the one hand, women were told their biological clocks were ticking and they had better make finding husbands a top priority. On the other hand, they were being told their chances were slim. One story even dramatized the situation by saying that unmarried women over 35 had a better chance of being kidnapped by a terrorist than finding a mate. While the media may be obsessed with women's marital status and the number of children she is producing, they are not as concerned about her making the news.[34]

"Women remain under-represented both as subjects and as reporters of news, according to a 'Women, Men and Media' project at New York University," wrote Rita Ciolli for *Newsday*.[35] In the latest survey, they examined 20 newspapers and three networks and found that men were written about or quoted 85 percent more on the front page than women. Men wrote 66 percent of the leading news stories and 74 percent of the opinion and commentary columns. Men reported 86 percent of the stories on ABC, CBS, and NBC. In fact, the number of stories by women is decreasing rather than increasing. "Women are not sought out for their expert opinions," observed Junior Bridges, author of the study.

Coined phrases like: "the man shortage," "the biological clock," and the "mommy track" all stereotyped women and assumed the author knew what was important to women. "The mommy track" was part of Felice Schwartz's, founder of Catalyst, prediction that women would trade growth and compensation in the workplace for flexibility and freedom from long hours. It was never proved that women actually would trade growth and compensation for more flexible hours, but that didn't stop the flood of stories on working women and working mothers and how they would corrupt the family with their selfishness. As women became financially responsible for children as single heads-of-households or went to work because the family needed the dual income, media stories continued to suggest she should be at home raising children. The paradox continued, as the media often prescribes one thing for women, but real-life demands dictate another.

Ways Advertisers Can Win with Women

Women care about more than the product and the price. They care about how they are portrayed in the company's advertising. She wants to know: What does the company think about me?

"By last year women were suddenly saying, 'It matters to us what your company is saying and how you're portraying women—if we don't like the message, we'll buy elsewhere,'" said Barbara Feigin, head of research at Grey Advertising. According to Linda Kaplan, creative director at J. Walter Thompson, this quote, along with the growing knowledge that there is a difference in the way men and women communicate, reinforces the new direction of advertising and the new concern for the sensitivity of women. Articles like "You've Come a Long Way" in *Advertising Age* only reconfirm how important it is for marketers to understand the new professional woman consumer.[36]

Below are just a few tips to consider when creating advertising aimed at women:

1. Stay in touch with your market. Conduct research. Use focus groups. Do pre-tests on the ads.

2. Hire female creative directors or copy writers. Make women a part of the strategic development team. Get a woman's perspective.

3. Portray real women. Most women aren't 20 years old with 20-inch waists.

4. Eliminate sexist ads. Sex is overused in advertising. When it sets the tone or creates the mood, that's fine, but when women are used strictly as decor, the ads need to be rethought.

5. Women shouldn't have to feel inadequate after watching a commercial or a series of commercials.

6. Women should connect with the message. Be sure to include things that are important to them.

7. The copy should communicate that the company recognizes her as an intelligent, astute shopper. Condescending, chauvinistic phrases can kill the entire message.

8. Get feedback from women. Listen to the comments.

9. Understand that small things are big things to women, even in advertising. Men view things differently, have a different sense of humor, and react to ads differently than women. Even the importance of various features of a product differs between men and women.

10. Utilize good advertising rules—strong visuals, attention—grabbing headlines, and informative copy sell to women as well as men.

11. All advertising to women doesn't have to have a woman as the spokesperson, but it only makes sense that women would usually identify with another woman more than a man. If you have a series of ads, or ads with a group, the people in the ads should be diverse. They should reflect your target—men, women, young, old, and various ethnic minorities.

12. If you use a woman or women in the ads, make sure the usage is appropriate for the product and your market.

13. Look at winning ads that also have increased sales substantially. Analyze what makes them so successful. Learn from others.

14. Position the ads in the proper medium.

15. Be aware of trends and how they affect your advertising. As women's roles and lifestyles change, advertising must reflect their current status.

16. Campaigns shouldn't be offensive to any segment of the population. Advertising to women should portray socially accepted values, unless it is a spoof, and then caution is recommended.

17. Don't let too many rules inhibit clever copy. Understand the guidelines, but imagination and creativity are recognized by nearly everyone.

Notes

[1]Betsy Sharkey, editor-at-large, *Adweek*, interview with author, 11 August 1993.

[2]Kimberly Barta, curator, American Advertising Museum, interview with author, 11 August 1993.

[3]Sharkey.

[4]Barta.

[5]Bob Garfield, editor-at-large, *Advertising Age*, interview with author, 10 August 1993.

[6]Cooper-Hewett Museum Exhibit, August, 1993.

Ellen Lupton, *Mechanical Brides*, Cooper-Hewitt National Museum of Design Smithsonian Institution (Princeton: Architectural Press, 1993).

[7]Ann Armbruster, "Mechanical Brides: Women and Machines From Home to Office," *Working Woman* (September 1993): 92–93.

[8]Betsy Sharkey, "You've Come a Long Way, Madison Avenue," *Lear's* (March 1993): 93–101.

[9]Leonard McGill, "Fashion Magazines: Ad Pages and Circulation—The Model of Health," *Advertising Age* (4 April 1985): 17, 31.

[10]Rochelle Lazarus, president, Ogilvy & Mather, interview with author, 23 August 1993.

[11]William Sever, director of marketing, Upjohn Company, interview with author, 14 October 1993.

[12]Sharkey.

[13]Jeffrey Scott, "Advertisers Put 'Real' in Pitch to Women," *San Gabriel Valley Daily Tribune* (16 July 1993).

[14]Jack Reitman, "Sex Sells Pool Products That Women Buy," *The Wall Street Journal*, Marketing and Media (17 August 1993).

[15]Chuck Hipp, assistant manager passenger car advertising, Chevrolet Motor Division, interview with author, 28 July 1993.

[16]Dorthy Miller, president, Miller Agency, interview with author, 27 August 1993.

[17]*Sports Illustrated*: "The American Male '91", conducted by Lieberman Research, Inc., (New York: The Time Inc. Magazine Company, 1991).

[18]Cyndee Miller, "Publisher Says Sexy Ads Are OK, But Sexist Ones Will Sink Sales," (23 November 1992): 8.

[19]Martha Moore, "Debate Brews Over Selling Beer With Sex," *USA Today* (15 November 1991): B–1.

[20]Martha Moore, "Debate Brews Over Selling Beer With Sex," *USA Today* (15 November 1991): B–1.

[21]Martha Moore, "Michelob Shifts Pitch to Women to Boost Flat Sales," *USA Today* (3 February 1992): B–5.

[22]Bruce Horovitz, *Los Angeles Times* (24 March 1992): D1–6.

[23]Carol Christie, group creative director, D'Arcy Masius Benton & Bowles, interview with author, 3 September 1993.

[24]Daniel Howard, associate professor of marketing, Southern Methodist University, interview with author, 14 September 1993.

[25]Kevin Goldman, "Sony Changes Tune," *The Wall Street Journal* (1 September 1993).

[26]Daymon Muehl, advertising promotions manager, Exxon USA, interview with author, 10 August 1993.

[27]Amy Zipkin, "Marketing to Women: Lifestyle Ad Boost Banks, Insurers,"*Advertising Age* (7 March 1988): S 10.

[28]Susan Faludi, *Backlash: The Undeclared War Against American Women* (New York: Crown Publishers, Inc., 1991), 75–111.

[29]Lynn Folse, "Magazines Join Movement," *Advertising Age* (12 September 1985): 36–38.

[30]Katherine Bell, editor-in-chief, *Lear's*, interview with author, 15 August 1993.

[31]Charline Allen, "Radio Listens to an Increasingly Female Audience," *Advertising Age* (13 October 1983): M–32.

[32]Hugh Morgan, "Women Readers," *Editor & Publisher* (13 October 1992): 13.

[33]C.D. Bohon, "When in Doubt—Advertise!" *Dealer Business* (July 1993): 20–26.

[34]Faludi, *Backlash.*

[35]Rita Ciolli, "Women, Men and Media Project," *Dallas Morning News,* from *Newsday* (7 April 1993).

[36]Warren Berger, "You've Come a Long Way" *Advertising Age,* 21–25.

Part III

Demographic
and
Psychographic
Differences

Chapter Seven

Segmenting the Marketplace:
Single, Married, and Working Women—
How They Buy

There are many segments within the woman's market. In many cases, she is the purchasing agent for the family. In this role, she buys for herself and for others. Today, many single women are primary buyers. They are the ultimate consumer who will use the product or service. In the business world, the corporate buyer, discussed in Chapter 9, is also a purchasing agent. She buys for her company rather than for her own personal use.

This chapter delineates products more generally purchased by specific categories, and provides statistical data that clearly defines these various segments.

Single Versus Married

In the last 20 years, the number of single adults has nearly doubled. Today there are more than 73 million singles, the majority of which are women. Young women put off marriage for careers; middle-aged women get divorced, never marry, or become widows.

In 1985, 36 percent of the women in the United States were single with no children, 9 percent were single heads-of-households with dependent children, 28 percent were married but had no dependent children at home, and 27 percent were married with children (Figure 7-1). Interestingly, 72 percent of women believe they can have a complete and happy life if they remain single; 23 percent disagree. However, 57 percent of

173

women think men must be married to be happy. The vast majority, 94 percent, saw a combination of marriage with a career and/or children as the ideal lifestyle.[1]

Within the singles group are many subsegments. There are teenage girls, young women in their twenties, baby boomers, single professionals who have never married and probably never will, divorced women of various ages, single parents, and widows.

Young single women are a marketer's dream. They have discretionary income and few responsibilities other than themselves. They are often considered more selfish because their spending emphasis is self-centered.

"Single women have more time. They browse in stores more. It is an entertainment and social experience, where they feel comfortable and powerful," said Janice Leeming, editor-in-chief of *Marketing to Women*.[2] Generation X women seem to worry less about the recession, are less concerned about planning for the future financially and love to travel.

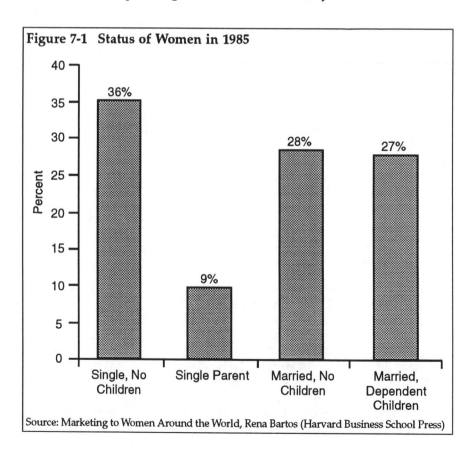

Figure 7-1 Status of Women in 1985

Source: Marketing to Women Around the World, Rena Bartos (Harvard Business School Press)

"Travel is very important to younger singles," stated Leeming. "They like to travel abroad, are more adventurous, and enjoy everything from the beach to mountain climbing. Fifty-one percent of the time, women in their twenties prefer to vacation in new places they have never been, compared to the overall average of 43 percent." As single women begin to age, their priorities change. Baby boomers are beginning to plan more for the future, and are more concerned about money when the economy is in a recession. As they mature, retirement planning, IRAs, and mutual funds take on more significance to them.

The singles market is an untapped segment for life and disability insurance. Selling to single women is an excellent way to build a new dimension into a company's or agent's customer base. Generally, these women are underinsured and have a more positive view of insurance than men do. Too frequently, the market is overlooked because there isn't a male head of the household buying insurance to protect his family. Insurance agents need to rethink their marketing strategies and target this undiscovered group.[3]

When young women marry, their priorities change. Their lifestyle becomes more traditional. Their new emphasis is on family and the children they plan to have. Saving for a house becomes important. When they become parents, they have more demands on their money, and their purchasing patterns shift dramatically. When a married women with children becomes a single parent, another major shift takes place. She is totally unlike the carefree single woman with no children. Young, single, working women who enjoy the freedom of their own income and the material things they can buy with it are diametrically different from struggling-to-get-by young, single mothers.

Single mothers are among the poorest group in America, and this segment is growing. Today, 75 percent of the nation's poor are woman and children. White women and children represent 51 percent of those in poverty. Blacks, Hispanics, ethnic minorities, and white males make up 49 percent.[4] These women count every penny. They comparison shop and use a lot of coupons. Married women redeem and collect coupons even more than single women do, although both groups are significant users.[5] This group often works on a very tight budget because women as a group earn less, frequently pay more for basically the same product or service than a man does, and are usually the caretakers of small children.[6] "As family and traditional values continue to play a predominant role in our society, even women without children will spend more on children," claimed Leeming. "They will buy for siblings, for friends' children, and for extended family members."

While married women, especially young wives, have returned to the basics and enjoy cooking from scratch, single women eat more frozen dinners than their married counterparts and eat in restaurants more often. Many food companies are recognizing the phenomenon of the single-person household and are repackaging their products in single servings. Frozen gourmet dinners, microwave breakfasts, smaller cans of soups and juices, and one-serving coffee packets have all appeared on store shelves. Salad bars have become a staple at grocery stores where a single person can purchase variety without waste.[7] Single women between 18 and 24 make fewer food-shopping trips than married women or women with children. While other categories average eating out six times a month, single women eat out nearly nine times a month.[8]

Married women make more major food shopping trips than single women. But, the biggest difference is the amount of money spent weekly by married and single women for food. Forty-four percent of married women spend $100 or more per week, while only 16 percent of single women spend that much. Conversely, only 15 percent of married women spend less than $50 per week, while nearly half of all single women do.[9] While only three-fourths of single women cook very often, 94 percent of married women cook most of the family meals.[10]

Singles of both genders have entered the real estate market. According to home builders, 25 percent of first-time home buyers are single, and 54 percent of condominium purchasers are single. Like those in other industries, home builders have found out that women who live alone want security, services, and social opportunities. Many companies that design and manage health clubs choose multi-residential buildings for their facilities that have a high percentage of singles.[11]

In the automotive industry, 61 percent of new cars buyers under 25 are female according to the Motor Vehicle Manufacturers Association.[12] Women between 25 and 34 will be the buyers of 1.6 million imported cars and 1.9 million domestic cars according to a report by *Cosmopolitan* magazine entitled, "The Changing Course of American Women." Women between 35 and 44 will purchase 1.5 million new import cars and 2.2 million domestic cars. These two age categories represent 46 percent of all female new car buyers.[13]

The majority of first-time female car buyers are single. "The image of the car is more important to young, single women than the female population as a whole. Like their stylish clothes, they see cars as a reflection of themselves—who they are," said Leeming. Single women, or women with no children, are more likely to buy a sportier car, while married women with children tend to buy more practical vehicles including minivans and sports utility vehicles.

Lifestyle changes created by working women have affected most industries. While greeting cards may not be as visible a sign of changing times as automobiles, card companies, nevertheless, have undergone transitions in the marketing of their products. With sales flat, greeting card companies began to look to new markets and ways to spur their growth. Hallmark, Gibson, and American Greeting cards began creating cards appropriate for announcing divorce as well as marriage. Many have added cards about dieting, dating, congratulations to fellow employees, and other contemporary topics to their line. With women buying 90 percent of all cards, it isn't surprising that astute marketers would concentrate on that market. Some have hired women writers and psychologists who can create sayings and designs that speak to women.[14]

Card companies aren't the only businesses focusing on the more than 20 million Americans who live alone, triple the number in 1960. Between 1970 and 1986, the number of singles living alone between the ages of 25 and 34 increased 346 percent. Singles between 35 and 44 rose 258 percent.[15] As single-person households increase three times faster than other households, they become a ripe target for many companies. The diversity of the live-alone single includes young women just out of school; baby boomers; and divorced, widowed, and never-married women. More than 60 percent of those living alone are women.[16]

Since loneliness is a by-product of living alone, many companies have developed strategies aimed at this emotion. As the singles bar scene faded, video dating services like Great Expectations have sprung up and have prospered. Located in nearly 50 different cities, Great Expectations has signed up thousands of singles searching for that perfect mate, or at least a fun companion. Dating services are a big business in the 1990s. Technology has picked up where humans have failed. Computers access thousands and thousands of files in their quest to match compatible partners. Trade show organizations have also cashed in on this trend with Singles Fairs that travel to various cities annually.

Managerial, Non-managerial and Non-employed

According to *Working Woman* magazine, businesswomen do more and spend more than other women.

Employed women buy more suits, coats, blazers, jackets, dresses, blouses, sweaters, accessories, and shoes than non-employed women. Working women are more active in sports than non-working women. They exercise, jog, and play tennis far more often. They ski, dive, and sail more. All these activities generate equipment, clothes, and travel purchases. Working women make purchases from catalogs more often and for higher dollar volumes than non-working women.

Managerial and professional women were the decision makers approximately twice as often when new import or luxury cars were purchased than non-professional women. They also purchase financial services far more often. Buying securities and mutual funds was even higher by professional women than professional men. The life, home owners, and automobile insurance buying patterns were similar for both professional men and women.[17]

Judith Langer, president of Langer Associations, Inc., a market research company, knows women's attitudes are changing.[18] According to Langer, women have more interest in financial services, spend more money on clothes, and are buying different types of clothes. Departments that cater to the professional woman have sprung up in many stores.

"Women are a complex segment that can't be marketed to as a single unit," acknowledged Langer. "They are a growing segment. Both the number of working women and their purchasing power are increasing."

Career-oriented women pay for their purchases with credit cards more often than the general population. Forty percent of career women have travel and entertainment credits cards such as American Express or Diners Card, compared to 29 percent of the adult population. Fifty-eight percent of career-oriented women have bank credit cards compared to 41 percent of the adult population; 61 percent have department store credit cards, compared to only 43 percent of other adults. More career women have checking accounts, invest in securities, and in general have a higher level of sophistication in financial matters than non-career women.[19]

Career women are developing new skills both in the workplace and outside it. Along with a more savvy approach to financial matters, they also are concerned with developing tools to help them be more effective in their jobs. Golf is one tool the new professional woman is using.

As more women become interested in golf as a business development tool, golf shops and manufacturers need to recognize that managerial, professional, and entrepreneurial women are the largest growth segment in the industry. Organizations such as the Executive Women's Golf League have a national presence as well as local chapters in numerous cities. Started in 1991 to provide for the growing needs of women golfers, the organization expects to have 2,500 members in 40 cities by the end of 1993.

"Women are getting angry at the patronizing ads that depicted them as non-serious golfers," warned Patricia Dixon, president of Dixon International Inc., dba Empowered.[20] Empowered is a women's golf store with a new concept and marketing strategy. "I got tired of seeing clothing manufacturers' ads that indicated all they think women care about is how cute they look on the golf course, or going into a store and the salesmen saying 'What can I help you with, little lady?' " said Dixon. "Women are out to play serious golf, just like men." Dixon, in partnership with LPGA golf pro Mary Lou Crocker, offers women golfers a haven from male ridicule and demeaning treatment. Together, they plan to offer private and group lessons, mini-clinics, and travel opportunities in addition to selling golf equipment and apparel. "We also have the capabilities to figure handicaps for women who don't belong to a country club, so they can play in tournaments." Dixon will also be marketing to corporations to assist executive women in becoming proficient golfers. "Men have done deals on the golf course for a long time. It's time women had the same opportunity." Empowered also has a management consultant who works with executive women golfers to develop golf profiles of their behavioral styles. "This will make them a better team player at work, as well as on the course," predicted Dixon. "The assessment will make them more effective managers and employees."

Dixon believes this business-to-business marketing approach is unique for a golf shop, as are the other services they offer. They intend to do targeted direct mailings and cross promotions with other events or businesses whenever there is an opportunity. Dixon and Crocker expect their concept to really take off. "We saw a niche in the market that wasn't being addressed, and we decided to do something about it." Golf manufacturers, retailers, and marketers just weren't hitting the market.

Other people must agree. Another store that is targeting the woman's market at the other end of the spectrum is the Lady Pro Golfer discount store. Effectively marketing to women golfers will increase any current golf-related company's bottom line tremendously this decade and in the future. Not targeting or successfully attracting this market will mean sales revenues will probably remain flat or decline.

Narrowly focused publications that cater to the needs of the managerial and working woman have flourished. *Women in Golf, Working Woman,* and *Working Mother* are three examples of publications that have evolved to meet the needs of this female segment. Because of the rising number of women professionals, about 50 regional publications were started between 1982 and 1986. While many were tabloids, some were glossy magazines such as *New York Woman* published by Esquire Magazine Group Inc. and *Boston Woman* produced by a group of private investors.[21]

Even magazines once thought of as male publications are seeking to increase their women's readership. *Esquire: The Magazine for Men* has approximately 30 percent per year female readership. *Esquire* has increased the "female covers" to four—up from the one "Women We Love" cover in August—written more serious profiles of women, and added more women staff writers.[22]

Age

Age, like any other demographic, divides the group into categories by specific criteria. In this way, marketers can determine the size of their market. While size is often a measure of what can be expected from a specific group, it isn't the only criteria that determines a company's success within the market.

Adult women need many services, but they vary as women enter different phases in their life cycles. Publications such as *Lear's*, which targets the over 40 affluent market, have drawn new attention to this group of women. A few years ago, a panel made up of Grace Mirabella, publisher of *Mirabella*, Frances Lear publisher of *Lear's*, Evelyn Lauder of Estee Lauder Inc., and Shirley Young, then a marketing executive with General Motors, addressed this market. They had 550 attendees. "There are more than 24 million women over 45 with an aggregate household income of $729 billion dollars," attendees were told. That amount of money is worth getting a marketer's attention. Many products and companies that could market more successfully to this segment, either forget or ignore it. Lauder mentioned that fashion institutions now use mannequins of mature women. Saks Fifth Avenue illustrates to women that they can be attractive and fashionable, without trying to imitate youthful fashions. Lear emphasized the importance of this market by saying: "Women over 40 are the fastest growing and likely the sanest segment of the population." With baby boomers aging, and women living longer, the over 40 market segment will continue to grow for some time.[23]

Realizing that young women as well as the more mature woman could be a lucrative market, fur retailers began to reposition their product. In the past, the snob appeal of the luxurious fur coat attracted many women. Most received a fur as a reward for their accomplishments or as a gift from a man. As marketers began to create commercials and advertisements that showed real people wearing furs in everyday situations, furs began to appeal to young professional women. Seeing an attaché case dangling from the sleeve of a fur coat, or furs on ski slopes caught the younger woman's attention. They began to see furs as fun, not as a product for older women. To accommodate this market, new channels of distribution had to be developed. Young women were less likely to frequent a posh, exclusive furrier, than to shop for furs at a department store or specialty store in a mall. Today, fur buyers make their first purchase around 26 years of age, and their second by 35.[24]

Women between 25 and 44 read more publications than other age categories, with women between 25 and 34 being the heaviest readers.

While women between 25 and 34 watch a lot of television, the largest group of viewers are women over 65. Obviously, as has been mentioned previously, along with age, other demographics must be taken into account. Working women in all categories watch less television than nonworking women in the same age group.[25]

As would be expected, older women are the predominant users of hair coloring, with women over 65 being the primary users. Divorced and widowed working women who have no dependent children are the highest consumers. Working married women comprise approximately 20 percent of the market. In 1990, 68.7 percent of the cosmetic market was between 18 and 44. Women between 25 and 44 comprise nearly half of the facial-moisturizer market, while fragrances appeal more to a slightly younger group. Women between 18 and 44 represent 61.7 percent of the female fragrance market.[26]

Women between 18 and 34 are large purchasers of over-the-counter drugs. They purchase more gastrointestinal medication, products for hair and skin problems, and products related to reproductive complaints. Younger women want immediate benefits in order to maintain their active lifestyles and feel better quickly. Women over 35 are more concerned about preventive care.[27]

Many other products are sold in much higher numbers to younger women. According to store owner Marcia Kahn, 65 percent of Condom Sense's customers are women, mostly between 18 and 39 years old.[28] "Women in relationships frequently buy massage oils or other items that will make the evening a little more romantic for their significant other," said Kahn. While Condom Sense does a big business with gifts and novelty items for bachelor/bachelorette, office and birthday parties, a large number of their sales are condoms. Sexually transmitted diseases have become so prevalent in our society that young people who are sexually active need protection. "It's very hard for young people, even those in their thirties, to go into a grocery store or pharmacy and buy condoms. There is a tremendous difference in the products, and we offer a lot of information as well as a fun, comfortable atmosphere," explained Kahn.

Kahn, along with a lot of manufacturers and marketers, saw a woman's niche in what was once considered strictly a male product. Men used to be the primary, if not the only, purchasers of the product. That's not the case today. In an attempt to capture this new market, manufacturers have changed the package design, and several companies have entered the market with novelty items such as gold coin earrings that house a condom in each earring, or condom cases for women to carry in their purses that are a little more discrete than the traditional packaging.

While Trojans, Ramses, and Sheiks still retained their masculine names, the package designs have changed dramatically from the original helmeted warrior, Egyptian symbol, and male figures used respectively on these major brands. They now show couples on their packages in romantic, but not sexist settings as they realize that, with the need for birth control and fear of disease, their product has appeal to both genders. Condoms are easily accessible, located frequently on the aisle with the feminine hygiene items, early detection home pregnancy tests, and other contraceptive products. This placement makes it easier for women to pick up condoms and throw them in their shopping basket with other grocery or drug items.

In the mid-1970s, only 15 percent of condom buyers were women. Between 1982 and 1987, the number of unmarried women using condoms almost doubled to 2.2 million, or about 16 percent of the sexually active female population.[29] The more than $200-million-a-year industry is enjoying rapid growth as more women are concerned about sexually transmitted disease (STD). But this growth segment is definitely under 40. As women become widows or divorced and re-enter the dating world, they can't quite add condoms to their list of getting ready-to-go-out items. "It's appalling to me that some of my friends don't use anything. They think if they date upscale, nicely dressed men, it's not necessary to have safe sex," exclaimed Kahn. "The very young and the more mature seem to feel they are somehow immune from STD. Condom makers are not addressing the issue and educating these market segments properly. Older men aren't much better than women, but I do have more seeking information than I do women over 40." Reaching women, particularly older women, and convincing them to buy the product could have a tremendous impact on the bottom line of a company and the industry as a whole.

The prevention of pregnancy has always been a major reason for using condoms. Now, the prevention of sexually transmitted diseases has brought condoms into classrooms, on television, and in print. That, coupled with their wider distribution system, makes them more accessible to women. "Women are buying more condoms because it is easier. The grocery store is the fastest growing segment of the business," according to Kim Leffler, product manager for Safetex.[30] "Our package doesn't show couples like some of the other brands. We produce a blister-pack with either three, six, or 12 colored coins. The condoms inside the coins are the same color as the coin," said Leffler. "The 12-packs are popular with store owners because condoms are the number one shop-lifted item." Leffler speculates that one reason for the high incidence of shop lifting is that people are still embarrassed to buy them.

As advertisers and marketers continue to target women, they mustn't neglect a very large and growing segment—mature women between 40 and 65. Often, these women have achieved greater success and have more discretionary income than the more youthful segment. Advertisers in the past have not used older models except for products specifically created for them. Today that is changing, and women in their forties and fifties are being seen advertising everything from Calvins to Nikes.

Unfortunately, one industry that hasn't neglected the female youth market, and that is experiencing much success, is the tobacco industry. Young women, including teenagers, are the fastest growing segment of cigarette users. Even though overall smoking among adults is on the decline, among adolescent and young women, it is on the incline. More female high school seniors smoke than males. Surveys show that 18 percent of collegiate women smoke, compared to only 10 percent of college men. Estimates show that as many as 60 percent of young females start by age 14. Billboards and magazine advertising usually appeals to either the young woman's need for independence or her concern about her weight.

Since the introduction of Virginia Slims in 1968, the first cigarette targeted specifically to women, the cigarette industry has continued to prosper from the woman's market. It is now estimated that women make up approximately 25 million or 50 percent of the cigarette market. Young, less educated women are the target, according to most reports on the topic. Dakota, an RJR Nabisco cigarette, is aimed at the 18 to 20-year-old-woman.[31] The names themselves depict the image—slims, thin, light, and long.

In 1987, for the first time, more women died of lung cancer than breast cancer. More than 126,000 women die each year from smoke-related deaths.[32] In retaliation for the successful efforts of cigarette marketers, health agencies have launched campaigns to persuade young women not to smoke. Many are targeted at advertising executives who create the campaigns or the companies for exploiting young women for profits.[33] "Tobacco companies spend $3.3 billion per year on advertising and promotions, while the Department of Health and Human Services spends $3.5 million on anti-smoking campaigns," said Surgeon General Antonia Novello (in 1990).[34]

Women of Color

There are 10 million black women in the United States. Many have a better education, higher income, and greater self-confidence than previous generations. As recently as the late 1980s, there were few marketing efforts aimed at this group, even though their spending power is increasing as is white women's. Two products, liquor and tobacco, have targeted this segment successfully.[35] RJR Nabisco was forced to change their strategies of marketing Uptown cigarettes to the minority community because of the number and types of complaints.[36]

According to Marcie Brogan of Brogan & Partners in Detroit, Michigan, two of the primary target markets for cigarettes are African-American females and teenagers.[37] Their agency developed an awareness campaign for the Michigan Department of Public Health that targeted African-American women and children 10 to 13 years old. The message was simple: to let women, especially black women, know that smoking wasn't as glamorous as the tobacco companies portrayed it.

Just as the workplace has begun to address the issue of diversity, so must the marketplace. Cars, retail establishments, and any number of other businesses are beginning to communicate diversity in their advertising. While many cosmetics have been created to appeal to women of color, often marketing to this segment is lacking. Even though research shows that Hispanic women's usage of beauty and cosmetic products is high, most cosmetic firms haven't created Spanish ads to run on either radio or in print media.[38]

Marketing to the diverse population is very important. Ethnic minorities, the mature and graying population and children are each unique marketing segments. It is beyond the scope of *Targeting the New Professional Woman* to address these segments. Each could fill a book of its own.

Men's Versus Women's Buying Habits

Traditional marketers have thought of men as the purchaser of big ticket items such as cars, financial products, and travel. Women bought fashion, cosmetics, and household products. However, the reality today is that 81 percent of married couples share the decision when buying major household appliances, 77 percent share the decision on how to save or invest, and 87 percent do financial planning together.[39] Obviously, women's influence is no longer relegated to only "female products."

Even though women frequently do their homework better in a buying situation than men, in general, each gender has specific products that they are more interested in learning about. Men want to know more about new car models, whether they are anticipating a purchase or not; whereas, women learn about cars when they are ready to buy. Men are more interested in home entertainment products and in learning more about new beers, wines, and liquors. Women, on the other hand, are more interested in new food products, healthcare, apparel, and hair styles.

Even though women's interest in new food products is a third greater than men's, a little more than 50 percent of men still want to learn more about new food products, according to the *Sports Illustrated* "The American Male '91" report of a survey conducted by Lieberman Research, Inc. in New York City, of 1,117 men and 1,203 women, 18 years and older.[40]

Women are the predominant purchasers of clothing. Besides occasional gifts, women buy almost all their own clothes and most of their children's—at least, until they become teenagers. According to Gail Duff-Bloom at J.C. Penney, they also buy between 75 and 80 percent of all men's clothing. The cosmetic and fashion industry is still very much a female domain.

However, men are in charge of household fix-up projects nearly twice as often as women, but women are frequently the purchasing agents for the materials used. Men use half as many cents-off coupons as women.

Women and men are interested in different sports. Men enjoy football, basketball, boxing, auto racing, and golf. Women, on the other hand, prefer ice skating. When marketers are selecting programs on which to advertise or events to sponsor, they need to be cognizant of which sports attract which gender as spectators.[41]

According to Nye Lavalle, managing director of Sports Marketing Group-Dallas, there is growing popularity among women for a number of sports besides ice skating and gymnastics.[42] "During the past three years," said Lavalle, "the NFL has grown in popularity 45 percent with women and only 1 percent with men. The NBA has grown 70 percent with women, 10 percent with men; and major league baseball's popularity increased 40 percent with women and only 7 percent with men." One reason for the disproportionate growth among women is that the Next Generation, or Generation X, has a greater interest in sports than previous generations. "It used to be taboo or unfeminine for a woman to be interested in sports. She would be called a 'tomboy.' Today, men are more attracted to women who are active and participate in fitness or sports programs," noted Lavalle.

Title IX has also affected the sports scene. As more girls were allowed to participate in accepted sports programs at school, their interests developed differently than those of their mothers.

"Utilizing sports is an excellent corporate marketing strategy. People get emotional over a game. It's a good motivator. People love to identify with sports teams whether they are a high school, college or pro team," continued Lavalle. The Dallas Cowboys are an excellent example of how people react to sports and the personalities involved. Lavalle said his research indicated that while many people are turned off by traditional advertising and the messages they convey, a company can use sports as a vehicle to reach its market in a positive way.

Despite women's growing interest, sports is still more of a man's world than a woman's. The Winter Olympic Games is the only major sports event watched by more women than men. In 1988, the Winter Games in Calgary, Alberta, consistently had more women viewers, regardless of the time of day.[43] In participatory sports, men play baseball twice as often as women play softball. They like hunting, basketball, football, racquetball, and scuba diving more. Women are far more involved in aerobics.[44]

These figures are important to sports marketers of equipment and apparel, sports and fitness centers, and other sports-related items.

Equally important to a manufacturer's marketing strategy is the development of programs to deal with a declining sales slope, rather than an increasing market segment. The beer industry's sudden interest in the women's market is not because they are altruistic and want to do the right thing. It has more to do with good business. As distributors and marketers watched consumption fall from 194.9 million barrels in 1990 to 190.7 million barrels in 1991, they had nowhere to turn but to women to boost their sagging sales. Even though brewers have ignored women for years, with the decline in consumption over the last 10 years and the introduction of low-alcohol and low-calorie brands, women have caught beer marketers' attention.

While beer manufacturers are still trying to sort out if women are their market, or if they can be, the statistics still indicate that men decide nearly twice as often as women what brand to buy in a given household. They also influence the brand of liquor more than women do. Of course, changing their advertising and selecting a premium and a light beer to target to women could change those demographics, as breweries are discovering. Women will never be a major consumer of beer if commercials continue to be patronizing and designed to appeal only to the male drinker. According to Steve LeResche, director of public communications at Anheuser-Busch Co., things are changing. Brewers definitely have an interest in marketing to women because of their greater buying power.[45]

But it hasn't been a smooth transition for beer manufacturers as they try to gain an edge on this untapped market. Marketing efforts aimed at women have caused concerns by health organizations, just as the increase in cigarette usage by women did. Because beer drinkers are traditionally a younger market, critics complain that they are targeting women of childbearing age.[46] Marketers need to understand there is a middle ground. Ads that the growing number of women beer drinkers don't find offensive can be targeted to their primary audience—men.

Should Marketers of Traditionally Female Products Market to Men?

Identifying growth segments is a very important aspect of a marketers' job. Many companies have identified women as a growth market and have made inroads into securing their business. Others have only paid lip service to the concept that women are a very distinct market that must be addressed by every industry hoping to maintain their market position in this decade.

Procter & Gamble has always considered women its major market for household products. As I watched two of their laundry detergents' advertising and promotional strategies shift, I thought they really were attuned to the changing demographics of the marketplace. Not so.

I questioned Lynn Hailey, Procter & Gamble spokesperson, about All-Temperature Cheer.[47] I noticed that their ads always included males: a mother teaching a son going off to school, a boyfriend-girlfriend, or two people of the opposite sex in a laundromat. Obviously, P & G had concluded that as more women went to work, married later, and got divorced, men would be doing more laundry. In other words, just as women were buying more cars and gold jewelry, men were buying traditionally "women's" products as well. But according to Hailey, that wasn't the intent. Too bad. Men are a great untapped market that could have been expanded into a really profitable market segment.

Next I asked about Tide. With its bright orange and yellow colors splashed across NASCAR race cars and crew uniforms, Tide was targeting the 43 million women who attend NASCAR events, as well as the millions more who view the sport, I was told. There is nothing wrong with this new venue, and many other products aimed at women are seeking this outlet. However, I believe deliberately targeting the male attendees would be an excellent idea. What other avenues could be used to capture the single male customer's business? Just as General Motors has learned it must market to women, so should P & G and other companies that have primarily targeted women develop campaign strategies aimed at capturing the emerging male market.

As more women are looking for convenient, quick meals, and other time-saving products designed with the busy, professional woman in mind, manufacturers should take advantage of the secondary male market that would provide a whole new segment to their demographic mix.

Staying in tune with your customers, modernizing your products to reflect the lifestyle changes that are happening with your primary customer, and looking for new, income-generating secondary markets are vital to the growth and prosperity of many companies in this competitive marketplace. Change is not gender bias. Both men's and women's lifestyles are in transition. Astute marketers are reacting quickly to the changing demographics and buying patterns of today's men, as well as today's women.

Summary

When trying to market to a new segment, marketers must meet the challenge by examining the target market, evaluating its potential, developing a fresh perspective, and exploring the attitudes and needs of the new segment.

As has already been established, men and women react to information differently. When segmenting the market, marketers need to remember that although there are numerous differences depending on the age, income, occupation, lifestyle, personality style, and a whole range of other factors, women still have certain innate characteristics, and these should be considered when creating effective marketing programs. Campaigns are a mass media effort and, while individual characteristics should be addressed, general traits must not be forgotten either.

As marketers use demographic information, patterns and trends become obvious. In 1990, the population of the United States was slightly more than 250 million. It is projected that by 2000, it will be 268 million, and by 2050, it will be 309 million. As baby boomers continue to mature, they will skew the age demographics upward. For instance, in 1970 there were only 17.7 million women between 30 and 44. In 1988 there were 26.3 million women in that age category. In addition, women are marrying later, and having their children at a later age. The number of childless women between the ages of 25 and 29 has risen from 31 percent in 1976 to 41 percent in 1988. Today, one out of every four babies is born to a woman over 30.[48]

As marketers develop new programs, promotions, and product strategies, they need to be cognizant of how the lifestyle of the new mother is different when she gives birth to her first child when she is 31, not 21. What kinds of products and services do these women want? How will the fact that they have been in the work force for a decade or more affect their buying patterns? Will they be returning to their careers? What is the most effective way to target them with their now even busier lifestyle?

Old questions and outdated premises just won't work anymore. Marketers need a fresh approach and a comprehensive look at the woman's market. The demographics of age, sex, income, and occupation are certainly aspects to consider in formulating marketing strategies for the late 1990 and the next century. But marketers need to include the human element as well.

Notes

[1]Rena Bartos, *Marketing to Women Around the World* (Boston: Harvard Business School, 1989) 58–66.

[2]Janice Leeming, publisher and editor-in-chief of *Marketing to Women*, interview with author, 1 September 1993.

[3]Barbara Solomon, "Guidelines for the Agent in the Singles Market," *Manager's* (February): 13–16.

[4]Dallas/Fort Worth National Association of Women Business Owners, "Women Owned Businesses: Decidedly Disadvantaged," April 1993.

[5]Conducted by Liberman Research, Inc., *Sports Illustrated*: "The American Male '91," (New York: The Time Inc. Magazine Company, 1991): 35.

[6]Frances Cerra Whittelsey, *Why Women Pay More: How To Avoid Marketplace Peril* (Center for Study of Responsive Law, 1993): 51.

[7]Betsy Bauer, "A New Way to Reach America's Good 'Ol Girls," *U.S. News & World Report* (29 June 1987).

[8]Prepared by Battelle, *The Cosmopolitan* (Seattle: Human Affairs Research Centers/Hearst Magazines): 17.

[9]*Sports Illustrated*, 37.

[10]*Sports Illustrated*, 43.

[11]Bauer, "America's Good 'Ol Girls."

[12]Ibid.

[13]Battelle, *The Cosmopolitan*, 11.

[14]"How Working Women Have Changed America," *Working Woman's Venture* (November 1986).

[15]Alexander Hiam, Charles Schewe, *The Portable MBA in Marketing*, (New York: John Wiley & Sons, Inc., 1992): 147.

[16]Bauer.

[17]"How Working Women Have Changed America."

[18]Judith Langer, president, Langer Associate, Inc., interview with author, 30 June 1993.

[19]Bartos, *Marketing to Women Around the World*, 203.

[20]Patricia Dixon, president, Dixon International, Inc., interview with author, 2 September 1993.

[21]Lois Therrien, "New York Woman, Meet Boston Woman, Meet Michigan Woman ...," *Business Week* (Industrial/Technology Edition), (8 September 1986): 86.

[22]Mary Huhn, "Woman at Her Best?" *Mediaweek* (22 March 1993): 16.

[23]Melissa Sones, "Panel Focuses on Power of Women Over 45," *Los Angeles Times (UPI)* (9 December 1988): Pt. 5: 25.

[23]Michael. P. Sullivan, "Bank Marketing Strategy: Courting the Older Woman" *Bankers Monthly* (June 1991): 36.

[24]Battelle, 10–11.

[25]*Working Woman* (January 1987): 48.

[26]Battelle, 13–14.

[27]"Survey: Women's Health Needs Are Not Being Fulfilled," *Marketing News* (4 July 1988): 8.

[28]Marcia Kahn, president/owner, Condom Sense, interview with author, 3 September 1993.

[29]Dick Thompson, "Packing Protection in a Purse; Condoms are becoming part of a Women's Sexual Survival Kit," *Time* (15 August 1988): 65.

[30]Kim Leffler, product manager, Safetex Corporation, interview with author, 8 September 1993.

[31]Matthew S. Bromberg, "Critics Fume at Cigarette Marketing," *Business & Society Review* (Spring 1990): 27–28.

[32]Shari Roan, "Under Fire: Women and Smoking," *Los Angeles Times* (17 April 990): E–1.

[33]Ed Stych, "Anti-smoking Ads Say Women Exploited; Tobacco Firms Are the Butt of a Campaign" *Philadelphia Inquirer* (AP), (5 September 1992): A–2.

[34]John Monk, "Cigarette Ads Aimed at Women Draw Fire from Surgeon General," *Philadelphia Inquirer* (5 October 1990): C–3.

[35]Sheila Gadsden, "Seeking the Right Tack in Talking to Blacks," *Advertising Age* (12 September 1985): 18–21.

[36]Bromberg, "Critics Fume," 27–28.

[37]Marcie Brogan, president, Brogan & Partners, interview with author, 9 June 1993.

[38]Michele Conklin, "The Question Is Raised Why Cosmetic Companies Show Little Interest in the Hispanic Woman's Market," *Madison Avenue* (October 1986): 50–51.

[39]Bartos, *Marketing to Women Around the World,* 197–199.

[40]*Sports Illustrated,* 33.

[41]*Sports Illustrated,* 55.

[42]Nye Lavalle, managing director, Sports Marketing Group–Dallas, interview with author, 14 September 1993.

[43]Lee Winfrey, "CBS Will Court Women During '92 Winter Games," *Philadelphia Inquire* (5 June 1991): D-3.

[44]*Sports Illustrated,* 55.

[45]Steve LeResche, director of public communications, Anheuser-Busch Company, interview with author, 26 August 1993.

[46]Joanne Lipman, *The Wall Street Journal* (6 April 1992): B1–8.

[47]Lynn Hailey, spokesperson, Procter & Gamble, interview with author, July 1993.

[48]Hiam, *The Portable MBA in Marketing,* 139.

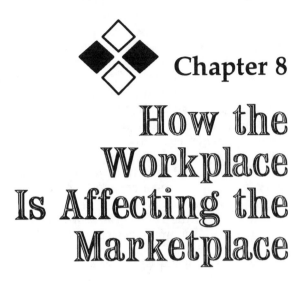

Chapter 8

How the Workplace Is Affecting the Marketplace

T here is a direct correlation between the changes taking place in the workplace and in the marketplace. As more women go to work, they have more discretionary income and less time. The transition that has occurred in their lives has affected *what* they buy, *where* and *when* they buy, and *why* they buy.

The New Professional Woman

The transformation from the part-time working woman to the full-time career woman has had a tremendous influence on the marketplace. Fewer women are entering the workplace on a temporary basis. Most are there for a lifetime and will never again be full-time wives and mothers. They will experience things their mothers never did, and as a result, they will make purchasing selections based on different criteria than any generation before them.

Women are more educated and more astute consumers today than in the past. As part of the work force, many have learned to research products, handle multi-million dollar budgets, and demonstrate leadership and management styles all their own. When in the marketplace, they expect courteous, professional treatment. They don't hesitate to leave when retailers and sales personnel don't meet their expectations.

In order to totally understand the significance of the new professional woman in the marketplace, businesses must first gain a thorough knowledge of the statistics that support what has happened in the workplace. Three elements will be considered: the educational level of women, and how that affects the workplace; the types of professions and jobs women are training for; and the increasing numbers of women, both married and single, that are entering the labor force.

Education is a critical factor in the work force. Only 21 percent of the women who have eight years or less of schooling are in the work force. Of women with up to three years of high school, 40 percent work. When a women graduates high school, her chances of being in the work force increase to 59 percent; with up to three years of college, 66 percent work; with four years of college, 71 percent; and with five or more years of college, 77 percent work.[1]

In 1990, of the 117,914,000 workers in the United States, 53,533,000 were female. Women are entering all fields today:

- ❖ Nearly 9 percent of the construction industry is made up of women;

- ❖ Well above half of those in finance, insurance, or real estate are women;

- ❖ 8 percent of all engineers are women, but 17 percent of graduating engineers today are female;

- ❖ 21 percent of lawyers and judges today are women, but 40 percent of current law school students are women;

- ❖ 36 percent of scientist are women;

- ❖ 36 percent of all mathematical and computer science graduates are women;

- ❖ 36 percent of medical school students are women, but in 1985, only 15 percent of all physicians were women;

- ❖ 9 percent of dentists are women, but 23 percent of new dental school graduates are women;

- ❖ 11 percent of police and detectives are women; and

- ❖ Approximately 50 percent of all accountants are women. In 1979, about one-third of all accounting graduates were women. By 1985, 49 percent were, and by 1992, 52 percent were, according to the American Institute of Certified Public Accountants.

Between 1965 and 1982, women receiving degrees in accounting increased more than 2,000 percent. In the same period, women earning degrees in medicine increased 700 percent; in law, 2,800 percent; and in engineering, 5,600 percent. Between 1965 and 1985, the percent of university and college students that were female grew from 33 percent to 55 percent.[2]

Today, women are serving in the military in greater numbers and are going overseas as combat troops, rather than nurses. They are pilots, fire fighters, and CEOs of Fortune 500 companies. They are serving in local, state, and federal government posts, both as appointees and as elected officials.

Corporations and smaller companies are beginning to recognize the potential of the female employee in the workplace in many areas that for so long have been thought of as male fields. Consolidated Edison (Con Edison) fills 30 percent of its engineering jobs with women.[3] These women understand the intricacies of today's products and how they work better than many men do. When in the marketplace, they demand respect. When they ask a question, they want a full answer—one equal to what a male would receive if he asked a technical question. As more women enroll in technical and specialized fields, once thought of as areas only for men, they expect the marketplace to recognize their proficiency and accord them treatment in line with their achievements.

While fields involving a high degree of science and technology still have a low percentage of female employees, girls are beginning to be directed into what were once primarily male classes. Soon there will be more gender balance in these fields.

In 1870, only 17 percent of the labor force was female, compared to nearly 50 percent today. The increase has been gradual until recently. Nearly half a century ago, only 33 percent of women between the ages of 18 and 64 worked. By 1980, 51 percent did, and by 1990, 58 percent were working. In the late 1980s, 56 percent of all married women worked. Women with young children have entered the work force as never before. Fifty percent of mothers with preschoolers work today. Women contribute 30 percent of the household income.[4] It is projected that by 2000, 65 percent of all women will be employed full-time.

Between 1985 and 2000, women will be the largest single segment entering the work force. Some will be "just-a-job" statistics, but many more will be corporate executives and entrepreneurs. In the 1980s, female entrepreneurs grew 82 percent. They grew nearly 300 percent in the five years between 1983 and 1988. Revenues from women-owned businesses rose 129 percent accounting for approximately $278 billion. By 1992, women owned more than 6.4 million businesses. They employed more workers than all the Fortune 500 companies combined. It is projected that by 2000 women will own nearly 50 percent of all small businesses in the country.

"Women business owners say they are actually more competitive in times of recession because they emphasize quality and service," explained Gillian Rudd, chair of the National Foundation for Women Business Owners (NFWBO) in a statement released by the Foundation.[5] When you add to this their insight, compassion, and hard work, women entrepreneurs are a challenge that many businesses, corporations, and professional services need to recognize as both viable competitors and strong contenders.

In a survey conducted by NFWBO, one-third of the respondents own full corporations, 44 percent have gross revenues of $250,000 or more, and 18 percent have sales of more than one million dollars. The vast majority of women business owners, 75 percent, are between 30 and 49 years old. Two-thirds have a bachelors' degree, and 40 percent have done some post graduate work.

While many women hit the "glass ceiling" and chose to open their own businesses rather than try to buck the system any longer, others have persisted and are slowly inching up the corporate ladder. In 1990, 45 to 50 percent of mid-managers were women. While these women still haven't shattered the "glass ceiling," they are at least putting cracks in it. They are beginning to be visible on corporate boards and in top-level managerial positions. The momentum is there. Women have paid their dues in middle-management and are ready to take the reins with greater responsibility and more power. Today women are career oriented, professional, skilled workers. They are no longer content to just get coffee and provide clerical support. In every industry, women are seeking managerial positions that carry substantial responsibility.

If they are not given the opportunity to progress within the corporate environment, these women will leave the corporate environment to compete on their own using their initiative and education to propel them ahead. Corporations are already feeling the impact of this competition and realizing their lost resources.

Women have fought for everything they have gained in the workplace, including respect. They will settle for nothing less in the marketplace. Their dollars are now sought by many industries that have taken notice of these new consumers and their buying power. More than 10 million women earned in excess of $30,000 in 1990, and 2.1 million had salaries in excess of $50,000. However, women still earn far less than their male counterparts in most areas. As more women move into executive positions in corporations or vie for entrepreneurships, they will fight for their fair share—many out of virtue, a sense of fairness, others out of necessity—as they become the single source of revenue for themselves and their families.

Fifty-seven million women are now working, receiving paychecks, and sending a loud message to corporations, retailers, and others about what they need and want.

These highly successful, well-educated women are smart shoppers who aren't going to spend their hard-earned money with any company that is patronizing or doesn't treat women as valued customers. Those businesses that listen to women and understand what they are saying will thrive and grow during the next decade. Those who ignore the message will continually lose market share or cease to exist entirely.

As more women enter the workplace, climb the corporate ladder, and become entrepreneurs, many services and products have had to adjust their marketing strategies, even though women have always been their targeted audience.

Bringing Services and Products into the 1990s

KinderCare, a day care center begun in 1969, has seen some revolutionary changes during the last 25 years. Offering a safe and wholesome environment for children of working mothers isn't enough anymore.

"As more families have became dual-career couples, we began to notice that these women were probably the busiest people around," reported Becky Gober, marketing communications manager.[6] "They had to balance a job, family, home, and a number of other activities. We wanted to do something to help ease their path." KinderCare did a series of focus groups over a year-and-a-half period to determine what would make their families' lives easier. "One thing mothers told us was that it was really difficult with all the errands and things that needed doing on Saturday to take the children to get their hair cut. If the day care could provide that, it would help immensely." KinderCare arranged to have that service available at a number of their centers. The centers contracted with a local shop to come in and cut the kids' hair. The parents pay the shop directly, not KinderCare. Another service that has been contracted for at some locations is dry cleaning. Parents can drop off the clothes when they leave the child and pick them up that afternoon or the next day. Around the holidays, the lines at post offices or mailing centers are always a problem for people with limited time. KinderCare arranged with UPS to pick up packages that parents leave and also be a drop-off point for incoming packages. Some KinderCare centers even have frozen take-out food, for last-minute menu planning.

"All our programs are designed to help save time for our parents," said Gober. "Each center is different. They survey the parents to see what services are wanted most in a given area and try to implement those." Gober is fast to point out that their primary focus is, and has always been, on the child. "We provide quality child care. That is our job, and our main focus."

Another popular item that many locations offer are extended hours. The centers don't all have the same hours. It depends on the needs in a particular community. At least once a month centers offer extended hours, usually on a Friday. They are open until 9:00 p.m. so that parents have an opportunity to enjoy a quiet dinner together, or single parents can have an early dinner date.

The growing trend is for office parks, large office complexes, and shopping malls to provide on-site child care for workers and shoppers; KinderCare has met that challenge as well. Their KinderCare at Work Division helps design and manage day care facilities in many corporate developments, on university campuses, and in hospitals.

KinderCare's innovative marketing approaches and interest in staying in tune with the needs of today's women has been rewarding. Since the inception of its first facility in Montgomery, Alabama, in 1969, they have expanded across the country and now have 1,200 centers serving thousands of children and their families annually.

Adequate child care has become a national issue as more women with children return to school or begin careers. It is no longer a private concern addressed by only a few. Cities like San Francisco, Seattle, Boston, and Pittsburgh have all changed the city's zoning codes to include day care centers in new office or shopping complexes of any significant size.[7] Businesses that recognize the needs of women, design services and products for these needs, and implement a successful marketing effort will capture a large share of women's dollars.

Tom Fitzpatrick's business also identified the working mother as a market. Champion Sports Club, a New York-based company, ferries kids to and from sports practices and games.[8] "We pick kids up at school and take them to activities; then, drop them off at their own door. This way, kids get to participate in the sports with their peers, and their mothers don't have to worry about them being safe," explained Fitzpatrick, co-owner of Champion Sports Club. "We are seeing a lot more single parents now. They want more punch for their bucks. Several years ago, parents just enrolled their offspring in athletic activities for the fun of it. Now, there is a lot more competitiveness in sports, even for kids as young as six," commented Fitzpatrick. "We organize the teams, get the facilities, coach, referee—the total package."

Many businesses have developed or grown in response to the needs of working women. Seeing that their families are taken care of, even when they aren't there to oversee the process, is of prime importance to mothers. Fitzpatrick said that the majority of their business is from word-of-mouth referrals, mothers telling other mothers, or the kids spreading the word. As has been consistently mentioned, women's networks can help build a business. Tom Fitzpatrick's profitable company is an excellent example of that.

Motorola has taken advantage of the changing marketplace by repositioning its pager. Once thought of as a product men used in business, the pager has become a much more utilitarian product. As more mothers enter the work force, the availability of a product that offers them peace of mind is important. They know that if they were needed, they would be able to be reached no matter where they were.

"I used to have voice mail," said Julie Greene, manager of marketing services for Motorola Paging Products Group.[9] "One day after I finished a meeting, I checked my messages and my son's day care had called hours before that he was sick and needed to be picked up. He had to remain at day care sick because I didn't get the message. What I like about the pager is the instant access."

Greene went on to say that Motorola has done a series of focus groups and discovered that there were numerous ways the pager was improving busy people's lives. Obviously, working women, especially when they travel, is one market. But couples leave the pager number with a babysitter when they go out in the evening as well. Parents of college students know the frustration of trying to reach them. "They are never in their rooms" was one comment of the focus group participants, Greene said. In this case, the students carried the pagers so that the parents could reach them. With the "sandwich generation" growing, women like having the pagers so they can be reached by their elderly parents as well as their children.

Single women also said they used it when they meet someone and didn't want to give their home or office number; they would just give the pager number. The diversified usage of the pager is important to Motorola and its future.

The pagers come in a palette of colors including translucent pink, purple, and blue as well as clear, neon yellow, navy, and the standard black. A snap-on cover is available in a range of colors for those who prefer the professional black casing during the day and a more fun image at night. Black is still the most popular by far. Clear is in second place followed by translucent blue and translucent pink.

In an ad in *Good Housekeeping*, June 1993, the pager was pink. According to Greene, the ads have different colored pagers in them. Since the reader may only see one ad, it should have an assortment of colored pagers in it so the reader doesn't assume that Motorola thinks "pink" is the way to market to women.

The spectrum of businesses affected by the new professional woman cannot be overstated. The Greenhouse, a luxurious spa facility originally known as the Neiman-Marcus Greenhouse, catered to the same exclusive clientele that the store did. Wealthy corporate wives, socialites, and celebrities made up nearly all of the client base. They came for a week of pampering and to experience dieting in the most luxurious manner. As more working women became professionals, rather than clerical workers, they had the discretionary income for such an extravagance. Attorneys, physicians, CFOs, and corporate executives began to be an increasingly larger percentage of the guests—women who had the means to experience a week of total luxury and pampering that was stress free.

"Our guests frequently come to get away from their managerial tasks and day-to-day decision-making. We have everything brought to them so no stress is involved at all," said Trish Donaldson, director of public relations for the Greenhouse.[10]

While luxurious dieting is nice, many women don't have the discretionary income required to stay at the Greenhouse and have selected another weight loss system. Weight Watchers Inc., founded in 1963, caters to an entirely different clientele than the Greenhouse. As more housewives went to work, Weight Watchers witnessed their primary stay-at-home customer base shrink. In 1984, Weight Watchers began a program to recapture their customers who no longer had the time to come to them. The "At Work" program now functions at more than 4,000 companies. The goal of the program is to help people on the job reduce stress, eat more nutritionally and, in general, lead more productive, healthy lives. "To inform people of our new direction, we did business-to-business advertising, direct mail and, in 1993, went to consumer advertising," remarked Linda Bruno, marketing manager for the At Work program.[11] "People can participate in the program during lunch or before or after work." Weight Watchers believes this new program is in keeping with the times by being responsive to its customers' needs for flexible time parameters and programming.

Shopping

Shopping has also undergone some significant changes as more women work. No longer is shopping considered a leisurely, social activity with a few friends. Women are turning to mail-order, cable shopping, and ordering by telephone. Convenience stores, a quick way to pick up a few necessities, are what busy women often seek. Extensive comparison shopping is done by only those on strict budgets, because time is so valuable to working wives and mothers. Already cooked, take-out gourmet meals are available in many high-end grocery stores or in small shops in strip centers. While-you-wait shoe repair, one-hour cleaners and other types of instant services are also springing up in neighborhood centers and malls.

Retailers such as Neiman Marcus, with a reputation built on service to the affluent couture client, have restructured their marketing strategies to incorporate the female business executive. As part of their program, they are sending women's professional organizations letters in hopes of speaking at one of their monthly meetings or providing a seminar for its members.

Grocery stores, pharmacies, gas stations, beauty salons, and other businesses are adopting longer hours and adapting their schedules to fit their customers. Doctors and dentists offer more evening and Saturday appointments. Car repair shops, banks, and other institutions have implemented extended and weekend hours.

With women watching less daytime TV, advertisers have taken their message directly to the marketplace. Coupons and information appear on the back of the check-out receipts at many grocery stores. Ads dangle from the handles of the shopping carts.[12]

By the end of this decade, many additional instant services will appear. There will be more pick-up services to accommodate families where both adults work. Shopping has undergone some major transformations, but it will endure more the next few years.

Summary

Women have revolutionized both the workplace and the marketplace. Their style of leadership and management, along with the impact technology is having on many businesses, will dictate a different work environment in the future. Women will be at the helm of multi-million dollar corporations; they will be operating robotic equipment; and they will be participating in space missions. They will die in the line of duty, and they will lead local, state, and national governmental bodies.

Notes

[1]Rena Bartos, *Marketing to Women Around the World* (Boston: Harvard Business School Press, 1989), 29.

[2]Daniel Evan Weiss, *The Great Divide: How Females & Males Really Differ* (New York: Poseidon Press, 1991).

"How Working Women Have Changed America," *Working Woman* (November 1986).

[3]Diana Kunde, "Companies to Give Parents a Break With Day-Care Projects," *The Dallas Morning News* (23 December 1992): D–4.

[4]*Dallas Times Herald* (10 February 1989).

[5]Sharon Hadary, National Foundation for Women Business Owners, news release, 1993.

[6]Becky Gober, marketing communications manager, KinderCare Learning Centers, interview with author, 30 June 1993.

[7]Ken Zapinski, "An Urban Day-Care Incentive: Building a City Around Day-Care Needs," *The Dallas Morning News*: C1–7.

[8]Tom Fitzpatrick, owner, Champion Sports Club, interview with author, 30 June 1993.

[9]Julie Greene, manager of marketing services, Motorola, interview with author, 22 September 1993.

[10]Trish Donaldson, director of public relations, KRI Greenhouse, interview with author, 29 June 1993.

[11]Linda Bruno, marketing manager, Weight Watcher International, interview with author, 19 May 1993.

[12]"How Working Women Have Changed America."

Part IV

The Marketing Environment of the Future

Chapter 9

Women Speak Out

Across the country women are voicing their opinions on political issues, healthcare concerns, education, violent crimes especially those against women, employment inequities, and marketing insensitivities. As women speak out in the media and in the marketplace, their voices will be heard and their concerns addressed. Women no longer intend to do business as usual. Some out of necessity, others from a moral or ethical belief, have abandoned the "I will be taken care of" attitude and have joined together to forge a future for themselves and their children. They are demanding products and services, as well as fair and equal treatment, and they will put political and financial pressure on those who aren't hearing their message.

Women don't have to form a coalition to boycott companies that are treating them unfairly. They have chosen other means. When poorly designed products are sent to market, when sexist advertising is used to convey the sales message, when they are patronized or spoken to in condescending terms, they no longer just accept it. Some share their feelings publicly on radio, television, or in print. Others walk out of showrooms or never enter certain ones.

Whether in the spotlight speaking to millions or quietly telling a few friends, women are getting their message out to each other and to manufacturers, marketers, and retailers. Some marketers are listening; others aren't. The companies that recognize the woman consumer and address her needs will prosper as we approach the year 2000; those that don't will have a tough time. While the survival of those heedless companies is in jeopardy, the new professional woman will be thriving and growing, becoming an even more discriminating shopper.

Marketing to Women: An Academic Point of View

Like corporate America, academia is slow to change. The premise that women and men are different, that women are independent beings making major purchasing decisions on their own and that marketers should pay close attention to this prominent component of the consumer mix is a concept that hasn't quite been accepted by universities in this country.

"When I wanted to do my dissertation on this subject," recalled Lynne Jaffe, professor of marketing at Northeastern University, "it was hard at first to even get the topic approved by the faculty in charge."[1] But her convictions were strong, and her dissertation was accepted.

In 1991, Jaffe showed 200 women mock ads to determine which ones were more effective. One ad showed women in traditional home-maker/mother roles. The other featured professional women in a more modern setting. The later ad depicted a woman with a briefcase waiting for a plane and a woman in a business meeting with several men. The second ad drew a much higher rating from professional women. Traditional women had no clear preference. When shown ads using the super-woman concept versus a more equalitarian arrangement, women overwhelmingly favored the equalitarian ad. "I plan to research these two ads with men, as well, but I haven't done that yet," reported Jaffe. Marital status didn't influence the way a woman responded as much as income level. Her conclusion: companies that portray women in more modern situations will earn more money.

Jadish Sheth, a professor of marketing at Emory University, agrees with Jaffe on many points.[2] He believes businesses must recognize the economic clout of women and change any stereotypes they are using in their advertising. "Today, consumers are looking for value. Manufacturers and service-oriented businesses need to understand that women aren't going to continue to pay more for basically the same product and services that men get cheaper," said Sheth. He acknowledges that changes are occurring. Citing the fact that advertising used to feature only young, sexy models, he points out that today marketers are using more mature women as well. He contends that, with the population aging, this is an essential move for marketers. He also recognizes that manufacturers of many products, such as automobiles, have begun to apply ergonomics to the design of their products. Marketers must see a woman as the purchasing agent for herself, not just for the family. With the high divorce rate and the number of women marrying later, women's roles have switched from family purchasing agents to single consumers. Lastly, he thinks marketers must re-examine their channels of distribution and look at women's lifestyles today. Products may not sell as well in grocery stores or malls as they have in the past. Direct mail, 800 numbers, and other alternative distribution channels are going to be crucial.

What Angers Women?

Many things the government, bosses, husbands, boyfriends, marketers, advertisers, manufacturers, retailers, and salespeople do make women angry. Sometimes it's something small and is easily forgotten. Other times, it affects sales. When women are scorned or shown only as sex objects in ads, women get angry. When manufacturers insist that pink is what women want in a product, anger often results. When they are ignored, talked down to, or called honey, rage is probably the better descriptor. When they aren't listened to or given credit for an idea, disappointment and resentment result.

Debra Kent's article, "What's Making You Mad?" listed a few things that make women angry.[3] "Men who trade in their wives for younger women. Beer commercials that blatantly portray women as sexy, but stupid. Women's restrooms without enough stalls. Men's restrooms without diaper-changing tables. Clothing designed for women built like teenage boys. The pressure to be physically perfect. Tobacco companies that try to persuade us we're empowered if we smoke. And that's just the beginning."

Recognizing a woman's anger is easy in some circumstances, but not in all. When 524 women were surveyed, 62 percent said they talked the problem through with the person involved; 30 percent said they withdrew.[4] In other words, if a salesperson angers a woman buyer, she may not always lash out at him as he expects, but may quietly and silently disappear. However, she will not remain quiet—she will tell her network about her experience. Understanding what makes a woman angry and how she shows it are important to marketers and salespeople. Nearly 70 percent of the women who responded were angry about being portrayed as sex objects in the media the week they were surveyed. That same week, 68 percent were angry that politicians think they have the right to make decisions about a women's reproductive rights. Marketers and politicians should remember that more women vote; more women buy; and more women influence purchases than ever before. Angry women are not good customers.

Whose Responsibility Is It?

On a local radio station the other morning, Max Morgan a female DJ, was talking about the problems she was having with her car and the Pontiac dealership where she had taken it for service.[5] Morgan was frustrated, not only because her car kept dying, but because they kept telling her they couldn't find anything wrong with it. In fact, as she verbalized to the entire Dallas/Fort Worth Metroplex, after they again "found nothing wrong with it," the car died as she attempted to drive off the lot.

When she queried, "What do you recommend I do now?" The reply was, "I don't know what to say, Ma'am."

The service advisor might not have known what to say, but Morgan sure did. She couldn't believe that the manufacturer didn't provide better training in both the area of product knowledge and customer service. "How can they tell me they don't know what to say?"

Morgan is quick to mention that she praises extraordinary service on the air when she receives it, as well. "I didn't mention the name of the dealership, I just want people to be aware of what's happening and what they can do about it. They never tell you about things like secret warranties. You have to have enough savvy to ask about them. Most people don't know to ask. That's why I point out issues like this on the air."

While Morgan never mentioned the two dealers to whom she had taken her car, she did tell me that after the broadcast another Pontiac dealer called her and said he would be happy to take care of her problem.

Now that's good marketing!

Selling to the Corporate Woman

While the majority of this book deals with manufacturers, associated agencies, and retail establishments, one significant area that needs to be addressed is the corporate buyer. What happens when a male salesperson accustomed to selling to men suddenly finds that the new purchasing agent in charge of his product line is a woman?

Women aren't part of the "good ol' boy" network. While they do have their own network, it is markedly different from a man's. For one thing, when the gender of the salesperson differs from that of the customer, the salesman can't put his arm around the customer or slap her on the back in the same way he may have with a male customer. Telling off-color jokes is not recommended, and going out for a beer is less likely. Obviously, these scenarios reflect ongoing buying situations, rather than a one-time purchase, but in the corporate or business world, the purchase of services and products occurs at regular intervals.

Understanding how to develop a relationship with a woman buyer in a corporate position is as important as knowing how to build rapport with her in the store. Karen Swinehart, manager of certification for the National Association of Purchasing Management, believes that successful salespeople like dealing with people.[6] "They deal fairly with everyone regardless of race, position, or sex. They like to be helpful. Unfortunately, these are rare individuals," noted Swinehart.

Swinehart is a former buyer in the oil and gas industry. Service was an important part of the sale. The on-line buyers had to trust the salesman and know that, when he promised delivery, it would be there. "Otherwise, we might have to shut down operations, depending on the product."

Having both professional and personal experience as a buyer, she definitely thinks that corporate salespersons are much more polished than those in retail. Swinehart believes the relationship that exists between most sales reps and buyers is very professional. "Things have changed a lot the last five or ten years," she said. In the past, she has seen sales reps take buyers to bars to judge beauty contests, to strip joints and to country clubs that exclude women. Obviously, these are not places that they would, or could, take a woman buyer.

The field of purchasing has undergone a dramatic transformation the last 20 years as more women entered the profession. While the "good ol' boy" network may not be dead, it definitely has shrunk. With so many female corporate buyers, salespersons have to use different tactics than in the past. Keeping up with the changing times is important. While the social aspects of selling may have changed as more women became buyers, building relationships and trust hasn't changed. "If a salesperson treats a woman buyer in a condescending manner, he won't be selling to that company long. She will ask for another rep to handle her account." Women buyers do business with people they like and trust.

"When I started 23 years ago," recalled Jeanie Watson, purchasing supervisor for Universal Display & Fixtures, "there were very few women in purchasing, maybe 5 or 10 percent.[7] Five years ago, the ratio was more like 30/70. Today it is probably closer to 50 percent."

According to Watson, there has been a revolution in the industry. "Having more women buyers has really raised the level of professionalism. When I first started, nearly all the buyers were male. Companies would send out 'cute little girls' to get the orders. A salesperson today has to be knowledgeable about the product. We, as an industry, have raised our ethics and our standards."

Watson feels that today people are busier than they used to be. They don't have much time to visit at work. "I think it is important that a salesperson is respectful of my time; is prepared; and has something to offer me and my company. He should have done his homework. That's what's important to me." Watson feels that her manufacturing background prepared her well for her job as a purchasing supervisor. "I know I present myself in a very professional, business-like way." That message is clear to the reps who call on her.

Trudy Cohen, a buyer with J.C. Penney, also has seen changes during her 15 years in the business.[8] "Working with a company like Penney, I don't see much gender bias. We have a very good reputation in the marketplace, and many of the people who call on us are in top positions."

As the number of women employed in purchasing increases, new selling strategies are developing. Salespersons are adapting to the changing environment and are searching for effective ways to sell in today's competitive climate.

Cohen echoed the views of many of the women with whom I talked. It is important to know the company you are selling, its goals and philosophy and its competition. Being competitive is not just identifying your competition, but that of the companies you are pursuing. Another trait Cohen notices is that many salespeople have a propensity to talk more and listen less than they should. "A good salesperson is a good listener," she commented.

One of the differences between men and women Cohen mentioned is that men like sports more. That seems to be a common conversational topic between men. "Women just don't know the scores and statistics of the athletes like men do. Salesmen need to be careful not to ignore the woman buyer if they are in a mixed group, and the topic drifts to sports. There are many topics I can talk about with sales reps, such as current events, business, our industry, the economy, community issues, and kids. They shouldn't be uncomfortable if I don't want to discuss sports." In conclusion, Cohen said that in the professional arena it is much rarer for a salesperson to call the buyer "honey" or "darling" than in the retail environment. "But it does happen," she added. "That's a big mistake."

Beverly Miller, co-owner of Miller Bevco, has been in the wholesale distributing and packaging business since 1965.[9] "Now salespersons feel comfortable working with me, but in the early years, many preferred to work with my husband," recalled Miller. In the industrial environment of Miller Bevco, most of the buyers are men. But Miller said, "Women are looking for the same thing men are—good price, good product, and delivery on time. Today that's called TQM (Total Quality Management)."

Amy Brown, a product manager with Chief Auto Parts, also functions in a predominantly male industry.[10] As a buyer of interior and exterior automotive accessories, she believes it is just more pleasant to work with sales reps who respect her and don't treat her in a condescending manner. "I enjoy doing business most with people who behave toward me as if I have a brain; someone who knows I have the job because of my abilities and who shows no gender bias. It is very offensive to me when anyone calls me 'hon,' even on the phone. That doesn't happen as much as it used to, but it still happens," said Brown.

Sue Dielh-Sellman, a chemical buyer, also works for Chief Auto Parts.[11] "When I bought hard line items—clutches, fuel pumps, that type of product—I think I was the only female purchasing manager buying those products. The vendors were very traditional and many sold to wholesalers and middlemen rather than retailers. They were not at ease selling to retailers, so when they had a woman buyer too, they really didn't know how to react. Whenever I suggested something different, they would say 'that's the way we have always done it,' and that was the end of the discussion," remarked Dielh-Sellman.

Dielh-Sellman is in charge of promotions and advertising, financial planning, pricing strategies, negotiating dollar support for the proposed activities, and in-store displays for the chemicals, hardware, and head lamps areas. Because the automotive industry is so male-dominated, many salesmen haven't called on women before. "Those that are the most successful treat me as an equal. They are professional. I get along fine with all the sales reps, but when a factory man comes too, you can tell he is uncomfortable selling to a woman. Sometimes he will try to break the ice by handing me a joke he clipped. Usually, they are tasteless; they are either dirty, political, or racist."

Unlike Cohen, Diehl-Sellman loves sports and knows her interest makes it easier to communicate with most of the sales reps and factory men. "Sometimes we all go to dinner and, if it wasn't for the rep, I don't think there would be any conversation. The people from the factory just assume we can't communicate. That's not true. I can speak about any number of subjects. When a factory person or the sales rep calls me, what I really want to know is what they have to offer. I have certain standard requirements, and they should definitely know those before they even pick up the phone. If they want me to buy their line instead of the one I am presently carrying, they need to anticipate some of the questions I'm going to ask. I want a strong promotional idea or a new display for the product. The very successful reps offer more than is required," said Diehl-Sellman.

That marketing idea works in any industry. It isn't gender specific. It doesn't have to be expensive. All that is required is to offer customers more than they expect. It's a sure way to increase sales. As successful as this concept is, it is rarely utilized. (In Chapter 10, customer satisfaction is discussed in more detail.)

Jacqui Osborn owns Dolphin Commercial Chemical, Inc.[12] Seventeen years ago, when she first started, "Women weren't degreed in business or technical fields like they are today. Many who entered purchasing and sales came from nursing or teaching backgrounds. The industry is much more professional now. The women who are in sales or who are buyers have to know their stuff. They have to be good," said Osborn. "When I was new, the most adversarial sales rep I dealt with is now one of my biggest allies. I earned his respect though."

There are two keys to sales and marketing as Osborn sees it. "First, good sales and marketing strategies focus on the benefits of the product to me, not how much money I'm going to save. If the product doesn't do what I want, it doesn't matter how much I saved, I'll have to spend more money to get the job done," she said. "The second thing is that salespeople are often busier telling me what I need, than listening to what I want. Salesmen, especially with a woman buyer, need to listen. They need to be careful not to assume they are better equipped to know what her needs are or to imply that she doesn't understand what she needs. I never buy when that happens. When we were first starting this company, I knew what kind of trucks I wanted to haul the product. The first company I spoke with said that design wouldn't work, and I needed to carry the product differently. He as much as said, 'You don't know what you are talking about.' We found another designer and built the truck in 1984. We are still using that truck today," Osborn noted with a smile.

Both of Osborn's marketing strategies are apropos to the retail environment. Salespeople should provide products to fit the customer's needs, and they can only know what these needs are by listening to what the customer is saying. Ask questions, listen to the answers, and make sure the features of the product create a benefit to the consumer.

Molly Harvey, a buyer for the Anheuser Busch plant in Jacksonville, knows what it feels like to be called "honey" and "sweetie."[13] With a 13-year background in the shipyards, she has seen and heard a lot. "Frequently, I'm not taken seriously as the buyer because I'm a woman," remarked Harvey. But when Harvey signs the purchase order, it is as valid as any male signature. Harvey stressed that too often salespeople think the bottom line is the only determinant. That's not true. "We're not necessarily concerned with only the bottom line price on products—we're concerned with longevity. That's a big issue right now with organizations."

Harvey, Swinehart, Watson, and the other women mentioned above all echoed the same sentiments. Treat them as the professionals they are. Recognize they got their position by knowing the product and the job; they can continue the buying relationship with you and your company, or they can terminate you at any moment.

Derrick Schnebelt, manager for the media/public relations area of the National Association of Purchasing Management, Inc. (NAPM), surveyed purchasing agents from the association's 35,000 membership to determine what purchasers liked and disliked in their experiences with sales professionals.[14] The majority responded that outstanding service and customer satisfaction were the most important things. "Honesty and dependability, thoroughness and follow-up were attributes that were consistently mentioned throughout the interviews," said Schnebelt. "One woman purchaser said she enjoyed talking with her salespeople; however, she recommended that some of the male salespeople keep in mind that not all women purchasers are interested in hunting, fishing, and pickup trucks."

"My expectation of salespeople is that they have done their homework, uncovered some of our needs and probed to uncover other needs," stated Lynne Deegan, director of procurement with Raychem Corporation.[15] "Sales professionals need to ask more questions. Even with my time constraints, if they don't ask probing questions, then they aren't going to maximize the interaction." Just as in the retail environment, the purchasing agent, as the customer, wants to be asked questions, and they want the salesperson to listen attentively to their answers. Then, and only then, can the salesperson truly provide the best service and product for the individual customer.

Instead of telling the buyer what's wrong with the competition's products or service, sales professionals need to concentrate on what their products and services have to offer the customer. What are the benefits to me, the customer?

The Similarities Between Corporate Buyers and Retail Buyers

Whether in a corporate setting or a retail store, many aspects of selling are the same.

❖ When the buyer is a woman, it is imperative that the salesperson take her seriously and recognize her as the decision maker.

❖ Salespersons need to ask questions, listen, and react accordingly. Talking all the time is not good selling.

❖ Sales professionals know their product, their customers, and their competition.

❖ Good salesmanship emphasizes what's right about your product, not what's wrong with someone else's.

❖ The importance of building long-term relationships can't be minimized. It is far costlier to develop new clients than to maintain existing ones.

❖ Recognizing that price is a major component of the sale, but not the only one, is crucial to working successfully with customers. Women, particularly, are value-added customers who take many factors into account when making their buying decisions.

Businesswomen Speak Out

Joyce McLaughlin, national president of the National Association of Women Business Owners, said: "Marketing to, and doing business with women business owners is unique. We expect the playing field to be level, and we deal with those whose values include honesty, sound principles, and virtue. Women have been 'sharp shoppers' for generations and know how to get the most for our dollar. We are ever mindful of our bottom line and make our decisions accordingly, thereby contributing to the economic growth and stability of our community, our state, and our nation."[16]

McLaughlin voices the feelings of many women when she said women want to do business with people who share their values. Honesty, trust, and integrity are very important components in purchasing. No one likes to be taken advantage of or to overpay for a product. Good business decisions, including the selection of whom to do business with, are important for the continued success and growth of companies.

Marolyn Wright, owner of Program Resources, is married and runs a successful business in Louisville, Kentucky.[17] She makes most of the buying decisions for her family and company. "When I walked into an Acura dealership, I was ignored. They didn't take me seriously. When I confronted the salesman to ask a few questions, he suggested that I take the car home, show it to my husband and bring him back with me. It was my car. I didn't need him to tell me how to handle the transaction," said Wright. "He was very chauvinistic."

Women are loyal, good customers to manufacturers, stores, and salespeople who treat them with respect and intelligence. "When I was looking at a dictating system that cost several thousand dollars for my office, the salesman told me he would call back next week. 'I'm sure you want to talk this over with your husband.' When he did call back, he started the conversation with, 'Did you have an opportunity to discuss our system with your husband?' He never really tried to close the sale with me. He never asked me if I thought the equipment would be useful, or fit our needs."

Wright, like many women, was amused at the insensitivity of the salesman. "He kept making the same mistake over and over. He never realized what he was doing. He just didn't get it."

Women business travelers report they have experienced a discrepancy in the treatment they receive, even in first class. "I travel so much I almost always upgrade to first class," said Jeannie Baggett, former president of a New York-based holding company.[18] "I am usually ignored. The flight attendants are too busy paying attention to the male travelers to wait on me. I have even had to ask for coffee."

First-class travelers, regardless of their gender, deserve first-class service. In fact, airlines would be well advised to realize that there are other factors than price that make a difference. Especially if the price differential is nominal. They too often assume that no one, especially women, would pay more for better service. That's just not true.

Another story Baggett conveyed was a car-buying experience. "I met my husband at a dealership to look at a car. During the negotiations, he had to leave to go to work. The salesman became irate and said, 'He can't leave. We aren't finished yet.' When he realized that his only chance for the sale was me, he turned his attention to me and said, 'Tell your husband . . . ' "

These are just two of Baggett's buying stories. They happen to all women in all industries. Baggett's gross income exceeded 95 percent of the male population. She had a responsible job with a major New York company. Yet, like Wright, she was perceived as incapable of making a simple buying decision without assistance from her husband. Salespersons must begin to recognize the woman as the customer. They must look beyond the *glass wall* that divides them from her. They must reach out and secure her business. Or, they will become obsolete.

Summary

Women speak out in many ways. They buy elsewhere; they tell their network; they find a way to convey the message. Today's professional woman has earned the right to the power she has in the marketplace. With more discretionary income, her purchasing clout will have even greater significance on the marketplace.

Marketing departments at colleges and universities have a responsibility to provide students with the knowledge they need to become masterful marketers. Integrating a learning module on the female customer into consumer behavior classes is a must for academic institutions if they hope to remain competitive and to produce top-notch graduates. The rules are changing. As with the marketplace, academic institutions ought to re-evaluate their marketing principles and restructure the curriculum to fit today's diversified needs.

As businesses learn how to market and sell more effectively to the professional woman, so must universities seek wisdom from women to help guide them through these changing times.

Women business owners, female corporate executives, attorneys, doctors, and engineers—each has evolved into her own being. Each will verbalize her demands to manufacturers and salespersons. Their collective voice will echo loudly in the hollow buildings where businesses that failed to heed her message once resided.

Notes

[1]Lynn Jaffe, professor of marketing, Northeastern University, interview with author, 13 August 1993.

[2]Jagdish Sheth, professor of marketing, Emory University, interview with author, 1 September 1993.

[3]Debra Kent, "What's Making You Mad," *Special Report* (July/August 1993) 22–23.

[4]Kent, "What's Making You Mad," 26.

[5]Max Morgan, radio personality, Q102 Radio, interview with author.

[6]Karen Swinehart, manager of certification, National Association of Purchasing Management, interview with author, 18 June 1993.

[7]Jeanie Watson, purchasing supervisor, Universal Display & Fixtures, interview with author, June 1993.

[8]Trudy Cohen, buyer, J. C. Penney, interview with author, June 1993.

[9]Beverly Miller, president, Miller Bevco, interview with author, 23 June 1993.

[10]Amy Brown, product manager, Chief Auto Parts, interview with author, 2 June 1993.

[11]Sue Dielh-Sellman, product manager, Chief Auto Parts, interview with author, 24 June 1993.

[12]Jacqui Osborn, president, Dolphin Commercial Chemical Inc., interview with author, 23 June 1993.

[13]Molly Harvey, buyer, Anheuser Busch, interview with author, 30 June 1993.

[14]Derrick Schnebelt, media/public relations, National Association of Purchasing Management, interview with author, 30 June 1993.

[15]Derrick Schnebelt, "Turning the Tables: How Purchasers View Sales Professionals."

[16]Joyce McLaughlin, president, NAWBO, interview with author, 13 July 1993.

[17]Marolyn Wright, owner, Program Resources, interview with author, 28 July 1993.

[18]Jeannie Baggett, interview with author, 16 June 1993.

Chapter 10

Customer Service Is a Selling Tool

Manufacturers, designers, mechanics, clerks, waiters, cashiers, and salespersons all depend on the customer for job security. Without the consumers' dollars, marketers, advertising executives, media buyers, and CEOs wouldn't get a paycheck. The entire marketplace revolves around revenue generated and debits owed. Profitability and market share are what it's all about.

Accountants and comptrollers dissect financial statements, managers struggle with cost containment, and marketing strategists concentrate on the most effective way to get the message out. Engineers and designers create products, attorneys interpret the legal issues, and distributors and wholesalers make sure the product is available to customers.

When you get down to it, all of the various functions of a business are performed for the benefit of the customer. The focus of any business, or at least it should be the focus, is the customer. The marketplace and the workplace are both customer-driven. No matter how well the management team performs, without this one single entity, the business will cease to exist.

If this ingredient is so critical for business survival, why doesn't it get the same attention that other aspects of a business receive? Before I continue with some examples and suggestions, I have a few questions I would like you to answer:

❖ What do I think is more important than the customer?

❖ How much does it cost my company to get a new customer?

❖ Which is more cost-effective, retaining a customer or getting a new one?

❖ Who is easier to sell, a cold call or a referral?

❖ When a customer complains, how does my company handle the complaint?

Good Customer Service Is Just Good Business

When Lexus opened their first dealerships in 1987, they wanted to do it right. "We wrote the 'Lexus Covenant,'" confirmed Richard Chitty, corporate manager of parts, service, and customer satisfaction.[1] "The basis of the covenant is we treat each customer as if he or she was a guest in our home. We believe if you set high standards, people will live up to them. We wanted to have the best luxury facility, but still have it warm and homey, the best sales atmosphere, the best product, and the best after sales service," said Chitty.

Lexus's extensive training program helps insure that the owners, general managers, sales staff, and service writers all understand the company's philosophy and mission. The "Lexus Commitment to Perfection Certification Program" addresses many issues during the various training modules. While it doesn't spend a lot of time differentiating between male and female buyers, Chitty did acknowledge that it does point out different features of interest to men or women.

Chitty also stated that Lexus is constantly making adjustments in order to provide the customers what they want. "We have added 60 items to the cars as a result of input from our customers," noted Chitty. "For instance, they wanted an outside temperature gauge and a different horn tone." While many of the 60 items are little things, as I have mentioned, little things really make a big difference, especially to women. This response makes it clear to their customers that Lexus is listening to them. "We wrote 14 different guides for various jobs at the dealership," claimed Chitty. "It's not enough to tell someone to do something. You must tell them how to do it. No one enjoys doing a bad job. You have to create the environment for people to do a good job. It's really an easy formula."

The great thing is that Lexus shares what it has done with the Toyota brand. "We are a much smaller organization and can test and implement theories much easier," pointed out Chitty. But the bottom line is that when something works, it is passed on to the entire Toyota operation. Good service and customer satisfaction just might be contagious.

Carl Sewell, a Lexus dealer in Dallas, perfected the art of customer service prior to joining the Lexus team.[2] Sewell, who owns more than 12 franchises including Cadillac, Oldsmobile, and Buick, wrote a book on the fundamentals he has used over the years to build lifetime customers. Sewell's book, *Customers for Life: How to Turn That One-Time Buyer into a*

Lifetime Customer, describes a concept that more retail establishments should strive for. One thing he said that is constantly being quoted is, "Ask your customers what they want . . . they will tell you how to provide good service." Sewell believes it is important to exceed a customer's expectations. "Always give them more than you promise" is one of his philosophies.

Sewell knows that setting high standards and goals is important, along with raising them once they have been achieved. That's what keeps businesses competitive. He recognizes that how he treats his employees is reflected in how they treat customers. Good people have good performance and expect to be compensated accordingly.

There is no shortcut to extraordinary customer satisfaction. It takes constant work. In his business, he thinks holding daily quality meetings—not just with managers, but with the people who actually perform the work—keeps quality high. No one's perfect 100 percent of the time. That's why it's important to have established rapport, built a relationship and have some stored-up goodwill with customers so that when there is a problem, the customer understands if you handle it promptly. That's important when you're building customers for life.

Horror Stories You Should Fear

The next few pages will be actual accounts of how companies have treated their most precious resource. They are not provided for punishment or revenge, but to emphasize the need for businesses to listen to and respond to their customers. Therefore, in a few instances, I have blacked out the name and company. Who is guilty isn't my point, but rather what can and should be done. These stories are just the tip of the iceberg. What is really happening in the marketplace, and in the corporate environment is even more frightening. Imagine multiplying these stories by thousands of customers every day. Bad service, lost customers, and lost potential customers are daily occurrences in the marketplace. Could one of these stories be about your company?

Taken to the Cleaners

Debbie and Mike used the same dry cleaners every week. It was convenient to their house, and they were pleased with the work. Each week one took in the cleaning, and the other picked it up. Since they came frequently and spent approximately $125 a month, the cleaners knew them by name. One day Debbie went to wear an outfit she had recently had cleaned. She discovered that all the expensive buttons had been removed but not replaced. On her next trip to the dry cleaners, she took the outfit with her and asked that the buttons be replaced. She made it clear that the responsibility was the cleaners since they had lost the buttons. Upon returning to pick up her weekly cleaning, she was presented with a bill for an additional $8 for the buttons. Again, she explained to the cleaners that they were liable for fixing the outfit. She was astonished to be told, no, that it was *her* fault, not theirs. She took the clean clothes, paid the $8 and angrily left. Later, the $8 was refunded, but the damage was done: Debbie took her business elsewhere.

The moral of the story is obvious. The price for satisfaction was miniscule in relationship to the value of the customer. Who lost the buttons shouldn't have even been a factor. Yet the business chose to lose Debbie's business and her network, a ridiculously bad business decision over $8. However, I see this type of mistake every day.

Now, let's look at this example another way. Did the incident occur because Debbie was a woman? Probably not—but the fact that she is a woman still has a tremendous bearing on the story. When Mike was asked how many people he told the dry cleaning problem to, he replied, "none." And the answer would have been the same had he picked up the cleaning. When I asked Debbie how many people she had told, her reply was quite different. "During the week we argued over the $8, I told a bunch. Probably everyone I talked to." After the refund, she didn't bother to go back and tell her network she got her money back.

That's how the differences between men and women affect all areas of business, not just advertising campaigns, marketing strategies, and sales training, but the customer satisfaction philosophies as well.

Mike's friends will continue to patronize the cleaners, never knowing there was any difficulty. Debbie's friends and network, on the other hand, will shy away from the establishment fearing that they, too, will have a problem

A Gem of an Experience

Do you ever wonder what happens to a letter you took the time and trouble to write? I have. I wondered why no one took the same time and trouble to answer me. Below is a letter I wrote to the president of ▮▮▮ Jewelers. (The names have been blacked out to protect the guilty.) One that was never acknowledged by anyone. Could my negative experience have been turned into a positive one by responding appropriately? Of course it could have. Could he have converted me to being a buyer again? Maybe, maybe not. But, at least when I told the story, it would have a different ending. I wouldn't necessarily believe, as I do now, that customers don't really matter to ▮▮ Jewelers. I couldn't draw any other conclusion from my experience. You decide.

June 11, 1993

Mr.
President

TX 75060

Dear Mr.

On May 23, 1993, I left my watch at your store in Prestonwood Mall for a simple stem repair. I was told that this repair would take one week, and would cost $45. The only reason I agreed to pay this much for a repair I knew I could get elsewhere for $30 was the fact that I needed the watch back within one week.

Not only was my watch not ready in one week, but after four extra days of being told "maybe" and "probably" tomorrow, or the next day, I finally insisted that my watch be returned to me on Friday, June 4, repaired or not.

The watch was returned to me on Friday, and it was repaired. I was amazed at your staff's complete disinterest in my situation. They never once called regarding my watch, nor showed the slightest concern for the fact that it was almost one week late. I was charged the full price for the repair, although it was not ready when promised, and the stem I had requested was not used.

Professionally, I do a lot work in the customer service area. One very important thing I tell managers and owners is that you can't fix it if you don't know you have a problem. So, Mr. ▮, I'm telling you—you have a problem!

I am very sorry that I did not take the watch to Corrigan's, Kay, Whitehall or Bachendorf's—all of which are in the same mall. In the future, I can assure you, that is exactly what I will do.

Sincerely,

Gerry Myers

The "No-Response" Response

Unfortunately, the above jewelers isn't the only company that totally disregards letters from customers. How effective can the sales staff be if the corporate attitude is "We don't care what our customers think." Companies that think they are saying nothing by not responding are saying plenty—to me, to my network, and to every other customer who is ignored. Below are some excerpts from another letter I wrote.

February 3, 1993

Linda ▓▓▓
Sr. Vice President of Marketing
▓▓▓▓▓▓▓▓
▓▓▓▓▓▓▓▓▓▓
▓▓▓▓▓, TX 77002

Dear Ms. ▓▓▓

    I was appalled at a print ad ▓▓▓ recently ran in the *Dallas Morning News*. The ad, which I enclosed a copy of, ran Sunday, January ▓, as a full-color, full page spread. The photograph shows a woman in a swimsuit with three sailors not only ogling her, but one has his hands predominantly placed on her leg.
    While the theme is obviously nautical, I believe the ad is in questionable taste. I have received several calls asking me if I had seen the ad with various comments including, "After the tailhook scandal, how could they run an ad like that?" and "I almost cut up my credit card when I saw that ad."

The letter continued, but you get the general idea. Not only had I found it offensive, but for the next day or two, everywhere I went, someone commented to me about that ad. Recall was great. But would the ad sell to its market—women? No. They had totally missed the mark. Then, to further lower their image in my eyes, they simply ignored my letter.

Does a company realize the message a customer gets when she is ignored? Women immediately believe you don't value their opinions, you don't value them as customers, and all you are interested in is their money. The cliche "money talks" is true. And, when these women spend money with the competition, it will speak loudly.

Following is another letter the manufacturer obviously didn't think was worth a response, since Taunee Besson never received one.[3]

August 4, 1992

██████████

General Sales and Service Manager
███ Motor Division
██ E. Main St.
█████████████████████

Dear Mr. ██████

On June 1, I took my 1990 Riviera to █████████████ for a $650 body repair estimated by State Farm and the dealership to take four days. Five weeks later ██████ finally, the first and only time, called to say my car was ready. Unfortunately, an inexcusable lack of attention to customer service is something both I and my friends have experienced numerous times with American car dealers.

One other occasion when ██████ kept my car over two months to correct a $2000 sludge problem, I wrote to the corporate office for an explanation of how my engine could be full of sludge when I was following the recommended maintenance schedule. To my surprise and disappointment, ██████ sent me a form letter reply distancing itself from the problem because my car was out of warranty.

Against my better judgment, I bought another Riviera because it's the best looking car on the road. Before signing the contract, I told the general manager that ██████ and ██████ were both on probation. He assured me their service department had improved and the division was serious about increasing customer satisfaction. Yet, once again, I find myself writing to the corporate office. Is anybody out there? Does anybody care?

As a committed "buy America" consumer and a fourteen year owner of ██████, it angers and frustrates me to have to go through this again. I have a business to run, a family to raise and a variety of volunteer projects demanding my attention. Yet, I can't be complacent about our country's declining market share in manufactured products. We all must take responsibility for shoddy customer service and an antiquated system of quality control which fixes problems when they become critical instead of "doing the job right the first time." Neither you, nor I, nor ████, nor the U.S. can afford to have consumers sharing repair shop horror stories, shaking our heads at incredibly unprofessional treatment, and muttering, "They (dealers and manufacturers) just don't get it, do they?"

My friends and I are business owners, corporate managers, attorneys, and commercial salespeople who have the income to buy your highest margin models, but we're tired of being patronized and/or ignored. We pride ourselves on our relationships with clients, because we know our reputation for credibility and service is what keeps us in business. Naturally, we want to buy from suppliers who share this philosophy.

We don't want: a communication vacuum, discounts on botched jobs, empty excuses, buck passing, or platitudes. We want the job done right within the estimated time. If there is a problem, we want a prompt volunteered explanation, a proposed solution, and an ongoing update. If the problem is really big, we want attention from the boss, who will personally see to it that we are happy when we leave.

I hope this incident will receive your prompt attention. I'm looking forward to your personal response.

Sincerely yours,

Taunee S. Besson

P.S. If you want a chronology of events and responses by ▮▮▮▮ and the zone office, see attached.

Good Responses Save Customers

Following is my letter to American Express after months of trying to straighten out my account, which had never been properly credited for airline tickets for a trip I didn't take. Mr. Robinson didn't call me back, but his secretary did within 48 hours of receiving my letter. She informed me she had been given the letter and was going to look into the problem. In less than a week, she called me back. She apologized, sympathized with what I had been through the last several months, and assured me she had it taken care of. She also wanted me to know that she had credited my account for the $55 annual renewal fee, due shortly, to partially make up for the time I had spent on this problem.

Four years later, I still have my American Express card. They told me they cared. They let me know I was a valued customer. They took the time to resolve the problem. Then, they went one step further. They insured my staying a customer. They not only gave me a token gift to show their appreciation for what I had been through, but they tied me to them as a customer for another year. They had a full year to prove that they would continue to provide me with the type of service I had experienced in the past. Can you maintain a customer by handling their complaint no matter how angry they may be at the time they write? Obviously, yes.

June 23, 1989

Mr. James Robinson, CEO
American Express Cos.
World Financial Center
American Express-Tower C
200 Vessey St.
New York, NY 10285

Dear Mr. Robinson,

While I may not be your biggest account, I hope I am your angriest. Otherwise, you have a multitude of unhappy customers.

No one in your company has been able to properly credit my account with the $227 due me from the American Airlines flight ticket I did not use in January. I trust that, while this is not your primary function, somewhere in your organization there is a person capable of handling this simple procedure. If so, please see that my account is properly credited and that the credit remains there.

If not, consider this my last transaction with your company.

Sincerely,

Gerry Myers

P.S. Review my file since January. It will provide you with a condensed glimpse of the trouble your company has put me through.

These letters are just a couple of the millions of letters consumers write annually expressing disappointment, anger, and rage. Each consumer is sharing vital information with the company—information that all the sophisticated market research data won't give the manufacturer or business. Demographics and psychographics are limited in what they can provide a company. The information you receive from customers' letters versus market research is as different as the information gathered from open-ended and close-ended questions. Reading the letters, hearing the message and responding can:

❖ Provide valuable insight to the corporation or business about the customer that can be gathered no other way;

❖ Can save a customer relationship that is on the brink of disaster.

Below is an excerpt from the "Comment" column in *Automotive News*.[4] I couldn't agree more with what Mary Ann Maskery, the *Automotive News* bureau chief in Tokyo, wrote. "People can argue over the price or even about the job itself. But what can really make or break a future sale is the attitude of the people the customer deals with." She goes on to say that a survey was conducted in Japan, and they found that the customer had more loyalty to the dealership than the brand of the vehicle. "In other words," she surmised, "if the dealer were to switch brands, his customers would come back." Her comments concerned a minor repair she was taking care of for her family while she was in Michigan visiting them. The rearview mirror had fallen off the windshield. She called the closest Chevrolet dealer and asked if she could bring the car in. "Not today," she was told. "Tomorrow morning would be okay."

To facilitate matters, she planned to drive the car over late that afternoon so it would be there first thing in the morning. When she arrived, she received her next, "We can't do it. . . . " Obviously, unlike the Infiniti service manager I mentioned in Chapter 5, who taught her service advisors that the answer was "yes," these service advisors had been schooled in: "We can't do it, no matter what it is you want."

When Maskery asked about leaving her car, he quickly replied,"No." In fact, at that point, he told her to bring it back later in the week. Remember, the repair was for a rearview mirror, not a complex electrical problem. "When she again mentioned it was scheduled for service the next day, he became irritated and told her to bring it in later in the week.

"I can't do that—I leave for Japan tomorrow," she replied.

"And then came the heavy sarcasm: 'Well, I guess you really need the car.' "

The article continued, and, yes, she eventually did get the mirror fixed, but would she return to that dealership to buy, lease, or service another car?

A few weeks after she returned to Japan, she had a problem with her Nissan while out driving. She drove to a dealership on a Saturday, without an appointment. While she waited for them to fix it, they brought her a glass of iced coffee. After about 20 minutes, they returned to say it was more complicated than they had originally thought. Could she leave it over the weekend? They drove her home. When she returned, it was washed and the interior wiped clean.

If these two dealers were a block apart, which would you do business with?

Providing Good Service Pays Off

Sometimes you are so happy to get good service, you want everyone to know. That's because, unfortunately, it's so rare. When my daughter was getting married, there were so many details to handle, so much to do, so many people you had to rely on to make one of the most special weekends of our lives perfect. That's a really scary thought. You would think any smart businessperson in a competitive environment would not only strive to meet, but to exceed, the customer's needs. As we all know, that's usually not the case. Too bad. It would really give a business the edge over the competition. Instead of playing price wars until someone goes bankrupt, it would be a better strategy if the company provided extraordinary service, with a smile.

Below is a letter I was happy I had the opportunity to write.

October 28, 1992

Gil Walton
County Line
6159 Westheimer
Houston, TX 77057

Dear Gil,

Last Friday night, I hosted my daughter's rehearsal dinner at your restaurant. I have arranged and coordinated many dinners and events both personally and professionally over the last several years, and I have never had a more pleasant experience.

Linda and Rob were superb. The service was outstanding and the food delicious. Both waiters were always available and eager to help in any way they could.

On a wedding weekend, when so much is happening, and every detail needs to be taken care of, I really appreciated your staff's attention and service to our guests.

Thanks so much for making this very special weekend so much more special.

Sincerely,

Gerry Myers

Did it cost Linda and Rob, our waiters, anything to be so pleasant? No. In fact, it enhanced their gross. The tip was much better, and I think they really enjoyed the evening, too. Even if I hadn't taken the time to say thank you, all my guests, many of whom entertain for business, experienced the service we received. Some have even told me since then that they have hosted dinners there. Does customer satisfaction, or exceeding what is expected, pay off?

There were other great people we worked with on the wedding. Debbie still orders all her flowers from Corbett Designs/Plantiques, the florist she used. He has received hundreds of additional dollars from her, as well as a number of referrals. In return, she still receives wonderful service *and* value for her dollars. Like Sewell, Corbett believes in providing more than is expected. Good customer service continues to pay big dividends to those who understand its importance.

- ❖ Which of the businesses described above would you like to do business with?
- ❖ Would you like to do business with *your* company?
- ❖ What type of letters do your customers write?

If you can't say that the letters your company receives sound like the last one, then you had better rethink your customer satisfaction policies.

The Cost of Customers

The good news is that the most common offenses can easily be remedied. The bad news is that no one seems to care. Even worse news is that American companies are losing billions of dollars in potential sales and wasted advertising, and they are neglecting to build a base of happy, satisfied, loyal customers in the process.

The majority of cities in America today are never going to return to the general store concept where everyone knows everyone and personal service, along with friendly conversation, is commonplace. Consumers have more choices and are less loyal to brands and retail establishments than in years past. Yet, with good marketing and customer satisfaction, a certain level of loyalty and retention is possible.

T. Scott Gross, author of *Positively Outrageous Service*, stressed that standards of excellence start at the top of the organization.[5] "Businesses often concentrate on the minute percentage of customers who might take advantage of a situation. They should be serving the vast majority of good customers."

Gross is emphatic about positive, memorable moments. He believes customers should enjoy being in your place of business, and that they will if the people who wait on them enjoy being there. Good customer service is impossible if employees aren't motivated to be the best they can be, and that desire comes from within. Training can make someone good much better; it can't make a person with a bad attitude good.

Customers, especially women, are eager to find stores stocking products designed with them in mind and well-trained salespeople to help them. Continually having to replace lost customers with new ones leads to a slow, painful death. Make no mistake, while this trend can be reversed, without proper intervention the situation will eventually become terminal. It is just too costly to continually market to and satisfy new customers if you are failing to keep the existing ones happy.

Nothing worthwhile comes cheaply. Hopefully, manufacturers, marketers, and retailers will feel that customers are a worthwhile expenditure. After all, billions are spent annually in advertising dollars to bring them into the store to purchase your products. What percentage of your advertising/marketing budget is being spent to train the employees or sales force who have direct contact with the customers?

Do you know:

❖ It costs five times as much to secure a new customer as to keep an existing one?

❖ How many people your customer is going to tell her experience to?

❖ How little sympathy I have when I read about companies that are losing market share, especially if I have had a bad experience there myself?

If retailers took the time to figure out how much an average customer spends on a weekly, monthly, or annual basis, and multiplied that by just 10 years, they would be amazed at the gross revenue they are throwing away. For instance, if Debbie and Mike spent an average of $125 per month at the cleaners, they would spend $1,500 a year, or $15,000 in 10 years. A pretty good customer for a small neighborhood dry cleaners. If they recommended three friends who became customers at only $50 per month, that would be another $1,800 per year. All it would have taken to keep this profitable business was to handle the problem promptly and professionally. The total cost to keep the customer was $8. The cost of losing her was thousands of dollars.

Management must train employees. It must empower them to make decisions that will maintain good customer relationships, and it must hold them accountable for their actions.

Customer satisfaction is very definitely one of the components in today's marketing mix—price, place, product, and promotion just aren't enough. In fact, the 4 Ps could easily be rewritten to be:

Prompt Professional Problem-solving = Profits

Notes

[1]Richard Chitty, corporate manager—parts, service and customer satisfaction, interview with author, 21 September 1993.

[2]Carl Sewell, president, Sewell Village Cadillac, interview with author, 24 September 1993.

[3]Taunee Besson, president, Career Dimensions, interview with author, July 1993.

[4]Mary Ann Maskery, "Two Views of Dealer Service: Japan Wins," *Automotive News* (6 September 1993): 14.

[5]T. Scott Gross, president/CEO, T. Scott Gross & Company Inc., interview with author, 27 September 1993.

Chapter 11

Facts, Figures, and Sales Trends— What It All Means

T wo things are certain: The marketplace will continue to change and women will become an even bigger factor as a result of the economic growth they will experience. Breaking the "glass wall" and reaching out to women consumers in the marketplace will be as important to manufacturers and retailers as breaking the "glass ceiling" is to women in the workplace. Both will have to happen for a company to grow and prosper in the twenty-first century.

Unlike the era when women went to work to fill jobs vacated by men who had gone to battle, today, when American armed forces are called on to fight for and protect citizens of other countries, women don't replace men in their jobs but go to battle along with them.

The military is just one facet of the continually changing environment in which we live. The *traditional family*, the *extended family*, and *housewives* are all terms that will be found more in historical accounts than in today's vocabulary. The traditional family—a father, stay-at-home mother, and children—only exists in about 19 percent of American households. The extended family of nearby aunts, uncles, and cousins has given way to the mobility created by corporate America in the 1970s and 1980s. Women no longer see their roles as wives and mothers, but as partial or total breadwinners for the family unit. As women's roles changed, so did the type of products they purchased.

During this and future decades, women will play a more significant role in the development of products. As more women are involved in the design phase, the needs of women will be better addressed. They will not

231

be segregated out by *pink* products, but will be part of the total production effort. Women's needs are not the same as men's, and never will be. Women are not smaller males. They have legitimate concerns about the ergonomics of the product and their stature.

Just as companies have adjusted their product design to women, so will they have to adjust their management styles. They will no longer operate on theories that, in essence, try to put square pegs in round holes. In other words, they will recognize that women bring a style all their own into management and product design. Male-dominated corporations will acknowledge there is a difference in the way men and women think, communicate, buy, manage, respond, and interact, and this realization will be felt in the boardrooms and showrooms of America. Women won't be thought of as a niche market but a market that has its own set of needs, just as the male market does. Within the female market segment are specialized requirements. Businesses must address the commonality of women, as well as their diversity.

Along with quality service, value—which has always been an important factor to women consumers—will become an even more major component in buying decisions. "Value-pricing" and "value-added" will be terms used by corporations in their marketing strategies. Established companies such as Procter & Gamble have even abandoned their familiar "new and improved" and replaced it with "value price."[1]

It is projected that by the year 2000, women will purchase 60 percent of all vehicles, they will comprise 50 percent of all business travelers, and 50 percent of the work force. Congress will have more female members in both the House and the Senate, and women will have climbed the political ranks to be top office holders in many state and local governments.

By the end of the decade, even more changes will become apparent. Women will continue to enter the professions of law, accounting, and medicine in large numbers. Their numbers will grow in high-tech industries and other science-related fields. Construction, law enforcement, and the military will all attract more women. Women will begin to crack the "glass ceiling" and become a part of upper management in many corporations; women-owned businesses will grow and prosper. As women take on more leadership roles, the structure of corporations will change. In concert with the economic necessity to diminish layers of hierarchy in corporations, women will implement a more circular management style, gathering input from many areas and dispensing data the same way.

These transitions affect a number of industries. Child care will continue to be an important element, and more corporations will offer the option of on-site child care as part of the benefit package. Professional adult care will also thrive as women seek alternatives to home care for elderly parents. Adult drop-in facilities will become more commonplace.

Health industries—fitness and sports equipment, health clubs and workout apparel—will continue to be a growth market among women. Maintaining a professional, healthy image will be a priority. As women travel more, work longer hours and experience more stress in the workplace, they will turn to healthy foods and other means to maintain their physical and mental balance.

In health care, women have demanded to be a part of the research and part of the diagnostic process. Research will lead to the development of additional pharmaceutical products for women because that market has proven to be very lucrative. Businesses are offering more medical services to women. Companies such as Zeneca Inc., Adolph Coors, American Cast Iron Pipe, and Merck have begun to offer mammogram screening to women at work.[2] More companies will join this effort, as well as offering other on-site healthcare benefits.

The human element will play a bigger part in the research analysis phase of companies. Corporations will look at hard data, including demographic and psychographic information, but they will interpret the market and its needs by understanding the pressures, stresses, accomplishments, and thinking of the women to whom they want to sell.

Manufacturers will listen to what customers want and will work to fill their needs. They will no longer be able to control the marketplace unilaterally. Events will happen at a faster pace. Successful companies will have systems in place to respond quickly. Women will demand better service, and this will be a differential in deciding who they will patronize and who they won't.

When consumers don't receive the service they expect or don't find the products they desire, they go elsewhere, points out Faith Popcorn in her book, *The Popcorn Report*.[3]

In *Megatrends for Women*, Patricia Aburdene and John Naisbitt tackle some critical issues. Their book emphasizes how essential it is to be aware of the female market. They cite examples of retailers in bankruptcy and those with disastrous million-dollar advertising campaigns who either neglected or miscalculated the importance of the evolving women's market.

Aburdene and Naisbitt reinforce their beliefs by writing, "For venture capitalists, auto makers, pharmaceutical firms, food producers, advertisers, healthcare, computer and electronics firms—to name just a few industries—hundreds of billions of dollars are at stake if you are ignorant or lazy enough to neglect women and the changes they are experiencing and precipitating."[4] I couldn't agree more.

Hopefully, by now you are in agreement as well, and intend to make women a top priority as you create products, advertising, and marketing strategies that will position your company into the twenty-first century.

Automotive Industry

Women will be instrumental in the way the Big Three compete with each other and with imports. While trade policies and tariffs will certainly have a bearing on the industry and the price of vehicles, other factors will come into play. Women will be more involved in designing and marketing automobiles. The Big Three will have learned a bitter lesson and, hopefully, profited from it.

Looking ahead, recognizing what's happening and what's going to happen in the marketplace is key to survival in the twenty-first century. Ford, with a lower market share, has the upper hand and may well pull ahead of General Motors unless GM makes some dramatic and much needed changes in their corporate culture.

Ford has taken aggressive steps to integrate women into positions of power and influence. While Ford has a long way to go to take over the number-one spot, by successfully wooing the female market, it can dramatically increase its position. Much of its success in this endeavor will depend on the response General Motors makes. Ford, thus far, has been more responsive to the marketplace. Ford was the first to initiate the Total Quality Management (TQM) style in the U.S. automotive industry, even though it still trailed the Japanese.[5] Ford has led domestic automakers in leasing programs as well. If General Motors leaves the playing field wide open by not asking women what they want, by not hiring women, and by not using women consultants in their marketing and advertising, then Ford will walk in and grab the market in much the same way Jockey did.

General Motors is looking at innovative marketing strategies that will better position it for the future. Together with Hachette Filipacchi magazines, which publishes *Road & Track* and *Car and Driver*, GM will produce two episodes of "The TV Car Showroom" that will run on the Home Shopping Network in November and December 1993. The shows are currently being tested and are partially funded by General Motors. If successful, it might become a regular program by spring 1995.[6]

Manufacturers must take more responsibility for training their sales staff. The training must be a continual process, not a one-time or an occasional day program. The trainees must learn practical, easy-to-implement techniques that work. They must be accountable to the consumer, take responsibility for providing exceptional customer service, and be fully knowledgeable about the product. This standard will be expected. Training shouldn't be the stepchild of the marketing budget, but should be a prescribed percentage of sales, just as advertising is. One without the other is futile.

As the quality of domestic vehicles continues to improve and the price of foreign vehicles escalates in response to the fluctuating money exchange rate, the Big Three have an opportunity to again shine in the automotive industry. These factors, coupled with the revived spirit of patriotism and the fear of lost jobs to foreign companies, will keep the "Buy American" slogan alive.

Chrysler, the other Big Three player, has new challenges with Lee Iacocca resigning after his long reign and rescue of the company from bankruptcy. He has positioned Chrysler with a strong footing and positive momentum for the future.

The Big Three have consistently ignored consumer trends, and that just doesn't work any longer. "But what always amazes me the most are the companies that don't think they need to heed consumer trends. That it's only today, and not tomorrow, that counts. Usually those companies are located in Detroit," writes Faith Popcorn in her book, *The Popcorn Report.*[7] Today, industries must react to the changing marketplace. They must be cognizant of the world around them, and this includes appreciating the new status of the professional woman.

Advertising

Women will be portrayed as strong, powerful, independent, and intelligent, but with a warm, caring side. Women, as they become more immersed in the power struggles of corporate America and entrepreneurship, will not lose their nurturing, caring traits. Corporations will adjust their views to these standards, rather than vice versa. Successful advertising will be able to capture the essence of this accomplished, competent woman without creating another superwoman syndrome or a cold, all-business veneer. Women will, in reality, be able to fill the needs of the business community in a masterful manner, while still providing a human element not readily seen in corporate America today. As technology continues to dehumanize the workplace, reaching out person-to-person will be important.

Advertising messages will be diversified, better reflecting the marketplace. Fathers will continue to play a part in advertising and will be portrayed as single parents, as well as traditional husbands. Men will not be shown as weak in comparison to women but as equal partners in the day-to-day operations of either a business or family. Men will not be seen as more feminine or women as more masculine. Each will be comfortable with their own identity and sexuality.

Women will continue to succeed and achieve for themselves, as well as for the well-being of their families. Their self-esteem will be based more on their accomplishments than on their physical prowess. Advertising will reflect this.

Successfully balancing a family and career will be a top priority. Women will be more content with themselves and their ability to contribute to the business environment and the community.

The male-bashing of the 1980s and early 1990s will have disappeared. Working women will need the support of their mates, and vice versa. They will be a team in running the household and caring for the children, even though she will still control most of the household spending.

Some advertising will have a light, humorous approach, a brief escape from the tasks and responsibilities of the day. Companies will be more concerned that their advertising informs the consumer about the product rather than whether a women is the spokesperson. However, advertising agencies searching for appropriate female role models as spokespersons won't have to look far. They will have scientists, politicians, lawyers, doctors, researchers, computer programmers, and more to choose from. Having the husband in the ad refer to his wife as the doctor will not be considered unusual.

Women will always be more sensitive to their treatment than men, but as they become more respected for their accomplishments—their brains, not just their bodies—they will be less defensive and will relax in their reaction to advertising and sales messages. This is based on the premise that, when more women are involved in the creative process within the advertising agency or as the client, the industry will increase its current level of sensitivity. As more women are placed on creative teams, they will convince their clients that women in bikini-clad swimsuits are not appropriate for all products. Sex will still be a part of advertising, as it has for decades, but the message will have to be structured to be more seductive and romantic and less blatant and offensive. When sex is used to sell a product, it will have a sense of good taste that is not displayed in much of the current advertising. Marketers who use sexist advertising directed toward women who are the major consumer or influencer of the products will have to refocus their message. Women will no longer tolerate ads that are demeaning and patronizing, and they will make sure that any company that continuously creates this type of advertising doesn't survive their wrath. Neither will advertising agencies that insist on providing clients with sexist ads.

Cosmetic and fashion ads will have to begin to use more mature, real-life women in their advertising. This does not mean that the models shouldn't be attractive. When selling cosmetics and fashion, image is the name of the game. But wholesome, healthy, and confident will be more important than extreme thinness and exquisite beauty. With the graying of America, more wrinkle cream will be advertised, and if manufacturers want their ads to be believable by today's sophisticated female shoppers, they need to use an attractive women at least close to forty. A twenty-year-old spouting the virtues of wrinkle cream just won't sell. At the other end of the spectrum is the use of the elderly in advertising. Kevin Goldman, who writes on advertising for *The Wall Street Journal* recently commented on this trend. He cited several ads where companies have ridiculed or minimized the value of the elderly in their advertising.[8]

Stereotyping—women, blacks, Hispanics, the elderly—will have very negative effects on companies that produce such ads. Women don't like seeing any group stereotyped, and that includes portraying men as bumbling idiots. Advertising of the future will focus on positive traits rather than on negative stereotypes.

Beyond the gender issue, a future trend that enormously impacts advertising is cable television.[9] The interactive capabilities of the audience with the programming and the number of cable channel options available will make it more difficult for an advertiser to capture a large segment of the market. Interactive TV allows the viewer to watch only those ads they select. While this will affect all marketers and advertising agencies because both genders are free to zap the ads, women will definitely tune out ads that are demeaning, sexist, or that don't speak to them. With 500 channels to choose from, commercials will have to be entertaining, eye-catching, and provide information sought by the consumer.

Obviously, as on-line advertising becomes more prevalent, it will affect the marketing strategies of many industries. Advertising will have to be created with more individuality and tailored for very specific niches.

Cable opens many realms to advertisers. They will literally be able to create their own programs with infomercials supporting that programming. As Liza Schoenfein pointed out in *Advertising Age*, companies like Procter & Gamble could create a parenting channel that would be informative and capture its primary customer as its viewing audience. It would position its products as part of the program creating a very positive message.[10]

This is true for many industries. As Exxon and other oil companies seek to win the lucrative women's market, they might look at this concept instead of network or print media. For example, an astute company that wants to target women could produce a show on issues important to women. They could be business related, health related, or even sports related. The programming would depend on the marketing strategies and the products.

Financial Services

Women will become more knowledgeable about money and money matters. They will stop underestimating the value of their lives and the contributions they are making to the financial stability of the family. They will begin to buy more life and disability insurance as their incomes continue to catch up to their male counterparts. Disability insurance will no longer be thought of as a male product, but one that is sold to both genders. Insurance companies will develop new programs that better address the needs of women.

Financial planning for their future will take on a different perspective. Women will need retirement income even more than men, since they live longer. Women have realized they cannot be dependent on corporate America to provide the security it once did. They will have to provide for themselves. They will put little faith in social security or other government programs. They will not expect a husband to take care of them in the same way their mothers did. As a result, younger women will become interested in savings and investing. They will not consider investments totally from the perspective of retirement, but to obtain peace of mind, for both the immediate and long-term future. Taking care of herself and her children will be more prevalent in a woman's thinking, even at a young age.

Professional women will also recognize the importance of establishing good relationships in the financial community. They know a line of credit and a good banking relationship is essential. In turn, bankers will need to recognize the importance of the woman business owner, understanding that as women create a "good ol' girl" business network, it will affect who they and their network choose to do business with. As corporations continue to downsize, the financial community will no longer be able to count on corporate America as their prime customer. Their typical customers will be made up of smaller companies, rather than corporate giants. While large corporations will still play a very real role in American business and the development of products for the marketplace, their power and numbers will diminish, and small businesses will grow in number and in strength.

Women will also occupy more seats in financial institutions' executive offices. They will change many of the old rules and rewrite the image of women in the financial community. As women continue to receive more education and become more involved in the business world, financial services will need to be marketed a little differently. Education and experience will not eliminate the differences that exist between women and their male colleagues. What it will do is make her as desirable a client as he has been.

Politics

While *Targeting the New Professional Woman* is certainly not a study of women and their influence on the political scene, it would be a great omission not to include at least a comment or two on the status of women in politics and its effect on the marketplace. There is no doubt that women will continue to penetrate the political arena as they have every other area of American life. Women, as political candidates and office holders, will make dramatic changes in the way laws are written. They will determine what issues are before Congress. They will continue to aspire to hold political offices, and with each victory, they will take on greater power and responsibility. A woman will undoubtedly be vice president soon, and be elected president during the twenty-first century, although I'm not quite as optimistic as Patricia Aburdene and John Naisbitt in their prediction that a woman will be electable, or already elected, as U.S. president, by 2008.[10]

While this new entry into top-level government positions will have marked effects on the country, the issue of this book is the impact women will have on the political marketplace—not as politicians, but as financial supporters and voters. They will have a profound effect on the political party system as we know it today. Traditionally, the Republican party has been labeled the party of big business, and the Democratic party more concerned with small businesses, minorities, and "average" people. As women become more involved in business, they will have to make the choice, and they will put their values first. As women's issues play a larger part in political decisions, candidates who listen to women, respect their viewpoints, and aggressively develop strategies based on women's needs will lead in the polls. Women's issues are not mutually exclusive of men's. Women just prioritize some items differently. As in other markets and organizations, women's input will strengthen the system, not weaken it. Women will vote with their ballots and their dollars, and both will speak loudly to the candidates.

The Republican party had better learn a lesson from Detroit and heed the words of women before it's too late. Women's causes—reproductive choice, healthcare, and other social issues—will take on more importance and will become a major determinant in the vote. The "good ol' boy" Republican party is out of step with the times. The Republican party will continue to suffer until it understands the influence of the new professional woman and meets her needs. Her involvement in the political scene will only continue to grow. Women will give their votes and dollars to the candidate or party that is reacting to their issues. In the past, men constituted the majority voter. Not anymore. Women voters outnumber men 54 percent to 46 percent. In the 1988 presidential election, nearly 10 million more women voted than men.

Neither the Democrats nor the Republicans acknowledged the power women had gained and the control they had on the outcome of the election. By 1992, the Democrats had learned that not paying attention to women was costly. They didn't make the same mistake in 1992. The Republicans have yet to realize the need to sincerely court the woman vote with substance and issues of importance to her.

By examining just the last 10 years, the trend for the future in politics is clear.

In 1980, no woman even ran for governor. In 1992, three governors were women. In 1990, only two U.S. senators were women. In 1993, seven are—five are Democrats. In the 1991 primary, 42 percent of Republican women crossed party lines to vote for Carol Moseley Braun for Illinois senator. In 1991, 124 women ran for the U.S. House and won 28 of the 435 seats. Women hold 300 state senate and 1,075 house seats. Four of the ten largest U.S. cities—Houston, Dallas, San Diego, and San Antonio— have had women mayors.[11] Two women sit on the Supreme Court, the Surgeon General and Attorney General are women, and many more hold cabinet positions.

Politicians proudly boasted at their national convention that 1992 was the Year of the Woman. It was only the first year of the political woman. Many more conventions will heed her words as she continues to make her presence known—as an office holder and as a voter.

Retail

The retailing industry will continue to evolve to meet the needs of the professional woman. Mega-malls will become more commonplace. Small specialty boutiques will also occupy a spot in the retail industry in the next century. Home shopping via cable television or direct mail catalogs will garner a substantial share of the retail dollars, leaving neighborhood malls as the entity that will suffer the most as women find alternative methods to fulfill their shopping needs.

Ron Stegall, chairman and CEO of LiL' Things, created a store for the future.[12] "Our concept is very different from other retail stores. LiL' Things is customer, not product, oriented. We are a one-stop shopping for newborns to age six. Today's parents are better educated, have more discretionary income and less time than in previous generations. They are looking for convenience and value," said Stegall. LiL' Things has the broadest selection of merchandise for newborns to school-age children assembled under one roof. The 35,000 square foot facilities offer everything from $1.99 T-shirts and shorts "that are almost disposable" to designer outfits. In addition to apparel, they offer an enormous range of toys, from mass marketed toys available at stores such as Wal-Mart and Toys 'R Us to ones generally available only at exclusive educational toy stores. Haircuts, a portrait studio, furniture, an interactive play center, and a library are just a few of the services and products available at LiL' Things.

In the developmental stages, Stegall formed an advisory group of mothers. "We wanted a broad cross-section of moms," declared Stegall. "We assembled full-time and part-time working moms and stay-at-home moms. They were career-oriented, professional women and those with just-a-job. We also had a variety of ages of both the women and their children. They provided invaluable input into the design of the store, the types of merchandise we would carry and the pricing structure. Our guarantee is that every item in the store is the best price available for that product in the market."

The narrow focus, only newborns to six-year-olds, allows LiL' Things to have the widest assortment of merchandise of any one store in the marketplace. Stegall felt that if they continued into the school-age years, they would lose their focus. "When kids start school, there is so much more—school supplies, computers and other learning tools. This way we could provide everything except grocery and drug store items."

This decade will be a time for refocusing marketing programs in many areas. Retailers, as well as manufacturers of soft goods, will need to re-evaluate their positioning and make sure it is in sync with the lifestyles of women consumers.

Travel

Women will equal the number of men who travel for business by the turn of the century. However, many of the amenities that will be emphasized this decade are business related, not gender related. Some hotels are already offering in-room amenities including hookups for laptop computers, phones with multiple lines, fax machines, and voice mail. Radisson Hotels International are testing a "business class" room rate with special features they hope will attract this market. The in-room concept offers much more flexibility and appeal than the business centers hotels installed in the 1980s.[13]

Airlines and airports must become more service oriented and female friendly. They will find it necessary to offer programs to assist women travelers with luggage and other items. To stay abreast of the competition, they will have to provide more lighting in parking facilities and more secure and convenient parking or a valet-type system for women who arrive after dark. They should re-evaluate their food service and provide more nutritious, heart-healthy meals. While the ticket price will always be a factor, an industry paradigm shift is necessary so that airlines understand that it isn't the only factor. Service, customer satisfaction, convenience, and safety will play a far bigger role in the future. Airlines must ask their customers what they want and then provide it. Women will not be shy in voicing their dissatisfaction with the current system and the level of service provided.

Check-in at airports, hotels, and car rentals will be more automated and faster. Many hotels offer some type of express service. Some rental car agencies are already computerized to the point that you can slide a card through a machine and get the rental contract and the parking space number. Limousines and shuttle services will continue to expand as a way to get around in a city without renting a car. With the increased competition, rental car agencies and shuttle services, which have done little thus far to capture the female market, should look at this segment as a profitable marketing strategy.

Women also will be traveling on their own more for leisure and recreation. As was previously mentioned, young single women love to travel, but so do other segments. Many adventure companies are being formed by women to cater to female travelers. Sheri Griffith, owner of Sheri Griffith Expeditions, provides river-rafting adventures for women. Ms. Griffith believes that for women to reach their capacity, they can't depend on men to do the work. "When women are with men on trips, they often don't reach their potential. They defer to men. They allow men to carry the heavy stuff. They sit back and let men paddle the boat," said Griffith.[14] Other companies are providing exciting, out-of-the-ordinary, "women only" trips. With more single women having increased discretionary income, this trend will grow in the twenty-first century. Travel will be a way for women to relax from the stress of the office or experience the wilds of Africa in the company of other women.

Self-Protection

Firearms and self-protection classes for women will continue to flourish until crime is brought under control in this country. As women have more responsibility for themselves and their children, travel on business more, and work later at the office, they will make sure they are equally capable of taking care of themselves on the streets as in the boardroom.

Individual personal protection items, including guns, will become even more prevalent with women. Home security systems and private security services will continue to grow. Self-defense classes and other means of protection will be important to women. They will also make sure their children can defend themselves, as the number of latch-key kids increases, along with the spread of crime to outlying suburbs once considered safe. Personal protection will become big business.

Gaining a Competitive Edge

Women will be major players as corporations strive to gain a competitive edge. Their resources, skills, and visions will help propel many companies into the future. Their buying power will determine the prosperity of countless businesses. As more women become financial, production, design, advertising, and marketing executives, corporations will have more insight into the needs and thinking of this prime consumer. Understanding what women want in the marketplace requires competent women in management and expert consultants who understand this complex market segment.

Joel Barker, author of *Future Edge*, believes there are three keys to the future for any organization: anticipation, innovation, and excellence.[15] In the twenty-first century, customer satisfaction will have to exceed expectations. Products and services must be delivered with impeccable quality. Repairs will have to be done right the first time. Doing it over is too costly. According to Barker, anticipating needs is essential in the competitive marketplace in which today's companies exist. But corporations need to be careful not to assume that this means they should anticipate what customers want in lieu of asking them. Input from consumers will be a vital part of success well into the next century.

Reengineering the Corporation by Michael Hammer and James Champy describes how the technological revolution is affecting corporations.[16] The ability to align available technology with the services, products, and people within the organization in order to produce a more efficient system is the basis of reengineering. Reengineering looks beyond a specific task and dismisses the present organizational structure to focus on process in order to inter-relate activities. Reengineering takes information, raw materials, labor, and other input to produce outputs to meet the needs of the customer.

Just as technology has changed the workplace, the woman's revolution will have long-term effects on the marketplace. According to Gordon Dodson, an international marketing consultant, "As corporations deal with the concept of reengineering in the workplace, so must they become cognizant of the revolutionary changes that the new professional woman is making in the marketplace.[17] She is a fact and a trend, not fiction or a passing fad. Corporations must make paradigm shifts in their marketing efforts to women or risk losing one of the largest growth markets. There will be a few who will take decisive boardroom action and make the shifts necessary, while others will either take a 'wait and see' stance or deny the need for any such paradigm shift."

In Barker's book he explains that when one resides within their own paradigm, they know the rules and how to operate. When a paradigm shift occurs, there is often chaos and confusion. People knew the rules and then someone changed them.[18]

While the business world has been affected by changes in the economic climate in this country and globally—the influx of foreign-made products, downsizing, and numerous other internal and external factors—women have also played a significant role in changing the rules.

Notes

[1]Jennifer Lawrence, "Laundry Soap Marketers See the Value of 'Value!' " *Advertising Age* (21 September 1992): 3.

[2]Kevin Goldman, "More Women Get Mammograms at Work," *The Wall Street Journal* (17 September 1993): B–1.

[3]Faith Popcorn, *The Popcorn Report* (New York: HarperBusiness; A Division of HarperCollins Publishers, 1992).

[4]Patricia Aburdene and John Naisbitt, *Megatrends for Women* (New York: Villard Books, 1992), xiv–xv.

[5]Joel Arthur Barker, *Future Edge: Discovering the New Paradigms of Success* (New York: William Morrow and Company, Inc. 1992), 77.

[6]Kevin Goldman, "Car Shopping at Home," *The Wall Street Journal* (17 September 1993): B–6.

[7]Popcorn, *The Popcorn Report*, 101.

[8]Kevin Goldman, "Seniors Get Little Respect on Madison Avenue," *The Wall Street Journal* (2 September 1993): B–6.

[9]Joseph Winksi, "In Interactive, Consumer Taking Control: To Make An Impact, Advertisers Must Pique Curiosity or Extend Offer—And Personalize," *Advertising Age* (5 April 1993): S 1–8.

[10]Aburdene and Naisbitt, *Megatrends for Women*, 3.

[11]Ibid., 3–32.

[12]Ron Stegall, president/CEO, LiL' Things, interview with author, 29 September 1993.

[13]Pauline Yoshihashi, "Hotels Turn Guest Rooms Into Well-Stocked Offices," *The Wall Street Journal* (20 September 1993): B–1.

[14]Lisa Chase, "It's A Woman's World," *Dallas Morning News* (6 December 1992): G 1–3.

[15]Barker, *Future Edge*, 11–13.

[16]Michael Hammer and James Champy, *Reengineering the Corporation, Soundview Executive Book Summaries: Reengineering the Corporation*, vol. 15 no. 8 (August 1993): 2–8.

[17]Gordon Dodson, president, Dodson & Associates, interview with author, 20 September 1993.

[18]Barker, *Future Edge*, 30–41.

INDEX

About the Author

Gerry Myers, president of the Dallas-based Myers Group, is an expert in marketing and selling to women, particularly products and services which have been primarily sold by men to men. She manages day-to-day operations of the firm, provides speaking and training for major corporations, has served as an adjunct professor at Texas Woman's University in Denton, Texas and has been on the board of several non-profit and professional organizations including the National Association of Women Business Owners, Leadership Metrocrest and Girls Incorporated.

Myers has authored several articles and is frequently quoted because of her expertise in the sizable, influential and profitable woman's market. She has received the Matrix Award and was a finalist for the T.O.P.S. Award. Her background includes an MBA in marketing and 12 years in the advertising and public relations field.